Springer Compass International

Series Editors
Steven S. Muchnick
Peter Schnupp

P. Schnupp   C. T. Nguyen Huu
L. W. Bernhard

Expert Systems Lab Course

With 102 Figures

Springer-Verlag Berlin
Heidelberg GmbH

Peter Schnupp

InterFace GmbH, Arabellastraße 30/V, D-8000 München 81, FRG

Chau Thuy Nguyen Huu

InterFace Computer GmbH, Garmischer Straße 4, D-8000 München 2, FRG

Lawrence W. Bernhard

Soft & Hard Software, Kleine Klingergasse 6, D-8390 Passau, FRG

Editors

Steven S. Muchnick

SUN Microsystems, Inc., Mountain View, CA 94043, USA

Peter Schnupp

InterFace GmbH, Arabellastraße 30/V, D-8000 München 81, FRG

Title of the German original edition published 1987 in the series Springer Compass:
P. Schnupp, C. T. Nguyen Huu: *Expertensystem-Praktikum*

Cover picture: Pastel on paper (1984), John Pearson

CR Subject Classification (1987): I.2.1, J.7

ISBN 978-3-642-74305-4   ISBN 978-3-642-74303-0 (eBook)
DOI 10.1007/978-3-642-74303-0

Library of Congress Cataloging-in-Publication Data
Bernhard, Lawrence W.
[Expertensystem-Praktikum. English]
Expert systems lab course / L. W. Bernhard, C. T. Nguyen Huu, P. Schnupp. p. cm. --
(Springer compass international)
    Translation of: Expertensystem-Praktikum.
    Bibliography: p. Includes index.

1. Expert systems (Computer science) I. Nguyen Huu, C. T. (Chau Thuy), 1952-.
II. Schnupp, Peter. III. Title. IV. Series.
QA76.76.E95B4713   1989   006.3'3--dc20   89-6403   CIP

© Springer-Verlag Berlin Heidelberg 1989
Softcover reprint of the hardcover 1st edition 1989

Media conversion: Appl, Wemding
2145/3140 - 543210   Printed on acid-free paper

Preface

One learns to swim by swimming, to program by programming and to implement expert systems by implementing expert systems.

This is the reason for this book. It is a laboratory which introduces the software developer to new design and programming techniques that have emerged from knowledge-based data processing. The emphasis is placed intentionally on programming, and not on generating expert systems by filling a shell with expert knowledge. This is by no means a condemnation of such an approach. Indeed, the programmer can certainly simplify one or the other task by using such a metasystem as a "tool".

Our experience, however, has shown that good, user-friendly expert systems, which can be readily integrated into existing, conventional databases and applications, can typically be realized only when the programmer is able to program all the additional components which are either missing in the development environment (tools) or are not adequate for the purpose (unsuitable interfaces, etc.). In traditional machine construction the "tool and die maker" is the most sought-after and highly paid professional. In our trade it is not much different.

This is precisely the aim of this volume: to provide the software engineer with the necessary practical knowledge and experience, to enable her to either adapt existing tools for the development of quality commercial systems (and not just research models) or dispense with such aids altogether, and program the system entirely in a suitable high-level programming language, with the same success as with conventional software.

This brings us to the issue of programming languages. We use Prolog in this book. It corresponds to the Clocksin-Mellish standard, which is the basis of all Prolog implementations of any significance on the market. There are two reasons for this choice.

Firstly, we are convinced that Prolog is the most productive and, with respect to system resources, economical language currently available for implementing knowledge-based applications - far superior to its major commercial competitor, LISP.

Secondly, Prolog systems cover a hardware spectrum, from IBM-PCs and Apple Macintosh, up through VAX to Amdahl or Cray 2, comparable with, if not larger than, almost any other language. Indeed, if you are careful in your choice, you can even find extremely portable Prolog implementations, where the very same system, with identical syntax and functionality, is available on all the machines! This is important if you will be doing this lab on your work station, but intend, at some later date, to apply the results, unchanged, to some actual project on a mainframe.

That is the actual goal of the expert system laboratory and this book: practical experience. All the problems, techniques and procedures stem from genuine, industrial expert systems. We have merely taken the liberty of occasionally changing the superficial aspects, as in the case of the "Munich Transport Authority" example, to be able to concentrate on the functional and structural issues of knowledge-based programming, without the distraction of delving into complex, unfamiliar and, for the reader, conceivably irrelevant fields of knowledge.

A valuable by-product of this book is the comprehensive, well-documented collection of large Prolog programs. This should be of substantial interest even to those readers who do not intend to write expert systems in Prolog, but other types of applications instead. Indeed, many computer scientists are of the opinion that knowledge-based programming is not a special branch of software engineering, but merely a method used by professionals for planning and realizing programs.

We hope we have achieved the goals set and wish you much success – both in this lab and in the practical application of the techniques dealt with here in your daily work!

Munich, July 1989   Peter Schnupp
                                                     C. T. Nguyen Huu
                                                     Lawrence W. Bernhard

Table of Contents

1 Introduction

*Software is the Fate
which shapes the Life
of a Computer.*

Jost Niemeier
Der Computer neben Dir
(The Computer at Your Side)
Hanser Publishing House
Munich (1979)

Expert Systems Lab is conceived to provide you, by way of example, with practical exercise in the design and implementation of *knowledge-based software systems.* We are assuming that you fulfill certain prerequisites. Firstly, that you already have an idea of what an *expert system* is (otherwise you probably would not have purchased this book in the first place). Nonetheless, we prefer to briefly outline what we mean by expert systems to avoid any misunderstanding of the basic concepts and models. Secondly, we assume that you are familiar with the programming language Prolog and that you have access to it – otherwise our practical course will remain too theoretical. It is the basic software which determines just *what* you can reasonably implement on your computer and *how*. And the applications you develop shape the course of (many) a computer's "Life" – as a wall-flower or a respected and popular member of a successful team of workers.

1.1 What Do We Mean by Expert System?

"Expert system" is a buzz word increasingly used to promote many and varied software products. As such, one cannot assume that everyone is referring to the same conceptual idea. In the interest of fairness, let us define just what type of systems we intend to deal with in this book.

The etymology of the word provides some insight: an *expert*, colloquially, is someone who has a command of the *facts* and *rules* (likewise special terms to be elaborated upon later) relating to a particular area of knowledge or endeavor, which goes beyond that of the majority of people.

Similarly, an *expert system* is a computer system which can administer specific expert knowledge, storing and evaluating it in such a manner that it can provide targeted information to users, or can be used to dispatch certain tasks, e.g. managing a production process. Consequently, instead of "expert systems" one often speaks, perhaps more meaningfully, of *knowledge-based software.*

Just what "knowledge" is in this context shall be examined more closely in the following chapter. For the time being we appeal to your intuitive sense of the word. We should, however, emphasize that the user of an expert system is not always necessarily a layperson in that particular field. Indeed, more often than not an expert system serves as an aid to the specialist, e.g. a diagnostic system for the physician. One reason for this is that it is far more difficult to develop a meaningful and efficient dialog with a layperson than with a specialist. In the latter case one can draw on the special terminology, which even "human" specialists often cannot readily translate into everyday, "lay" terms.

By their very nature, most conventional data processing applications also embody some knowledge specific to a field. This is what makes it so easy to "sell" these applications as "expert systems" if the market demands it. Therefore, one needs additional criteria to distinguish the conventional software from the knowledge-based kind. The following are meanwhile widely accepted:

- The system operates on a *knowledge base* rather than the conventional *data base*. This contains not only *facts* but also *rules*, i.e. instructions for processing knowledge.
- It has components for maintaining and expanding the knowledge base, either interactively with the expert in the field or a *knowledge engineer*, or automatically, e.g. via statistical analysis of the results of previous consultations. This characteristic is often referred to as *passive* and *active learning ability*.
- Employing *heuristics*, i.e. special processing techniques and search strategies, the system can derive new knowledge from the facts and rules stored in the knowledge base. If this occurs based on its so-called *production rules*, we then have something referred to as a *production system*.
- The system is in a position to explain how and why it arrived at a given solution to a specific problem. Thanks to such an *explanatory component*, a good expert system can not only apply the expertise stored in its knowledge base, but can also serve to impart this knowledge to its users. Thus, it can be employed for training and educational purposes.

Not every expert system will fulfill all these criteria. Nonetheless, a software system should exhibit at least two or more of the above attributes to be considered a useful system.

The programming methodologies used to realize such systems differ substantially in many respects from those of conventional software technology. Consequently, most traditional, algorithmic programming languages are not especially suited for this advanced task. Our goal is to demonstrate, using what we believe to be the currently most suitable programming language for the purpose, how you can equip software systems with the above attributes so that they really qualify as expert systems.

In other words, we wish to introduce you to the technique of *knowledge-based programming*.

1.2   What Is Prolog?

Expert systems typically define the knowledge they administer in a "non-pro-
cedural" language. It was indeed the inappropriateness of traditional, algorithmic programming languages for the representation of "formal" knowledge
which led to the development of *knowledge-based programming*. This field of
endeavor is essentially shared by two languages.

   Lisp, one of the oldest of all computer languages, still plays the more important role, particularly in the USA, and *Prolog*, which is enjoying increasing popu-

```
/* Prolog : */

pop(usa, 203).
pop(india, 548).
pop(china, 800).
pop(brazil, 108).

area(usa, 3).
area(india, 3).
area(china, 4).
area(brazil, 3).

density(Country, D) :-
        pop(Country, P),
        area(Country, A),
        D is P/A.

/* Lisp: */

( Define pop lambda country
        ( cond  (eq country 'usa') 203)
                (eq country 'india') 548)
                (eq country 'china') 800)
                (eq country 'brazil') 108) ) )

( Define area lambda country
        ( cond  (eq country 'usa') 3)
                (eq country 'india') 3)
                (eq country 'china') 4)
                (eq country 'brazil') 3) ) )

( Define density lambda country
        ( div (pop country) (area country) ) )
```

Fig. 1-1. An example of Prolog and Lisp

larity in Europe and Japan (see [CLOC81, SCHN87]). The reason for this is that Prolog is a "very high level language" producing more compact, less system-resource-intensive and easier-to-read code. Moreover, it is easier to learn!

Fig. 1-1 illustrates this, based on a simple example taken from the Prolog textbook by Clocksin and Mellish ([CLOC81], S. 33), and implemented in Prolog and Lisp respectively. The problem consists in representing some "facts", namely the population (in millions) and the area (in millions of square kilometers) of a number of countries, plus a "rule" for determining population density based on such facts.

Prolog is based on formal logic as its language model: the name stands for "*Programming* in *logic*". In Prolog knowledge is formulated in *clauses*, i.e. the direct representation of *facts* and *rules* in *Horn clauses*, a special form of first order logic (see [KOWA79] or [KOWA85]). By comparison, Lisp is a "functional" language. Each of the three Lisp expressions in Fig. 1-1 is a function, returning, by definition, a single value.

This example should effectively illustrate the greater clarity of Prolog code: even someone not versed in Prolog probably would be able to "guess" what the code is doing, where the Lisp code is likely to prove more difficult.

Let us examine the Prolog clauses in Fig. 1-1 more closely. The statements about *pop* and *area* can be directly understood as a relation in the data model sense. Prolog calls them "facts", since they are "always", (i.e. independent of the validity of other statements), true. Rules, on the other hand, are dependent upon other statements, i.e. conditions. Thus, population density can only be calculated as P/A, if P is the population and A the area of a given country.

It is important to note that, in Prolog, one can arbitrarily combine facts and rules into a specific *functor*. Thus, one could catch the entry of an as yet unknown country with the rule:

```
pop(UnknCountry,P) :-
        write('The population of '),
        write(UnknCountry), write(' is unknown.'),
        nl, write('Please enter it here: '),
        read(P),
        asserta(pop(UnknCountry,P)).
```

One would simply include this rule at the end of the *pop* facts. Prolog would then request the population for an unknown country and, using the *asserta* predicate, add this fact to the existing knowledge base. In the future, it would no longer need to ask for this information for the particular country.

The example further shows how easily one can expand the knowledge base and thus implement a primitive form of "learning" or adaptation in a system written in Prolog. In Lisp, but even more so in more conventional languages, such capabilities are far more difficult to implement, because the knowledge is "packed" in functions or procedures and, consequently, not readily "updated".

1.3   Which Implementation of Prolog Are We Using?

A number of good Prolog systems are available on the market. Unfortunately, not all of them conform to the syntax and functionality of the defacto standard, defined by *Clocksin and Mellish*, and which we assume in this volume. It is advisable that you select your system with respect to this standard to avoid having to adapt our examples to your system's differences. This could be extremely time consuming and would reduce the effective use of this book.

Since *Clocksin-Mellish* implementations of Prolog are available for almost all classes of computers, from PCs upward, this should not prove to be a great stumbling block. In any case, we have taken great care to use only those language constructs which should be available according to the said standard.

One exception is the use of *floating point arithmetic* in a few examples. Implementations for PCs, in particular, often do not support it. The changes needed to run these few examples are, however, so minimal, that they should not cause any problems. Basically, you need only change the scale, e.g. from German Marks (DM) to Pennies (Pf), and the check predicate from *numeric* to *integer*. This is best done with a rule

```
numeric(X) :- integer(X).
```

in your knowledge base. Only the technical formulas in our last example, the "coupling expert", could prove to require a greater effort, if you should have to transfer them to a system without floating point arithmetic.

Prolog implementations strictly compatible with the *Clocksin-Mellish* standard are by no means necessarily the best for use in this lab or for programming "real" applications in general. For this reason, we have presented a "check list" of system characteristics which you should look for when choosing a Prolog implementation, even though we do not (explicitly) exploit them in this lab.

The **debugger**
> of your Prolog should provide not only a simple *trace* function, but should be screen-oriented as well. It should allow you to follow the activation of procedures with the concomitant unifications and the consequent backtracking. Without such an aid, you will be greatly handicapped when testing your programs and trying to follow complex processes. The flow of control in expert systems is often considerably more difficult to follow than in conventional algorithms.

A **compiler**
> should likewise be available for producing effective, practical applications. Since expert systems are typically dialog-oriented, reasonable response times are critical to user acceptance. Compiled procedures are usually anywhere from 10 to 30 times faster than interpreted ones. This means that a compiler can reduce an intolerable half minute wait to an acceptable 1 second response! Such improved run-time performance will

generally be achieved only by compilers which produce machine code and not intermediate code, e.g. P-Code or the like, which has to be interpreted anyway.

A C-interface

(or an interface to some other conventional programming language) is likewise essential for typical use, since most "serious" expert systems require access to data stored in an existing database or to program packages providing other services, for example standard numerical algorithms. We have intentionally avoided such practice in this lab so that your choice of suitable Prolog implementations does not become a serious limitation. Which is not to say that most Prologs do not offer such facilities. Many, however, do not really link the interface into the Prolog control flow, i.e. they lack a *backtracking* mechanism. Consequently, the procedures written in C or Pascal, for instance, are then ignored upon backtracking, in much the same way as the the Prolog built-ins for input/output activity. Such interfaces are then virtually useless in practice. You cannot even implement a simple exhaustive database query predicate, which picks out all the records satisfying given criteria, one at a time, via backtracking.

Exception handling,

for dealing with fundamental system errors, should also be at your disposal at the programming level. Moreover, you should not only be able to program your own response to system exceptions, but also be in a position to generate such exceptions from within your own procedures. If not, you will find yourself at the mercy of the system exception handlers, which typically respond to exceptional situations by aborting, an often unsatisfactory and unprofessional behavior.

So if you are planning to acquire a Prolog system for this lab, be sure to avoid such limitations which will only frustrate your efforts in future applications. We hope our advice will help you make a more informed choice.

1.4   How Is This Lab Structured?

Aside from a few chapters dealing with the fundamental structure and programming techniques of knowledge-based systems, we seek to explain various ideas, methods, etc. based on a few concrete, "real-world-oriented" expert systems. Indeed, many of these derive from systems actually in use. For example, the system for diagnosing defects in automobile heating systems is actually part of a larger package for automobile repairs in general. And the object-oriented knowledge base in Chapter 7 is used by *InterFace Computer Corp.* of Munich, West Germany to administer the licensing of IF/Prolog.

Since even "small" expert systems are often several pages of Prolog code, of which only a small percentage may be of particular interest for pedagogical purposes, we present only excerpts within the text, while the complete listings are to be found in the appendix.

Here, our notion is that each chapter enables you to learn the essential concepts and techniques based on the illustrative examples, so that thereafter you can, at your leisure, study the function embedded in the complete system.

If, at some later date, you should need to implement an expert system for some concrete task, you will likely find a suitable, related sample system in the appendix, to use as a framework for an optimal solution. As every practicioner knows, there is no better aid for program development than a working system that "does approximately the same thing". And it is for just such readers that this book is intended.

2 Characteristics and Components of an Expert System

Expert systems are a new class of application programs, intended to make the "knowledge" of an expert in some special field readily available to "lay" users via a computer driven, interactive, dialog-oriented system. The fundamental difference with respect to traditional programming is that the processing rules are stored in a *knowledge base* along with the "data" itself. The core of an expert system is an *inference engine*. It applies a particular strategy to draw conclusions from the knowledge stored, thereby producing new knowledge. Suitable *heuristics* must provide for targeted knowledge processing, so that a meaningful response to a user query can be produced within a reasonable amount of time. Naturally, not all tasks can (today) be managed by expert systems. Furthermore, depending on the area of application, one can distinguish between a number of different system types.

2.1 The Concept and Areas of Application

Expert systems form a part of those data processing applications which have gained notoriety in connection with the (rather unfortunate) buzz word *artificial intelligence*, or *AI*. Next to robot technology, expert systems are perhaps the most application-oriented branch of this otherwise somewhat "esoteric" field of research. They seek to "implement" the knowledge of an expert (just what that means shall be discussed in detail shortly) and make it available to even the non-expert user. Increasingly these are being designated, more appropriately, *knowledge processing systems* or *knowledge-based systems*. A summary discussion of these terms can be found in the books [HARM85] and [SCHN85].

There are a number of practical reasons for packing expert knowledge into computers. The following summary can serve as a checklist for determining if perhaps an expert system can solve one or the other organizational problem:

- Is there a shortage of qualified workers?
  An expert system cannot altogether replace such workers, but certainly can make the existing ones more productive, either by directly supporting them in their work, or by relieving them of routine tasks, so that they can devote more time to those which they alone can master.

- Do particular employees spend too much time helping or guiding others?
  A good expert system, with a powerful explanatory component, is among other things a *training system*, which can, at least partially, assume instructional tasks.
- Do bottle-necks occasionally occur, because certain specialists are not available, due to illness, vacations, retirement, etc.?
  "Canning" knowledge for emergencies is a common reason for developing expert systems.
- Are there small tasks involving many people, only because no individual has all the necessary knowledge?
  The communication and coordination problems in such cases can be greatly reduced, if not eliminated, if the person "in charge" of the job can get the necessary information from an expert system.
- Do problems or errors occasionally occur because the complexity of the solutions to specific tasks tends to confuse the persons responsible and certain aspects get overlooked?
  An expert system does not suffer from stress and does not "forget" things.

Of course, given the state of the art, not all expert systems imaginable are necessarily implementable. This is particularly true where economic factors are critical and a system is not being developed as a research project merely to push the state of the art to new heights.

What is needed are practical systems which run on hardware of the kind somewhere between a PC and a VAX and whose development time lies between a few person-months and a few person-years. At the present time, such systems are being developed mostly by the endusers themselves, e.g. the system for evaluating branch offices of the HYPO Bank in West Germany [GÜNT85], by consulting engineers, e.g. the "coupling expert" on a medium sized Data General computer, or by software companies, e.g. the model of a defect detector for automobiles which runs on a lap-top DG 1.

All systems mentioned were implemented in a few person-months on standard hardware. The avoidance of exotic, custom hardware is a prerequisite to the commercial success of such systems.

This brings us to a second checklist of conditions which must prevail if an expert system of practical import and commercial value is to be developed given the current state of the field.

- Is the task to be dealt with of a well-defined, narrow scope?
  Typically, problems which are not at least confined to a specific area of endeavor cannot be solved with only a few hundred rules and thus cannot be implemented at a reasonable cost.
- Does the solution to a problem require no *background knowledge* and no *general education*, i.e. the kind of knowledge which we assume every person to have as a consequence of human experience.
  This "common knowledge" can be garnered from essays, encyclopedias, etc., by recording all the information which is implicit in the understanding of such

explanatory writings. It has been estimated, however, that the task of gathering this information alone, excluding any structuring thereof into a useable knowledge base, would require some 200 to 300 person-years [ANON86].

- Is the solution independent of "feeling", "intuition", "common sense" or a natural sense of interpersonal relations?
  These human attributes are neither now nor will they be in the forseeable future, implementable with existing computer hardware and programming facilities.
- Does the task require no special sensory perception (smell, taste,...)?
  Even computer vision, the most highly developed "imitation" of a human sensory activity, is at a relatively primitive state of refinement. For example, such simple tasks as the recognition of individual nuts and bolts in a box of such parts is so costly as to be prohibitive for most purposes.
- Is the task neither extremely simple nor particularly difficult for the human expert, i.e. does it require somewhere between 2 hours' and 2 months' time? Or do certain time limits exist with which a person can hardly comply, such as a few seconds for a complex control sequence?
  This is a "rule-of-thumb" for determining the cost effectiveness of developing an expert system to execute the task. If neither of the situations apply, then an expert system would probably not be economically justifiable.
- Is the frequency with which given problems arise and the value of each solution determinable?
  These are basic considerations for an analysis of the cost effectiveness of developing an expert system. If there is no general, regular need for the services of the system, chances are that implementing it will cost more than the system will save in practice.

Now that we have discussed where and when it is sensible to use knowledge-based systems, allow us to define just what it is we mean by "expert knowledge".

2.2 Human Versus Machine Knowledge

Just how does the *knowledge* stored in an expert system differ from that which has already accumulated in data and program banks? This is not a trivial question. We must consider closely just what "knowledge" is and what very different forms of it are used in problem solving.

Probably the best taxonomy of human knowledge is one developed by the American anthropologist *E.T. Hall* (see [HALL59]). Figure 2–1 illustrates his system of classification. He distinguishes between

- informal,
- technical and
- formal knowledge.

Informal

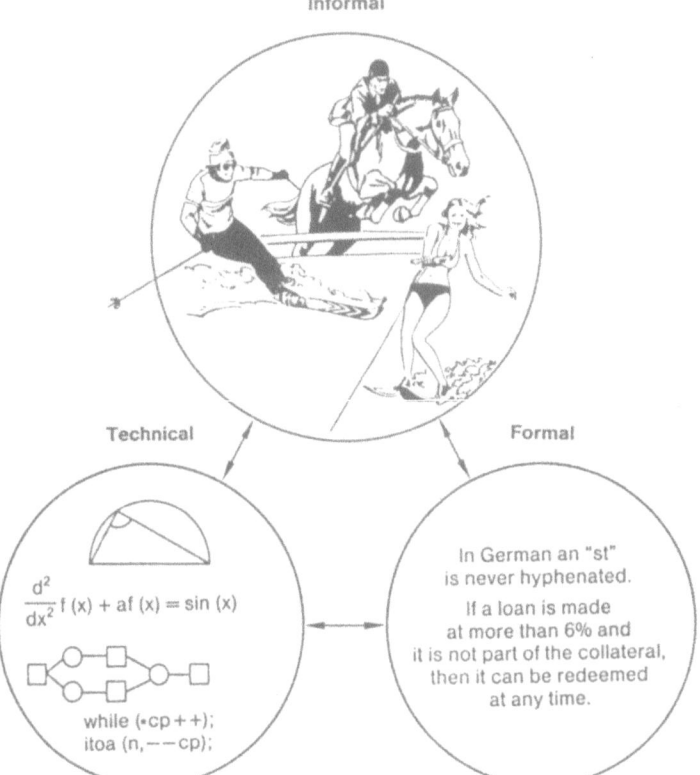

Technical

Formal

$$\frac{d^2}{dx^2} f(x) + af(x) = \sin(x)$$

while (•cp + +);
itoa (n, − −cp);

In German an "st"
is never hyphenated.

If a loan is made
at more than 6% and
it is not part of the collateral,
then it can be redeemed
at any time.

Fig.2 1. Taxonomy of human knowledge according to Hull

Informal knowledge is characterized by the fact that it is acquired by "observation and imitation". Learning to speak one's mother tongue, walking, dancing, sports are skills typically learned in this fashion. This is certainly not what we might consider to be "expert knowledge", but it is nonetheless of interest to us as data processors, since like tasks often form a part of the overall job in this field: for example, in the implementation of a natural language interface. And precisely for lack of a formalization of such knowledge the realization of such systems has been slow and tedious.

On the other hand, the rather unusual distinction between "technical" and "formal" knowledge is of great import in automatic data processing. Although both can be "formalized" in the sense that one can represent them as a framework of "facts" and "rules", a fundamental distinction remains with respect to the derivation of the formalization and, thus, how and in what form the knowledge is structured and which "updates" can be expected.

As a rule, *technical knowledge* is derived from "theories". The entire field of mathematics, the formulas of physics and technical calculations are exemplary of this class of knowledge. Our typical programming languages and methodologies draw from the same source. They describe *algorithms*, i.e. procedures of calculation, which allow one to model existing natural systems. Whether these systems are of a scientific, technical, economic or organizational nature is essentially irrelevant in this context.

In any case, it is just this class of knowledge which contemporary data processing generally deals with. Either the problems are by nature limited to such aspects or we do our best to "algorithmicize" them into "technical" tasks.

"Technical" formulas, being that they are derived from some theory, are not quite equivalent to scientific "laws": a different mathematical or programming approach can easily prove just as "correct" as the original. On the other hand, such formulas often embody a high degree of general validity. Typically they are "adapted" to some specific task via (numeric) parameterization.

This characteristic of technical knowledge and its method of representation has a far-reaching effect on current software technology. We tend to assume that changes in the data to be processed and in the task-specific parameters are more frequent than changes in the basic algorithms. This assumption is fundamental to the strictly observed separation of "data" and "program(s)" in modern software technology. The data is typically managed in the form of easily modified *data bases* and perhaps as *manifest parameters* in the form of "include" files. Programs, on the other hand, are formulated in one of the programming languages, most of which are difficult to modify, and then compiled into "objects" which are even harder to change. And all this is presumably done only after a complete specification has been made.

This process only makes sense as long as the problems being dealt with exhibit the "update"-characteristics of technical knowledge. Many of the problems observed in conventional data processing applications derive from the fact that the knowledge being dealt with is not of the "technical" type, to use Hall's terminology, but rather of a "formal" nature. This is particularly true in the legal, organizational and commercial fields.

In the case of *formal knowledge* the rules are not numeric "formulas" but rather expressed as formal, verbal "instructions" or *if-then clauses*:

"if we are dealing with a German language text, then ‚st' should never be hyphenated."

or

"if a loan is made at 6 percent interest and it is not part of the collateral, then a premature redemption cannot be contractually excluded."

Such knowledge is not the product of some law of nature; it is a convention which applies to a particular social group, e.g. for Germans living in West Germany it is the "law". In this sense, such rules are actually more binding than technical formalisms. Whereas many "correct" methods exist for the construction of a right angle or the description of an oscillation, it is impossible to make the aforementioned loan unredeemable in the jurisdiction of German law: any contractual agreements to the contrary are automatically invalid.

On the other hand, all aspects of formal knowledge are subject to change, if the appropriate authority deems it necessary. Thus, the German parliament can, at any time, make the redeemability of loans dependent on arbitrary conditions, whereby a change with respect to the numeric parameter 6 percent would be one of the least likely changes ("updates") to the rule mentioned. Correspondingly, the rules for hyphenating ‚st' (and any other such letter combinations) are determined entirely by the editorial management of the German Duden and a number of associated authorities.

The consequence for formal knowledge is that

(1) the usual division into *database* and *program library* becomes senseless,

(2) our algorithmic programming languages, as well as many of the methods and techniques of conventional software technology are no longer suitable, and finally

(3) modifications to the rules become as frequent as those made to the facts, i.e. the contents of our databases.

Knowledge-based software development, the programming technique of expert systems, seeks to provide better aids and methods for processing formal knowledge, much as *structured programming* has done for the processing of technical knowledge. Before we go into detail about the concept of the *knowledge base*, however, we should discuss one issue which is often overlooked.

As Fig. 2-1 already indicated, most practical problems rarely involve only one of the three types of knowledge which Hall distinguishes in his taxonomy (this in sharp contrast to many artificial intelligence research projects which often adapt the problem to be dealt with to the technique being studied). In practice a large base of technical knowledge often already exists, implemented on conventional hardware with the traditional programming languages and aids.

It would, of course, be foolish not to exploit these facilities. This is the reason why the authors of this book harbor a certain dislike for special *Lisp-machines*, special *AI programming environments* and all *AI languages* which do not allow access to existing operating systems and traditional programming languages.

2.3   Knowledge Base and Knowledge Bank

An expert's knowledge is for the most part of the formal type, i.e. it consists of a body of facts and rules, many of which are hardly of an *algorithmic*, let alone *numeric* nature. In the case of the previously mentioned fields of law, management and business this is probably obvious. It proves, however, to be true of much "technical" expertise as well.

One brief example: the coupling expert system mentioned earlier is meant to assist an engineer in the construction of couplings. The construction of technical units is done, these days, according to certain "conventions" guided by certain rules:

"If a coupling satisfying the given requirements already exists, then such a one should be used."

"If no coupling can be found satisfying the requirements, then one should (again according to some rules) look for one which can be adapted most easily to the said requirements.

Correspondingly, the *coupling expert* is an knowledge-based system whose facts and rules essentially embody a catalog of commercially available couplings and the means to effectively select individual models, based on *case data*, i.e. the requirements of the respective construction task. The analysis itself and the graphical representation for the engineer is conducted by a comprehensive applications package, which existed already in FORTRAN.

Thus, this particular expert system also provides a good example for the aforementioned interplay of technical and formal knowledge. Implementing it on "normal" hardware, with a Prolog system which can readily interface with existing, traditional software, made it possible to complete the job in a few person-months.

Perhaps the most significant feature of an expert system is the *knowledge base*, which, in contrast to the traditional *database*, stores all possible aspects of the necessary expert knowledge in an easily modifiable form. In large systems, this knowledge cannot always be held entirely in main memory (which is required by many of the existing expert systems, particularly those coming from universities and large research institutes).

Therefore, we prefer to speak of a *knowledge bank* – analogous to a *data bank* in conventional software terms – when we are talking about the entire body of knowledge which a system has available to it on secondary storage. We use the term *knowledge base*, on the other hand, to describe that portion of the total available knowledge which is currently being "consulted", i.e. has temporarily been moved to main memory. This distinction is by no means widely employed – probably because it is not considered especially relevant in academic situations.

Since the knowledge to be held in the knowledge bank tends to exhibit more variety of form than is usual in a conventional data bank, such knowledge banks cannot typically have a uniform structure. As a result, they always consist of a collection of different sub-systems for data administration, each of which is especially suited for the representation and processing of a specific knowledge type. The knowledge bank for the expert system shell *TwAIce* from Nixdorf is an excellent example (see [SAVO85] and [MENS85] for a sample application). It stores the the following types of knowledge:

Rule knowledge
consisting of the premises and conclusions, possibly with confidence factors (in per mil) to express uncertain knowledge. The rule knowledge is formal and thus represents the fundamental distinction from traditional data banks.

Tabular knowledge
corresponding closely to the usual relational data banks.

Procedural knowledge

representing what in the past was often referred to as a "methods bank". Specifically, these are algorithms in conventional programming languages, which are activated as needed (rule controlled) and return results (mostly numeric) to the rule which triggered them.

Taxonomic knowledge

describing objects and their attributes and hierarchies. This part of the knowledge bank has a strong resemblance to *data dictionaries*, both in structure and usage.

Natural language formulation knowledge

containing **substitute texts**, for use in conducting a dialog with the user. In an expert system long texts particularly should always be administered externally rather than in the context of the internal knowledge base. It is not just that such texts require a large amount of main memory. As *external text files*, they are more easily maintained and formatted than when directly embedded in rules or procedures.

Knowledge about user assistance

is like the knowledge about formulating natural language, i.e. a collection of substitute texts. The fundamental difference is that these texts are closely associated with the taxonomic knowledge and the objects and attributes defined therein. They are used to help the user assign a value to the attributes of given objects. For this reason they are administered separately from the general substitute texts.

In the following section we will concern ourselves primarily with rule knowledge, since the structure and use of the other knowledge bank elements would probably not offer much new insight for an experienced software engineer.

2.4   Rule Knowledge

Unlike procedural knowledge, which is easily expressed using the usual, algorithmic programming languages and describes the solution to a task as a series of operations to be performed, rule knowledge is a form of *declarative knowledge*. This means that all knowledge – and not as in the case of the algorithmic languages, only the "data" – is formulated in terms of *declarations*.

Rules can be understood directly as the internal representation of *if-then* statements. Figure 2-2 illustrates this based on an excerpt from the knowledge base of a system for diagnosing automobile defects (see [GSCH85]). We shall be discussing a similar system in a later example. The verbal formulation of the rules was composed in collaboration with an expert, an experienced professional automobile mechanic. The translation into the formal definition – in our example written in Prolog – was performed automatically using a small compiler.

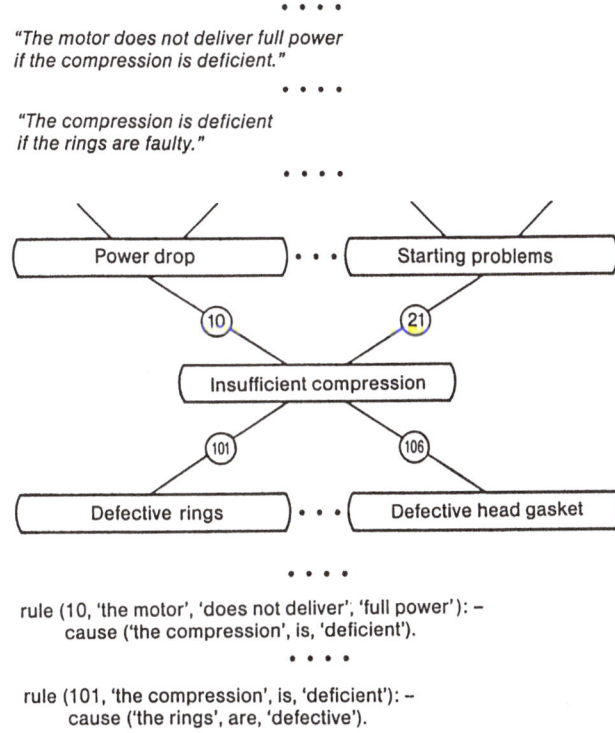

• • • •

*"The motor does not deliver full power
if the compression is deficient."*

• • • •

*"The compression is deficient
if the rings are faulty."*

• • • •

rule (10, 'the motor', 'does not deliver', 'full power'): –
   cause ('the compression', is, 'deficient').

• • • •

rule (101, 'the compression', is, 'deficient'): –
   cause ('the rings', are, 'defective').

• • • •

Fig. 2-2. Excerpt from the rule knowledge for repairing an automobile

The rules associate each particular condition with a (possible) cause, thus building a network of rules. New knowledge can be added to the network at any time by adding new rules, e.g. when new possible defects become evident or emerge as the result of remedial actions.

Since the rules, as declarative knowledge, merely define relationships without fixing any procedural structure, there must be a component which determines a meaningful application and evaluation of them. This component is classically referred to as an *inference engine*. It in itself represents special knowledge: one or more methods of knowledge processing and their appropriate order of application corresponding to a particular strategy for finding a solution. This component of the system is usually procedural in nature, implemented as a traditional program in some algorithmic language.

It is, however, possible to express the methods and strategies themselves declaratively, as general "rules for problem solving". In such a case, we speak of *metaknowledge*; this is a topic which will be discussed in the final chapter of this lab.

This higher level of description permits the implementation of expert systems which adapt themselves more flexibly to their particular tasks. It also enables such systems to achieve a certain degree of *learning capability,* so that the system can modify its own rule base for metaknowledge, based on its experience or direct queries to the user.

For the time being, however, we will be limiting ourselves to inference engines which work in a strictly procedural fashion.

2.5   The Inference Engine

A rule network like the one in Fig. 2-2 is used by the expert system to solve problems as defined via user queries and commands, e.g. to diagnose defects and give instructions as to how to repair them based on the case data entered by the user. In addition, the system should be able to guide the user through the dialog and explain why it is proceeding as it is, since a basic purpose of this expert system is to help the inexperienced mechanic in her efforts to determine and remedy the cause of some malfunction. And even an experienced mechanic may lack some knowledge with regard to a specific (aspect of a specific) model of automobile!

The system component for navigating the network of rules is the *inference engine.* By "inference", we mean "drawing logical conclusions": the inference engine derives new knowledge from existing facts and rules, which should lead to an answer to the user's question.

A *Prolog Interpreter* implements a Top-Down inference engine: it starts with the user query and attempts to "prove" its validity, based on the facts and rules found in a given knowledge base, using a special method known as *Resolution.* This allows one to write expert systems simply and compactly. The Prolog language model implicitly contains many components which in other languages, such as Lisp or other more conventional programming languages, must be "added in", with a corresponding increase of programming overhead.

Nonetheless, it is *not* true that Prolog is *only* capable of Top-Down resolution. It is possible, with moderate command of the language, to write a Bottom-Up inference engine in Prolog in a program less than a page long. Better yet, other techniques of knowledge representation and processing - of which we shall be demonstrating the more significant ones - can be implemented just as well, if not better and more clearly, in Prolog.

Why is it then that this resolution method and its implementation in the form of the inference engine is used merely as a "statement prover" and not as an interpreter for a generalized programming language? The reason is that one can interpret/apply an *if-then* rule either as

> **if** *Condition* → **then** *Result*

or

> **if** *Situation* → **then** *Action*

according to one's needs. The former is a *logical* interpretation, the latter a *procedural* one. The difference lies in the semantics of *Result* and *Action* respectively. If the *then* part is a *pseudo-predicate*, which causes some sort of *side-effects*, such as input or output or changes in the knowledge base, then the resolution of the rule is equivalent to a procedure call in a traditional language.

This is referred to as a *procedural interpretation* of a "logic" programming language. For someone familiar with a language like Prolog, switching from a logical to a procedural interpretation of program text occurs virtually subconsciously. We will therefore refrain from pointing this out explicitly in our sample programs. Inexperienced readers, however, are well advised to carefully consider if a Prolog text being explicated is either "logical" or "procedural" in nature. And if you should find a particular program or portion thereof difficult to understand, you might examine the possibility that you are applying the wrong "kind" of interpretation.

2.6   Instantiation of Variables

If the clauses stored in a knowledge base are treated by the inference engine as logical facts and rules from which an answer to a user query is to be derived, then such a query will typically include at least one variable: e.g.

```
?- density(china,X).
```

in the small "population"-knowledge base in Fig. 1-1 of the previous chapter. The system should instantiate the variable X with the correct solution and output

```
X = 200
```

To arrive at this result, the variables *Country*, P and A must be bound to the proper values according to the facts and rules applied from the knowledge base.

The *instantiation* or binding of variables with constants or with other variables or even arbitrarily complex structures is called *unification*. It is the fundamental mechanism, indeed the only one, by which a Prolog interpreter determines results. Prolog attempts, recursively, to match a *goal*, i.e. a functor with arguments such as

```
density(china,X)
```

with a fact or rule-head in the knowledge base, by finding acceptable values for the as yet uninstantiated variables both in the goal and the relevant clauses in the knowledge base. This pattern matching is the technique used to implement the search process in the knowledge base.

Unification is a more complex process than the typical value assignment of traditional programming languages, because firstly, the binding of variables to values may occur in either direction, i.e from goal to knowledge base or vice-versa, and secondly, variables can be (recursively!) bound to data structures of arbitrary complexity. Thus, unification is a more powerful mechanism than simple assignment, yet it is relatively easy to implement.

2.7   Applications Problems

The power of Prolog in the implementation of knowledge-based systems (but also for other applications, e.g. formal specifications or "normal" programming tasks) lies primarily in two characteristics of the language. On the one hand, it allows a direct representation of a particular problem in terms of formal logic. On the other hand, the resolution and unification mechanisms automate the search process for generating and evaluating solutions, so that the Prolog interpreter already provides the inference engine needed in an expert system.

Nonetheless, one should not be misled into thinking that programming in logic automatically solves all problems involved in developing expert systems. Prolog is a realization of a "General Problem Solver" (today one might speak rather of an expert system shell), such as was sought after in the 1950s as the basis for a general problem solving system. However, one cannot solve every problem "automatically" with Prolog simply by specifying it in formal logic. There are a number of reasons for this. The most important is the complexity of most problems. This complexity forces one to limit the solution-search process via suitable *heuristics*. These are strategies derived from the problem definition, previous knowledge and from experience or even "intuition" of experts, which lead to more expeditious knowledge processing.

If the search is totally unrestricted, the number of possible solutions grows combinatorially, i.e. as the factorial of the number of objects involved. Thus by 10 objects we have

$$10\ ! = 3\ 628\ 800 \text{ solution candidates}$$

and with just two more, i.e. 12 objects,

$$12\ ! = 479\ 001\ 500.$$

This means that as soon as the problems get "interesting" the naively programmed solution generator bursts due to combinatoric explosion.

Consequently, one must find applicable *heuristics* to reduce the "solution space" to be searched. Such heuristics are, however, typically problem-specific, thus rendering the "general problem solver" useful for only a specific area of knowledge or task. This departs in no way from human expertise, though, which also consists of knowledge about promising solution "paths", in addition to the usual facts and rules.

Figure 2-3 illustrates the use of heuristics to reduce the cost of finding a solution in the well known expert system DENDRAL. DENDRAL determines the chemical structure of complex, organic molecules based on empirical formulas and mass spectrographs.

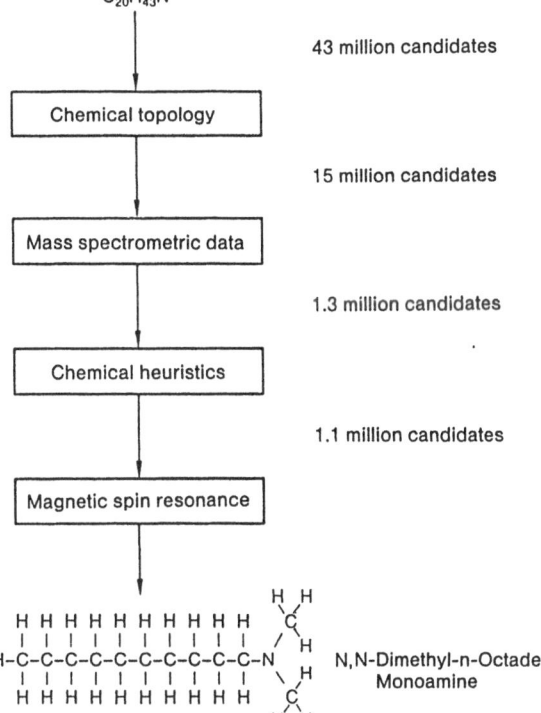

Fig. 2-3. Reducing the cost of solutions through suitable heuristics in DENDRAL (see [LENA84])

The complexity of knowledge processing, however, is not the only limiting factor determining the practical areas of application. Let us briefly examine a few others:

- Due to technical problems, as well as the disproportionate expense of collection and preparation, the size of a manageable knowledge base for a typical expert system is currently about a few thousand clauses, at most. This is several orders of magnitude less than the professional knowledge of an human expert. Consequently, today's expert systems tend to operate around sub-areas of knowledge and experience.
- For the same reasons, expert systems do not have a "world view" and do not embody "common sense". *Informal* knowledge is extremely difficult to represent and process. Thus, most people seem to store their *technical* and *formal* knowledge in an "informal", intuitive form, which each individual regards as her "experience".
- Sensory perception is such a well integrated aspect of knowledge processing that we tend to overlook it as a process in itself. The attempts to emulate it via peripheral hardware and software, processing events and data "into knowledge", are by contrast still most primitive. There has been some success in

speech and picture recognition, largely with great resource expenditure, while smell and taste, for instance, remain essentially unapproached.

- Much human thinking is based on analogies and associations; this seems particularly true in the case of expert knowledge. A major portion of scientific work, for instance, consists in building models and theories for new phenomena from existing knowledge – possibly from completely unconnected fields – which are then adapted to actual observations. Plausible software implementations of such thought processes are virtually non-existent.
- In this sense, expert systems cannot be "creative". Whatever the concept of "creativity" may be interpreted to be, the ability to make analogies and associations are vital components of human creativity, as are a sense of beauty and elegance or spontaneous ideas – all concepts for which computer science has not, so far, found adequate, implementable models.

And so, before one tackles new, as yet unsolved data processing tasks with the unquestionably powerful techniques of knowledge-oriented software development, one should consider whether the conventional approaches have failed due to one or the other of the above difficulties, since these are hurdles which expert systems overcome no better.

2.8   Classification of Typical Expert Systems

Even in the realm of problems which can be mastered with our current technology implementation problems do arise. These depend, among other things, on the area of application of the planned system.

Diverse requirements and difficulties demand different solutions to the problems of knowledge representation and processing, i.e. in the knowledge base and the inference engine. This is particularly true if one intends to implement an expert system using a *tool* typically referred to as a *shell*. The ideal expressed in many advertisements, that one need only "fill" this "shell" with the respective knowledge in order to build an expert system, presumes that the shell was designed for the same class of knowledge-based applications as the one which is to be realized (and even then things usually are not quite that simple). Thus, one can surely develop a system for diagnosing illnesses and maybe even a repair system for machines, using *MED1*, a shell for medical diagnosis systems [PUPP85], but it would be foolish to use this tool to implement a system for economic planning (and its authors would hardly recommend it).

Consequently, we shall define some of the more common types of expert systems as follows. Should you choose to use a shell as the basis of your system development, we recommend that you check if systems of the same type using it have already been implemented . If so, you should take a look at one to see whether their user interfaces, overall behavior, explanatory components, and scheme for knowledge input and maintenance seem acceptable.

Information systems

gather *case data* from the user via a dialog. This information is then used in conjunction with the system's knowledge to deliver specific information. Systems of this type cover a broad spectrum of applications: the selection of an optimal travel route or the best vacation bargain, the analysis of economic indicators or choosing between different technical processes. A simple information system will be demonstrated in the next chapter.

Diagnostic systems

are more ambitious and demanding information systems, which may be used in medical or technical fields to diagnose the cause of a given condition, based on measured values, disease or behavior symptoms and other relevant information. The distinction between information and diagnostic systems is somewhat fluid. A fundamental characteristic of *diagnosis* in contrast to simpler *information* is not only the greater number of rules and facts, but moreover the uncertainty involved. Consequently, such systems must include a mechanism for quantifying this uncertainty, particularly as it propagates throughout the process of drawing conclusions. We shall be presenting a sample diagnostic system in the course of our lab.

Repair systems

are an extension of diagnostic systems. They embody not only the knowledge needed to recognize the defects but also the information as to how to best remedy them. They are typically used to support maintenance personnel making repairs. Occasionally, e.g. in outer space or hazardous environments like atomic power plants, such systems control automatic repair procedures. Commercially, repair systems are commonly used in the maintenance of automobiles, aircraft, data and transport networks, computers and mechanical devices of many sorts.

Debugging systems

are a special class of diagnosis and repair systems, which are intended to support the search for and elimination of bugs in software systems. Unfortunately, there are still very few such systems in existence which are of any practical use. Probably the best known prototype of such a system is *Shapiro*'s [SHAP83]. A simpler example is a system for generating test-suites for Unix implementations [PESC85].

Interpretation systems

are used to analyze speech or images, evaluate signals and monitor measuring instruments. They interpret the input data in the sense that they provide a symbolic meaning for the condition encountered. If we include in this class those systems designed for translating natural languages, then it is probably the oldest one of them all. Nonetheless, such applications are among the most problematic and usually place enormous demands on system resources.

Predictive systems

derive developments expected in the (near) future from data about the present and previous conditions. The prognosis may be based upon mathematical, statistical or "experiential" rules. Applications are found in weather and harvest prediction, economic prognosis and such analyses as the development of traffic patterns or energy consumption, etc. Such systems are typified by a basic, dynamic, parameterized model of the system whose behavior is to be foretold. The parameters are satisfied by case data. The strength or weakness of such systems is to be found in the model being used. As the "real world" is too complex to be fully modelled, the system relies on much abstraction to achieve an acceptable level of implementability. Such simplifications or underlying assumptions, however, can and do lead to false predictions.

Planning systems

are used to support decision making when planning the execution of complex tasks, particularly in military and economic sectors. They are also used in other areas, such as the planning of scientific experiments. An excellent example of the latter is *Molgen* [FRIE85], which is used to prepare molecular genetic experiments.

Configuration systems

are a special class of planning systems. They make possible the technical construction and configuration of products from modular components (e.g. computing machinery and installations) or the layout of circuitry. Such systems are characterized by rules in the knowledge base defining the *constraints* limiting the possible results. A critical part of the process revolves around rules allowing for an optimization of the plan according to specific criteria, such as minimization of cost or production time or physical size or production material used. The last example in this book, an object-oriented implementation of a "coupling design expert", is a simple version of a configuration system, i.e. a *selection system*, which merely adapts a series of component units to a previously defined environment.

Monitoring systems

compare data derived from user input or measuring instruments with reference values and return information regarding the state of a given process, often indicating deviations and possible dangerous developments. A sub-class of such monitoring systems is the *assistant system*, which observes the input of a conventional data processing system – e.g. a text processor – and "as needed" provides some "intelligent" help or service, such as a spelling check. Some concrete approaches for such a system will be given later on.

Control systems

are an extension of monitoring systems. They build a closed control loop by automatically taking corrective action when a sub-optimal state has been recognized.

Training systems

are implementable on the basis of any of the above system types. Their goal is to simulate, for the student or professional to be trained, a concrete problem based on concrete data and then assist in its solution. If necessary, the user can be informed of the consequences of decisions via corresponding messages or - better still - graphic displays. A typical training system is STEAMER, developed by BBN for the U.S. Navy, for the training of engineers in the operation of marine engines. Such a system should store information about the user's actual state of knowledge, according to which it should then provide appropriate explanations and examples in the course of training.

If one chooses to develop an expert system directly on the basis of a suitable programming language, such as Prolog or Lisp, then one is generally not limited to the system types just listed. Nonetheless, the architecture and program structure for systems of different classes are quite different from each another. It is for this reason that we cannot illustrate the multitude of design strategies by stepwise elaboration of a single sample system in this lab. Instead we have selected a number of different systems to demonstrate different concepts and solution methodologies.

On that note, let us begin with the implementation of one of the simplest and perhaps most common types, an *information system*.

3 A Model System for Transit Fare Information

This is a small example in which we wish to demonstrate a few of the more important concepts and programming methods for building an expert system. The system is intended to advise the user in choosing the most economical public transportion when using the *MTA*, i.e. the Munich Transport System in Munich, West Germany. This is no simple task for a foreigner attending the Oktober Fest or one of the many trade fairs taking place there, as even the natives have their problems with the complex zonal system and its many fare variants for special classes of passengers. Our expert system asks the prospective passenger for some specific *case data* - e.g., how much money she has - and then recommends the least expensive, appropriate ticket. Even such a primitive expert system should have an explanatory component, therefore our *MTA Expert* notes the sequence of questions and answers in the ensuing dialog. Using this information, it can then explain, at any time, why it asked a particular question and how it arrived at a particular result.

3.1 The Problem

The author has this problem (among others): he is currently employed and living in Munich, has children too young to drive and has occasional guests from abroad who are also dependent on the public transport of the *MTA* (*Munich Transport Authority*). The MTA has a very complex fare structure involving many different types of tickets. The only simple thing about this public transportation (an honor system, with irregular checks made by non-uniformed controllers) is that a passenger found using it with an improper ticket is fined 40 Marks (approximately 23 US Dollars, as of 1988) and sometimes taken to court. Thus, an information system which helps select the most economical fare for a given trip is certainly "profitable" for the passenger, if not for the *MTA* itself.

Since the knowledge involved is certainly of the *formal* type, as per Hall's classification system of Fig. 2-1, and, furthermore, the rules defining the fare structure are subject to fairly frequent change, such an information system is a typical candidate for an expert system. Before showing you how the system is built, we must explain that we have simplified the fare structure somewhat, so that its many ramifications do not interfere with your understanding of the function and architecture of the software system. Had we, in the interest of greater truth, not done so, the probability is minimal that the rules governing the fare structure have not changed, by the time you read this!

The simplified rules determining a given fare are as follows. There are different ticket types (prices are quoted in DM = German Marks):

- The *Single Trip Ticket* costs 2.30 DM and contains 2 fields for cancellation.
- The *Multiple Trip Ticket-A* costs 6.50 DM and contains 7 fields.
- The *Multiple Trip Ticket-B* costs 12 DM and contains 13 fields.
- The *Kiddie Ticket* or *Short Route Ticket* costs 5 DM and contains 8 fields, each of which has a lesser value than the tickets described above.

Children are passengers under 15 years of age, or dogs, presumably because they do not usually live to be much older. To determine if a given trip constitutes a *Short Route*, one must consult a map of the transportation network, which is available at every bus, street-car and train or subway stop. For our purposes, any route less than 5 kilometers is considered a Short Route.

Our first task is to formalize this information into *clauses* which we can maintain in our knowledge base.

3.2   Transit Fare Rules

Figure 3-1 shows an excerpt of the fare knowledge base. With the exception of the "Kiddie Ticket" rules, the clauses initially check merely whether the prospective passenger has sufficient cash. In the case of the childrens' tickets, an additional check is made to see whether the passenger is really a child or the route is really a short one.

The ordering of the rules for the different ticket types intentionally places the most economical first and the most expensive last. The Multi Trip Ticket-A has a per field cost of 0.929 DM compared with the Multi Trip Ticket-B, with a cost of 0.923. In the case of a Single Trip Ticket, a field costs 1.15 DM.

This sequence plays an important role in the strategy applied by the system when examining the different possible solutions. We shall discuss this in greater detail shortly.

The clauses in Fig. 3-1 differ from those of the final implementation in two respects:

- They assume that the respective *case data*, i.e. the age and financial status of the enquirer, are known to the system.
- They do not furnish an *explanation* of the questions and conclusions of the system, which we consider to be so vital an aspect of a good expert system.

If the system is to conduct a dialog with the enquirer in the form about to be presented, we must supplement the rules in the knowledge base in two ways.

A means of *collecting case data* must be provided, so that missing facts can be acquired from the user and added to the knowledge base.

```
is_a_Kiddie_Ticket_possible :-
      status(cash,Money),
      Money >= 5,
      status(age,child).

is_a_Kiddie_Ticket_possible :-
      status(cash,Money),
      Money >= 5,
      status(distance,near).

is_a_Multi_Trip_Ticket_B_possible :-
      status(cash,Money),
      Money >= 12.

is_a_Multi_Trip_Ticket_A_possible :-
      status(cash,Money),
      Money >= 6.50.

is_a_Single_Trip_Ticket_possible :-
      status(cash,Money),
      Money >= 2.30.
```

Fig. 3-1. The simplified rules for calculating fares

Furthermore, every rule invoked must be recorded such that the system can, at any juncture, reconstruct how it arrived at a particular conclusion and thus give the enquirer a reasonable explanation of its behavior.

This is best illustrated with a few sample dialogs.

3.3   Conducting a Dialog

The information system should, based on the fare rules, indicate to the user how to apply this information optimally. This typically occurs implicitly, as the system interactively prompts the passenger for the appropriate data as the particular situation becomes increasingly better defined. Still, the user should have the opportunity to make inquiries to the system. To find out just what sort of options the passenger has in this regard, the user can enter

```
?- assistance.
```

To start with, the system introduces itself:

```
I am a small Prolog program, my name is MTA.
MTA stands for Munich Transport Authority.
```

```
My job is to help you select the proper ticket
for travel in the central city zone.

You must cancel 2 fields of a ticket for a single trip.
The following tickets are available:
- Single trip tickets, with 2 fields for 2.30 DM,
- Type A multiple trip tickets, with 7 fields for 6.50 DM and
- Type B multiple trip tickets, with 13 fields for 12.00 DM.

In addition, for persons under 15 or pets, we have
- Kiddie tickets, with 8 fields for 5.00 DM.

Passengers travelling less than 5 kilometers can
use a kiddie ticket regardless of age.

If you would like my help in selecting a ticket, enter "mta."
With "restart." you can start a fresh session, i.e.
any recorded facts will be forgotten.
```

?- assistance.

```
Possible questions are:

- mta.
- is_a_Kiddie_Ticket_possible.
- is_a_Multi_Trip_Ticket_A_possible.
- is_a_Multi_Trip_Ticket_B_possible.
- is_a_Single_Trip_Ticket_possible.
- must_one_ride_without_paying.
- must_one_walk.
- restart.              -> deletion of old data.
- tree(Step,Rule).      -> show tree.
```

We shall discuss the last alternative later, since we have included it only so that
we can, in our lab, easily observe the processing steps involved in our system, i.e.
a sort of trace function. We shall limit our discussion here to the normal interactions possible. In addition to the dialog for acquiring user data, we shall be
demonstrating some of the explanatory components, e.g. what the user gets in
response to such inquiries as *why* or *how_come*.

```
?- mta.
How much money do you have ?   20.
How old are you ?   why.
```

```
I know that you have more than 5 DM.
Consequently, if you are under 15 years of age,
you can buy a Kiddie Ticket.
So I would like to know if you are under 15.

Now: How old are you ?    18.
How great is the distance ?    why.

I know that you have more than 5 DM.
Consequently, if you are making a short trip,
you can buy a Short Trip Ticket (Kiddie Ticket).
A short trip is less than 5 kilometers.
So, I would like to know how long the route is.

Now: How great is the distance ?    10.

You should buy a Type B Multi Trip Ticket for 12 DM.
And remember to cancel two fields!

yes
?- restart.

yes
?- is_a_Kiddie_Ticket_possible.
How much money do you have ?    why.

To buy a Kiddie Ticket you must:
- have at least 5 DM and
- be under 15 years of age.

So I would like. to know if you have at least 5 DM.

Now: How much money do you have ?    2.

no
```

The following example is intended to show that a dialog is not restricted to tedious inquiries about money, distances and age.

```
?- mta.
How much money do you have ?    none.
Are you daring ?    why.

I want to know if you are willing to take
a risk to get to your destination quickly.
```

```
Now: Are you daring ?    why.
```

```
Since you do not have enough money for a ticket,
I must look for another solution.
```

```
Now: Are you daring ?    no.
```

```
You should walk.
yes
?- is_a_Kiddie_Ticket_possible.
```

```
no
?-
```

This sample dialog also illustrates how the system behaves when the user asks a new question; immediately following the last piece of advice, without having issued the "command"

```
?- restart.
```

beforehand, to clear the system of the information acquired in the dialog up to that point. In this specific instance, the system can promptly answer the last question based on the facts gathered, because it knows that the enquirer has no money and is not daring!

3.4   Control Structure and the Rule Interpreter

If we temporarily ignore the aspects of data collection and explanatory activity, processing a direct user inquiry, such as

```
?- is_a_Multi_Trip_Ticket_A_possible.
```

becomes rather simple – the Prolog interpreter merely activates the corresponding rules. Either one of the rules is successful, and Prolog (and subsequently, the information system) responds with "*yes*", or the whole effort fails and it answers with "*no*".

But if the system is to behave more like a live "consultant", as in the case when we enter

```
?- mta.
```

then our simple information system must include primitive elements of a *diagnostic system*: it must select among numerous possible solutions the one most appropriate to the "user's problem" based on knowledge permanently embedded in the knowledge base and/or facts gathered from the user herself.

Thus, this simple system differs from more complex diagnostic systems, such as those used in medical and other technical areas, primarily with respect to the number of rules involved. The structural aspects are fundamentally the same, as we shall see in other sample systems we show later.

The diagnostic aspect of the system is implemented as a *solution strategy*, which embodies specific *hypotheses* regarding the quality of given solutions with respect to specific criteria. In the case of a medical or technical diagnostic system, the strategy involves determining the relative probability of an illness or defect given a set of known symptoms. In our case, the criterion is user satisfaction with a given suggestion, the hypothesis being that the cheapest ticket provides the greatest satisfaction.

This is implied by the order of the alternative solutions in our case:

- the *least expensive* possible ticket which the user can afford, followed by
- riding mass transit *without paying* – this is an honor system – as the most expensive, being subject to a 40 DM fine if caught, and finally
- *walking*, which is cheaper but presumably not the user's mode of choice.

Figure 3–2 shows the correspondingly arranged Prolog clauses.

```
mta :- is_a_Kiddie_Ticket_possible.

mta :- is_a_Multi_Trip_Ticket_B_possible.

mta :- is_a_Multi_Trip_Ticket_A_possible.

mta :- is_a_Single_Trip_Ticket_possible.

mta :- must_one_ride_without_paying.

mta :- must_one_walk.
```

Fig. 3-2. The *mta* clauses as "hypotheses" about the transportation alternatives

Since Prolog processes a set of clauses like the one in Fig. 3–2 from the "top-down", this particular arrangement implicitly realizes the desired strategy: first a test is made to see if the cheapest ticket type, the Kiddie Ticket, is applicable, then the more expensive types, until the user, unwilling to risk a fine, is advised to walk.

Thus, from the point of view of the *rule interpreter*, our Prolog system, each *mta* clause is a *hypothesis* as to how the user could travel. And by ordering them according to diminishing satisfaction, i.e. increasing price, the "Expert" creating the system exploits Prolog's built-in top-down search for corresponding clauses in the knowledge base, to implement the information system's *strategy*. The first "successful" mta transport alternative is automatically the "best".

We emphasize this perhaps seemingly trivial aspect quite strongly, because many Prolog purists claim that the order of the clauses (as well as that of the *terms* in a clause) in the knowledge base has no, or at least should have no effect on the semantics of a Prolog program. This is based on the assumption that a "logic-oriented" programming language should enable one to define problems or tasks "in logic", or in the case of Prolog, as a set of logical predicates (*Horn clauses*, e.g. see [KOWA79]), and that drawing conclusions from the logically defined circumstances should be independent of the order in which the definition has been written.

The purist would argue that the *sequential* processing of the clauses in the knowledge base and the implications it has for the hypothesis testing, i.e. the knowledge processing strategy, is an implementation decision, which could just as well be made differently[1]. Nonetheless, we have just seen that the "sequentialization" indeed can be critical and thus consider it a fundamental characteristic of Prolog.

In our sense, therefore, Prolog is *not* a special implementation of a particular form of logic, but rather a practical tool for knowledge-oriented programming, a *rule interpreter*, an *inference engine*. It embodies not only the inference mechanism for each individual rule, *resolution*, but also an implicit rule selection strategy, i.e. the sequential, top-down search. This is quite acceptable for two reasons: it is a widespread approach in processes of many kinds and it is one whose implications are readily grasped by non-specialists: the more improbable or unacceptable a hypothesis is, the "further down" it should appear in the knowledge base.

The implicit top-down strategy in Prolog is also particularly advantageous for developing *adaptive programs*, which we shall be discussing later. In one particular form the behavior of the system is modified by changing the weight of the respective hypotheses according to statistical analysis of the acceptability of previous solutions or similar "experiences". Shifting the weights can be simply represented by reordering the clauses within the knowledge base. Thus, we shall assume the order of information in the knowledge base to be a fundamental semantic aspect of a program.

3.5   Gathering Case Data

The hypotheses implied by the *mta* predicates in Fig. 3-2, for example *is_a_Kiddie_Ticket_possible*, use certain *state information*, as illustrated in Fig. 3-1, to determine the applicability of a given hypothesis. Such information is formulated as binary *status* facts:

---

[1] Prolog implementations for *concurrent* processing of clauses, e.g. on several, parallel processors, do in fact operate independently of the ordering of clauses in the knowledge base.

```
is_a_Kiddie_Ticket_possible :-
       status(cash,Money),
       Money >= 5,
       status(age,child).
```

This assumes that such status information already exists in the knowledge base, which in general is not to be expected, insofar as this information depends on the current enquirer.

It is the job of a *data collection* module to gather the missing state information from the user interactively and store it in a "dynamic" section of the knowledge base. This means the system must recognize when specific information is missing. The *initialization* of the system lays the foundation by priming the knowledge base with the fact

```
status(_,unknown),
```

indicating that all possible states are currently *unknown*. Should the user reinitialize the system with *restart*, then this fact is restored, after all previously collected case data has been deleted from the active knowledge base using

```
abolish(status,2).
```

If a necessary status information cannot be found, the user must be queried, the response collected, checked and then registered in the knowledge base. The simplest implementation integrates these actions into the rules. Figure 3-3 illustrates such a technique, based on the hypothesis that a Kiddie Ticket is possible.

The order of the clauses in Fig. 3-3 yields an implicit control flow structure, whereby each successive clause increasingly constrains the solution according to the available state information for *cash*, *age* and *distance*. Preceding each clause which presumes the existence of a particular status information we have placed one which, should it as yet be unknown, requests this information from the user via the the predicate *ask*. After *ask* has checked the response for plausibility, *asserta* registers the information passed to it through the variables *F1*, *F2* or *F3*. Since *asserta* stores the new facts *above*, i.e. before all existing clauses in the knowledge base, we can be sure that it precedes and therefore *supercedes* any earlier facts, particularly the original

```
status(_,unknown).
```

As can be seen in Fig. 3-3, the clauses which perform the data collection always terminate with a *fail*. This causes control to flow automatically to the subsequent clause, where the facts just gathered are further evaluated. Figure 3-4 illustrates graphically this interaction between the rule base and the *fact base*, i.e. between the gathering and the analysis of the status information.

```
is_a_Kiddie_Ticket_possible :-
        status(cash,unknown),
        ask(cash,F1),
        asserta(status(cash,F1)),
        fail.

is_a_Kiddie_Ticket_possible :-
        status(cash,Money),
        Money >= 5,
        status(age,unknown)
        ask(age,F2),
        asserta(status(age,F2)),
        fail.

is_a_Kiddie_Ticket_possible :-
        status(cash,Money),
        Money >= 5,
        status(age,child).

is_a_Kiddie_Ticket_possible :-
        status(cash,Money),
        Money >= 5,
        status(distance,unknown),
        ask(distance,F3),
        asserta(status(distance,F3)),
        fail.

is_a_Kiddie_Ticket_possible :-
        status(cash,Money),
        Money >= 5,
        status(distance,near).
```

Fig.3-3. The rules for the possibility of using a Kiddie Ticket with case data collection

The rule and fact bases comprise the system knowledge base. This example is typical insofar as the rule base exists from the very start and remains unchanged, representing the primary body of "expert knowledge" stored in the system. The fact base, in contrast, starts with some initial information which is then subject to change based on information generated by the rule interpreter during its search for acceptable solutions.

You may have noticed, while examining the rules in Fig. 3-3, that the status values finally added to the fact base by *asserta* were not necessarily identical to the answers given by the user. The relevant *status* terms in the rules, such as

Processing the rule base

```
kiddie_ticket: -                          unknown
    status (cash, unknown),
    ask (cash, F1),                       F1 = 20
    asserta (status (cash, F1) ),
    fail.


kiddie_ticket: -                      Money = 20
    status (cash, Money),
    Money>=5,                             unknown
    status (age, unknown),
    ask (age, F2),                       F2 = child
    asserta (status (age, F2) )
    fail.


kiddie_ticket: -                     Money = 20
    status (cash, Money),
    Money >= 5,                           child
    status (age, child).       • • • •
```

Success: Kiddie_ticket is possible

Case data collection
```
                          • • • •
    status (age, child).
    status (cash, 20).
    status (-, unknown).ı
```

Fig. 3-4. Rule processing
with stepwise data collection
in the fact base

Building up the fact base

```
status(age,child)
```

or

```
status(distance,near)
```

clearly do *not* contain the numeric values input by the user, but rather the results of the analysis of her input, i.e. *child* or *adult, near* or *far.* In Fig. 3-5 you can see how such a check and analysis can be programmed. The system inquiry into the user's age is implemented accordingly.

The system inquiry about the distance to be travelled shows one way of dealing with answers like *do not know.* In this case we play it safe and assume a "great" distance.

The solutions shown in Figs. 3-3 and 3-5 are hardly complete, as they do not provide to the user any explanations as to why the system is proceeding as it is.

```
ask(distance,F3) :-
        write('How great is the distance ?'),
        read(Input),
        test_f3(Input,F3).

test_f3('not sure', far) :- !.

test_f3(Input,F3) :-
        numeric(Input),
        (       Input <= 5, F3 = near
        ;       F3 = far
        ).

test_f3(Input,F3) :-
        not numeric(Input),
        non_interpretable,
        ask(distance,F3).

non_interpretable :-
        nl,
        write('I cannot interpret your response.'),
        nl,
        write('Please re-enter your answer.'),
        nl.
```

Fig. 3-5. The distance inquiry with check and analysis

3.6   The Inference Tree and Protocolling

Before we deal with the implementation of the explanatory component, we should examine more closely just how the inference engine actually derives its solutions. After the system initializes itself and the user has entered

```
?- mta.
```

a dialog is conducted which can be represented as a three-level hierarchy. In Fig. 3-6 you will find a diagram of the *inference tree.*

Each hierarchical level represents a particular level of detail (constraint) with respect to the solution search and is associated with a different set of rules within the knowledge base.

Level 0 corresponds to the system initialization prior to assumption of a new dialog.

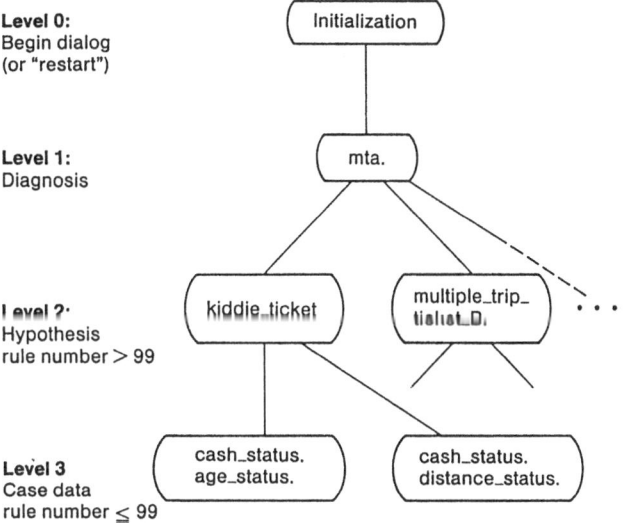

Level 0:
Begin dialog
(or "restart")

Initialization

Level 1:
Diagnosis

mta.

Level 2:
Hypothesis
rule number > 99

kiddie_ticket

multiple_trip_
ticket_D.

. . . .

Level 3
Case data
rule number ≤ 99

cash_status.
age_status.

cash_status.
distance_status.

Fig. 3-6. The inference tree

Level 1 the diagnosis of the user's problem is initiated by the rule *mta.*

Level 2 are the various *hypotheses* regarding possible ticket types which the system makes – as explained above – and then tests for applicability for the specific user.

Level 3 contains the actual facts, known to the system as "prior knowledge" or actively acquired as *case data* in dialog with the user.

The system should be able to easily recognize with which level a specific rule is associated. This is most conveniently achieved by numbering the rules according to some convention. In our case, we gave the rules from level 3 numbers less than 100 and those of level 2 numbers equal to or greater than 100.

The system makes a pre-order traversal of the inference tree, extending it as needed to accommodate data collected. The user's problem is solved as soon as the known or newly acquired facts in a level 3 node satisfy one of the hypotheses at level 2.

In order to reconstruct the path taken through the inference tree, for purposes of testing (tracing) the system and checking the plausibility of its dynamic logic, the MTA expert makes an *internal protocol* of the individual steps taken. This consists of a "trail" of facts recorded in the knowledge base, of the form *tree(Step,Rule)*. *Step* is the number of the respective action, beginning with "0" for the initialization, and *Rule* is the numeric ID of the rule applied at the given juncture. The latter implicitly indicates the level with which the rule is associated.

If we wish to see the "audit trail" of the last consultation we merely inquire *tree(Step,Rule)*, as mentioned earlier:

```
?- tree(Step,Rule).

Step = 0
Rule  = 0;

Step = 1
Rule  = 100;

Step = 2
Rule  = 1;

Step = 3
Rule  = 2;

Step = 4
Rule  = 4;

Step = 5
Rule  = 101;

Step = 6
Rule  = 7;

no
?-
```

The semicolon (";") input by the user in response to the system output causes, as you perhaps already know, the Prolog interpreter to present the next possible solution. In this particular case it proceeds to present the next *Step* and *Rule* recorded in the protocol *tree* until all have been exhausted and a *no* appears.

Using the knowledge base in Appendix A and the protocol above, you can trace the following path pursued by the inference engine during our sample dialog above:

```
restart :-
        abolish(status,2),
        assertz(status(_,unknown)),
        abolish(tree,2),
        assertz(tree(0,0)),                % <-- Rule 0
        set(step,0),
        set(level,0),
        set(increment,2).
```

```
mta :-
        enter_current_rule(100),              % <-- Rule 100
        is_a_Kiddie_Ticket_possible,
        recommend_childrens_ticket.

is_a_Kiddie_Ticket_possible :-
        status(cash,Money),
        Money == unknown,
        ask(cash,1),                          % <-- Rule 1
        fail.

is_a_Kiddie_Ticket_possible :-
        status(cash,Money),
        Money >= 5,
        status(age,Age),
        Age == unknown,
        ask(age,2),                           % <-- Rule 2
        fail.

is_a_Kiddie_Ticket_possible :-
        status(cash,Money),
        Money >= 5,
        status(distance,Distance),
        Distance == unknown,
        ask(distance,4),                      % <-- Rule 4
        fail.

mta :-
        enter_current_rule(101),              % <-- Rule 101
        is_a_Multi_Trip_Ticket_B_possible,
        recommend_multi_trip_ticket_B.

is_a_Multi_Trip_Ticket_B_possible :-
        status(cash,Money),
        Money >= 12,
        enter_current_rule(7).                % <-- Rule 7
```

Notice that the case data collection always records the second argument of the *ask* predicate as the rule number of the question asked.

```
ask(Status,Number) :-
        enter_current_rule(Number),
        set(level,3),
        ask(Status,Answer),
        asserta(status(Status,Answer),!).
```

set is a simple predicate for setting arbitrary state variables, i.e. facts.

```
set(State,Value) :-
        abolish(State,1),
        S =.. [State,Value],
        asserta(S).
```

Based on the protocol we can see that the attempt to suggest a Kiddie Ticket failed; the enquirer had enough money, but was too old and the distance too great for eligibility. Consequently, the inference engine returned to level 2 to try an alternative hypothesis, rule 101, a Type-B Multi-Trip Ticket. Since the prospective passenger had enough cash, as had already been ascertained via rule 1 and recorded as *status(cash,Money)* in the fact base, the hypothesis test (rule 7) at level 3 was immediately successful, without any further interaction being required.

Let us now take this example as a basis for studying the explanatory component.

3.7   Explanations

An essential characteristic of the *explanatory component* is a certain level of "intelligence". At the very least, when a user responds to an explanation by asking "why" another time, the system should "know" enough to not merely repeat its previous explanation, but rather offer an alternative response, perhaps more detailed, etc. This secondary explanation is in effect another level in our hierarchy of Fig. 3-6: the user wishes to know why the system has asked a particular question in another, "higher" or "meta"-context.

Just how such a multi-level, stepwise explanation might look is illustrated in the next dialog excerpt, based on the dialog which we just analyzed in the previous section.

```
?- mta.
How much money do you have ?    enough.
How old are you ?    'not sure'.
How great is the distance ?    why.

I know that you have more than 5 DM.
Consequently, if you are making a short trip
you can buy a Short Trip Ticket (Kiddie Ticket).
A short trip is less than 5 kilometers.
So, I would like to know how long the route is.

Now: How great is the distance ?    why.
```

Because a Kiddie Ticket is the cheapest.

Now: How great is the distance ?   **why.**

I want to find the least expensive ticket for your trip.

Now: How great is the distance ?   **why.**

How about fewer questions and more answers!

Nowı IIow groat io tho diɾtanœ ?   'whɴ knows'

You should buy a Type B Multi Trip Ticket for 12 DM.
And remember to cancel two fields!

yes
?-

The explanations in response to repeated "why" questions constitute a hierarchy, which, as Fig.3-7 indicates, corresponds precisely to the levels of the inference tree in Fig.3-6.

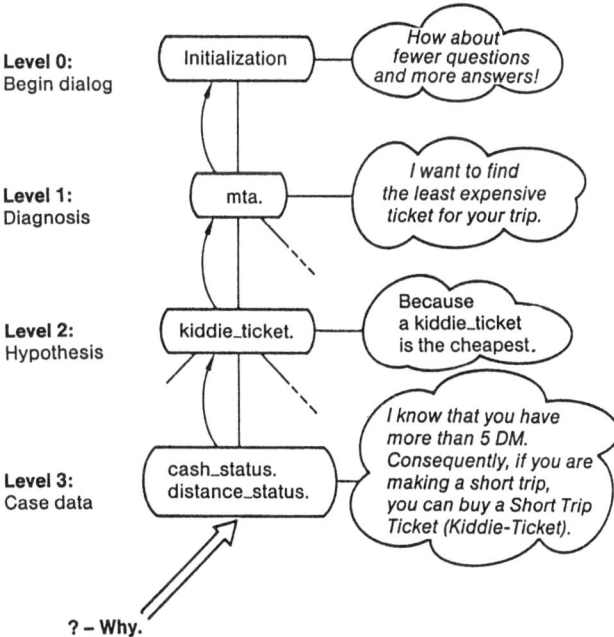

Fig.3-7. The explanation hierarchy of a diagnosis

The hierarchy of explanations always begins at level 3 because the user must be prompted for information before she initially asks "why" the data is being requested. Every subsequent repetition of "why" causes the explanation to refer to the next higher level – until "level 0" is reached, and no further sensible explanations are possible (since the system cannot know why the user turned to it for advice to begin with).

Consequently, the knowledge base must be supplemented by an explanation for every rule at every level, so that the explanatory component can respond accordingly. This is implemented in the form of clauses with a binary functor *explanation(Level,Rule)*. In our example they are defined as follows:

```
explanation(3,4) :-
    write('I know that you have more than 5 DM.'),
    nl,
    write('Consequently, '),
    write('if you are making a short trip'),
    nl,
    write('you can buy a Short Trip Ticket '),
    write('(Kiddie Ticket).'),
    nl,
    write('A short trip is less than 5 kilometers.'),
    nl,
    write('So, I would like to know how long '),
    write('the route is.'),
    and_so.

explanation(0,No) :-
    member(No,[1,2,4]),
    write('Because a Kiddie Ticket is the cheapest.'),
    and_so.

explanation(1,_) :-
    write('I want to find the least expensive '),
    write('ticket for your trip.'),
    and_so.

explanation(_,_) :-
    write('How about fewer questions '),
    write('and more answers!'),
    and_so.

and_so :-
    nl, nl,
    write('Now: ').
```

These clauses illustrate how variables, of the anonymous type as well as ones whose value is checked by *member* for validity, can be used to associate a common explanatory text with a variety of different rules. This can be extended to administer text excerpts which occur as part of many different explanations, thus reducing storage overhead and minimizing the initial typing effort. This latter was done in the case of *and_so*, which defines the text used to introduce the repeated inquiry after an explanation has been given.

The explanations themselves are displayed by the respective test predicate, which checks the user's response to inquiries made by the system, e.g.

```
ask(distance,F2) :-
        write('How great is the distance? '),
        read(Input),
        recognize(Input,Distance),
        test_f2(Distance,F2).

recognize(Input,why) :-
        member(Input,[why,'how come']),
        !.

test_f2(why,F2) :-
        !,
        write_explanation,
        enter_current_level,
        ask(distance,F2).
```

Two state variables, i.e. facts in the knowledge base, *step(Step)* and *level(Level)*, are evaluated with respect to the entries in the *tree* protocol to determine for which level and rule an explanation should be given:

```
write_explanation :-
        level(Level),
        step(Step),
        tree(Step,Rule),
        nl, nl,
        explanation(Level,Rule),
        !.
```

The *cut*, literally the "!" at the end of the rule intended to display the explanation, insures that only one explanation is made per level - otherwise the use of variables as explanation arguments in the database would cause problems.

After having given one explanation, the test predicate uses *enter_current_level* to decrement the state variable *level(Level)* and then calls itself (recursively). This causes repeated "why's" to successively invoke the next "higher" explanation.

Another problem arises in the design of the explanatory component and the implementation of the predicate *enter_current_level* to steer it through the respective hierarchical levels. The order, if not the content of the explanations to be presented in the event of repeated "why's" will typically depend on the initial query made by the user! Thus, the explanatory hierarchy in Fig. 3-7 is reasonable only if the user had requested a *diagnosis*, i.e. a dialog at the level 1 by entering

    ?- mta.

It is conceivable, however, that she merely wished to know if she could get by with a Kiddie Ticket and thus started off immediately at level 2 with the direct query

    ?- is_a_Kiddie_Ticket_possible.

In this case, the level 2 explanation

"Because a Kiddie Ticket is the cheapest."
makes little sense. Since the enquirer presumably knows why she asked the question in the first place, we would like the explanatory component to skip level 2 of the hierarchy in Fig. 3-7.

In our – admittedly not very high-powered – system we chose a rather simple solution to this problem: the rule responsible for decrementing the current level of explanation does so in units determined by a state variable *increment(Increment)*:

```
enter_current_level :-
        retract(level(Old)),
        increment(Increment),
        New is Old - Increment,
        assertz(level(New)).
```

The step unit derived through *increment* is initialized with each *restart* to the value "2" by

    set(increment,2)

The modification into a single stepping *increment*, like the one in Fig. 3-7, is made at the time when a hypothesis with a rule number greater than 99 gets added to the *tree* protocol:

```
enter_current_rule(Rule_Number) :-
        retract(step(State)),
        New is State + 1,
        assertz(step(New)),
        (       Rule_Number › 99,
                set(increment,1)
        ;       true
        ).
```

And, of course, that can only occur if the user starts the dialog at level 1 and not
level 2.

3.8   Equivalent Answers

An expert system should not only be able to give "intelligent" explanations; it
should also be capable of "interpreting" user responses to questions, such that
the user is not forced to give one and only one "acceptable" standard answer.

```
ask(distance, F3) :-
        write('How great is the distance ?'),
        nl,
        read(Input),
        (       recognize(Input,near),
                F3 = near
        ;       recognize(Input,far),
                F3 = far
        ;       recognize(Input,'not sure'),
                F3 = far
        ).

recognize(Input, near) :-
        member(Input,
                [near,'not very',short,'not far']),
        !.

recognize(Input, far) :-
        member(Input,
                [far,long,very,great,enormous,huge]),
        !.

recognize(Input, 'not sure') :-
        member(Input,
                ['not sure','no idea', perhaps]),
        !.
```

Fig. 3-8. Examples of synonym detection in user input

Natural language processing, even with a rather limited vocabulary, although desirable for such purposes, is too complex for this lab. Some simple *synonym detection*, however, is relatively easily implemented and provides an acceptable amount of flexibility. Figure 3-8 shows perhaps the simplest method for implementing this.

All the expressions or phrases considered to be equivalent – as for example in Fig. 3-8, those for the length of a route – are gathered into a list. The binary predicate *recognize* must then determine if the user's *input* is identical to one of the members of the *synonym list*. Should this be true, the user's input is considered to be equivalent to *recognize*'s second argument.

One particularly attractive aspect of this approach is that new synonyms are created by merely adding the particular phrase to the corresponding list.

3.9   Weaknesses and Possible Improvements

Our simple transportation information system has a number of weaknesses of debatable gravity. Let us summarize some of them. It would be a very worthwhile exercise to take the complete program code, to be found in Appendix A, and experiment with possible changes to make the necessary improvements.

- For simplicity's sake, the user interface was implemented directly upon the *interactive Prolog interface*. The "?-" prompt and the "yes" and "no" responses from the system, in the above examples, all are part of the standard Prolog "command interpreter". The "yes" response is often quite irritating, if not confusing, as it frequently appears after the user has already seen the specifically requested information. In a proto-type system we may be willing to live with this, but a professional product should shield the user from such superfluous interaction.
- It is absurd to demand that a user make a query such as

```
?- is_a_Multi_Trip_Ticket_B_possible.
```

A minimal improvement would be to request the enquirer to place her query in single quotes and thereby eliminate the need for the underline connectors:

```
?- 'is a Multi Trip Ticket B possible'.
```

Such a "phrase" is a legal *atom* in Prolog and can thus serve as a rule header as well. An even greater improvement would be to read the user query character for character into a list and then convert the list into an atom using the standard *name* predicate. In the same vein, one could exploit the syntax notation available in Prolog (see [CLOC81, SCHN87]) to make an infinitely higher performance (and infinitely more resource intensive) input analysis.

- A similar problem exists with the user responses which are not legal Prolog atoms. This applies to any responses beginning with uppercase letters, e.g. proper names, as well as answers consisting of more than one word, like "*who knows*". A normal user will hardly see the logic of having to place such "phrases" in single quotation marks, as we did. Clearly input predicates more sophisticated than the Prolog predicates *get* and *get0* are called for.
- The association of explanations with rules via simple, non-mnemonic ("magic") level and rule numbers is problematic enough, when you are programming the knowledge base for the first time. The maintenance of such a knowledge base, however, quickly becomes a nightmare, particularly as new rules, or worse yet, new levels get added. Consequently, it is preferable to integrate the explanatory component into the respective rule, i.e. to have *implicit* explanations rather than *explicit* ones, as in our example. How one might do that will be a topic in our next example.

These are some major shortcomings and you have probably already found some room for improvement elsewhere. We recommend that you now seriously consider how to go about implementing some of these changes.

4 The Representation and Processing of Knowledge

The Ticket Information System illustrated a number of different components and functions of an expert system: the knowledge base, containing the existing knowledge in a declarative form, the goal-oriented processing and case-oriented supplementing of this knowledge according to the control structure described and finally the explanatory element, which explicated responses and queries on the part of the system on demand, based on an internal, running protocol of the dialog being conducted. We are certain that this little system has left the reader with any number of questions. For instance, as to the *system architecture*: Where or how are the various data structures and functions localized, and how do they interact with one another? Or with respect to the representation and processing of the knowledge built into the system: Are there theoretical or practical "laws" or circumstances dictating the form of *knowledge representation* or the strategy for *knowledge processing* selected, or could one have just as well realized these quite differently. And finally, perhaps a question of technique: Does one design and implement an expert system in the same manner as traditional software or are other methods involved? This chapter will be dealing with these and related questions, laying the foundation for more complex sample systems to come.

4.1 System Architecture

What is the most significant difference between traditional and knowledge-oriented programming?

Conventional programs
> represent essential aspects of the knowledge embodied in them in the control structures used, i.e. the programmer defines the procedure(s), in an algorithmic language, whose behavior parallels that one would expect of a person with a given expertise. This requires a very in-depth, fairly complete, detailed knowledge –perhaps acquired through lengthy and repeated discussions with the authorities on the subject, or a *specification*, an unambiguous document defining all the properties of the task(s) involved and the solutions expected.

Expert systems,

on the other hand, separate the control structure from the knowledge to be processed. The specific expert knowledge is entered into the knowledge base in declarative form. The programmer building the expert system need only know how the knowledge is represented in order to formulate the generalized control structures for its processing. If the structure of representation and the manipulations to be made are sufficiently similar for different areas of expertise, then one can use the same control structures for different knowledge bases. That is the underlying principle of expert system *shells*, which are intended to be "filled" with the particular knowledge to be processed.

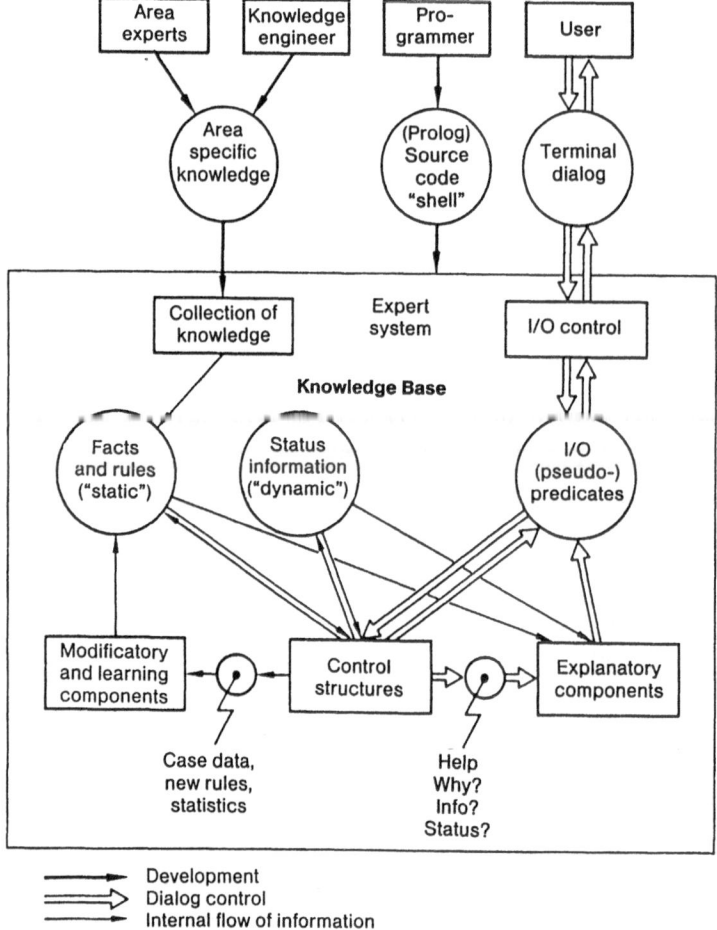

Fig. 4-1. System architecture of an expert system

This characteristic partitioning into declarative knowledge and procedural control structure, with the possibility of dividing the implementation task accordingly among competent persons or teams, was ignored in our simple MTA Fare Information System. Let us now consider this aspect in the context of our discussion of the system architecture of typical expert systems.

Figure 4-1 illustrates this architecture as a network of instances and channels (see for example [REIS85]). This is an unusual representation, insofar as it attempts to incorporate the developers and the users of an expert system as "instances" and their system interfaces as "channels".

To begin with we have the *end user*. She consults the functioning expert system by, as a rule, conducting a dialog at the terminal; we saw examples of this in the previous chapter. In contrast to conventional systems, however, we also have a second class of users, namely those persons responsible for implementing and maintaining the knowledge base: the *area experts* and/or the *knowledge engineers*. The final, relevant group consists of the *programmers*, who implement the actual system in the form of Prolog source code or as a shell. In smaller systems, of course, the functions of knowledge engineer and programmer often reside in a single person.

The structure of the source code and the basic concepts and techniques necessary for planning and implementing such programs are the topic of this chapter. We shall base our discussion on the architectural model presented in Fig. 4-1.

4.2 System Development

Knowledge-based programming is a relatively new branch of software engineering. The basic tenets of conventional software engineering remain valid with respect to developing high quality, robust programs. The primary difference in the development cycle derives from the fact that Prolog is (also) an excellent *specification language* [SCHN83a]. Consequently, when programming in Prolog, the most productive approach is the *evolutionary prototyping* method (see, e.g. [FLOY81]). The traditional *phase model* is not particularly suitable, as the strict separation of the specification and coding phases places artificial restraints on the typical Prolog programming techniques.

This is not to say that design or modularization considerations are any less important. To the contrary.

As *P.H. Winston* recommends in one of his many very good books [WINS84], the following methodological steps should always be observed when developing *artificially intelligent* software:

(1) identify the problem,

(2) select or develop a suitable representation,

(3) attempt to find "natural" constraints, laws and heuristics related to dealing with, i.e. solving, the problem,

(4) *and then* formulate procedures.

(5) Verify and validate your solution.

These principles do not, in essence, deviate from the rules of traditional software engineering. They are, however, not only formulated in the conceptual terms of artificial intelligence, but also demand a new approach to the development process.

Identifying the problem, for example, does not mean analyzing the data and the functional structure of the application. This emerges out of the knowledge entered into the knowledge base as it is being built. The implication here is more that of determining the type of expert system to be produced.

A good place to start is with the taxonomy we discussed in Section 2.8. It can, as we saw, help us develop a design framework taking into account the probable user community, the dialog structure, the type and structure of the knowledge bases to be built, sensible strategies for the inference engine, explanatory support and similar issues. At the same time one can begin to consider aspects of system integration, such as: Will the facts to be processed have to be fetched from external databanks at run-time, or are there existing software packages which are going to form part of the overall system (in what form?), performing specific services?

Finding a "suitable representation" implies establishing the underlying structure of the knowledge base. Can it simply be an (ordered) set of logical clauses, as in our MTA system? Or does one need more complex structures, such as *frames*, defining *objects* or *object types* among which, perhaps, dependencies exist, building *inheritance hierarchies*?

We shall be presenting examples implementing such complex representations in Prolog. This is, contrary to certain "myths" in the profession, easier than in most conventional programming languages. One must merely design the representational structures, and typically a few simple predicates for accessing and administering them, *prior* to beginning the coding process.

The *constraints* play a very significant role in knowledge-oriented programming, as these are ultimately the relationships and rules which reduce the number of possible solutions to be tested, limiting the *complexity* of the problem overall.

An exhaustive search of all possible solutions for a best fit leads, in "real world" situations such as for example all the possible games of chess, to explosive demands on computing resources, with drastic increase in response times. (See [SCHN85] for a simple explanation of this phenomenon of *combinatoric* or *exponential explosion*, or a textbook on *complexity theory* for a more detailed, mathematical discussion.)

To improve performance, expert systems typically employ two techniques for reducing the potential complexity, and for converting essential knowledge about the problem and its solution into an optimizing factor in the search strategies:

constraints,

> by applying known, *certain* prior knowledge, e.g. mathematical, physical or judicial laws, as well as

heuristics,

> by applying "rules of thumb" or more formally, *uncertain* information, e.g. experience, "common sense" and the like.

This knowledge is sometimes referred to as *metaknowledge,* i.e. "knowledge *about* knowledge and knowledge processing". This is sometimes not present as such in the knowledge base, but rather implicit in some structural form (for example, in the order in which the rules occur)!

Indeed, such metaknowledge is usually incorporated in the inference mechanisms driving the program. In Prolog this implies a special set of clauses, which define and implement the inference engine and its processing strategy. This metaknowledge should be maintained as a module independent of the knowledge base for the application and must be specified, if not implemented, *before* one begins to enter the expert knowledge into the knowledge base.

4.3   Modularization

Modularization is one of the most important techniques for structuring programs. It involves organizing source code into a number of individual, independent components, or *modules,* which are administered and maintained in separate files. These components are then linked, at some time prior to program activation, into an *object* which can be run. Traditional environments provide *linker-loader* utilities to do precisely that. Software engineering theory is not unanimous on the issue of how one best decides to break code down into modules. There are informal "rules of thumb", such as "all code, which logically belongs together and dispatches a particular task", or Parnas' principle of *information hiding*[1], as well as more formal concepts, such as that of the *abstract data type.*

Rather than go into great methodological detail about these techniques, we suggest you refer to some standard works on the subject (e.g. [KIMM79, INCE84]). We prefer to briefly deal with the specific methods for modularizing Prolog programs. We leave it to the software developer to decide what criteria should be applied in organizing her clauses into modules. In any case, those used in conventional software engineering certainly are a good place to start.

One of the common (but unjustified) criticisms made of Prolog is that the language provides no means for modularizing programs. This is simply not true.

---

[1] A module should "keep secret" one or more implementation decisions, for example a data structure or an access method. It should strictly provide a set of syntactically and semantically well-defined and implementation-independent functions.

Even our simple, little MTA expert system was implemented in modules. This is achieved through the use of the *consult* predicate.

If you look at the main module *mta*, located in Appendix A, which contains the complete source code listing for the ticket information system, you will see the usual method employed for this purpose. The first module consists of two clauses, each beginning with the unary operator ":-". This operator causes these two clauses to be "run" immediately when this module is read, rather than having to enter them into the knowledge base.

The first clause consists of a series of *write* and *nl* predicates, the latter yielding carriage returns in the output stream. Together they present the introductory explanatory text. The second clause then proceeds to *consult* a series of files, whose names are presented in the list notation with which you may already be familiar.

```
:-
        [
        controlling,
        dialog,
        explanation,
        aux_programs,
        rule_base
        ].
```

These files are the modules into which we have organized the remaining source code. The reading of the files effectively "links" the corresponding code into the program at run-time.

By dispensing with the separate, explicit linkage process the programmer enjoys the advantage of being able to *develop programs interactively*, i.e. testing and correcting the code as it is being written.

Direct, dialog-oriented programming merely requires that we write a simple Prolog predicate, which calls some arbitrary editor, e.g. in our Unix environment *vi*, with the name of the given file as its argument, and then *reconsults* the newly edited file. Figure 4-2 illustrates just such a predicate [SCHN87]. You can, of course, adapt the predicate by replacing "vi" with the available editor of your choice.

```
:- op(70,fx,vi).

vi ModuleName :-
        name(ModuleName,FileName),
        append("vi ",FileName,CString),
        name(Command,CString),
        sh(Command),
        reconsult(ModuleName).
```

Fig. 4-2. A Prolog predicate for calling the *vi* editor interactively

If you store this predicate in a file of its own, let us say *editor*, then all you have to do is load it, along with your application, when starting your test run. A good system allows you to do this via an option when invoking Prolog[2].

```
$ ifprolog -c editor -c mta
```

Whenever you see the Prolog system prompt, you can then invoke the editor to manipulate a module of your choice, for instance

```
?- vi rule_base.
```

Prolog starts the editor *vi* for the file *rule_base*, enabling you to modify its contents. As soon as you have left the editor, the *reconsult* terminating the predicate *vi* in Fig. 4-2 causes the new version of the module to be loaded, replacing the one previously in the knowledge base.

This style of programming, however, requires observing the following convention: All clauses with the same functor (and arity) must be placed in *a single* module and should not be scattered across several files, since otherwise the reconsultation will remove the ones read in from the unmodified files as well. This convention is a matter of "good Prolog programming style" anyway, and should be followed strictly, if only to promote the readability and easy maintenance of your programs.

Critics sometimes claim that this is not "genuine modularity", because "real" modularity limits the *visibility* or *scope of names* to a module, something which the *consult* predicates do not enforce[3]. This criticism is absolutely correct; however, the problem of scope is insignificant in Prolog. Not only are the programs generally more compact – usually containing a fifth of the total code compared with a like system written in a conventional programming language – but the number of "visible" names is altogether far smaller, because there are *no global variables* in Prolog! This reduces potential name conflicts to functors of equal arity.

In practice this occurs only rarely . And should you wish to avoid this, an excellent exercise is to write a short utility program which goes through each module and checks whether clauses with identical functors are defined in more than one file. This is a useful tool for insuring that the convention for localizing clauses has been observed.

---

[2] In a Unix or Unix-like environment you would probably prefer to automate the entire process by "hiding" the invocation of Prolog, including the options, in a script or batch file, e.g. *testprolog*.
[3] Compiling, in contrast to interpretative Prolog systems typically provide the means for limiting the scope of names. The compiled equivalent of *consult*, *load*, allows names to be *exported*, i.e. they have a local scope by default.

4.4   Knowledge Structures and Deductive Mechanisms

The most important design decisions affecting the quality of the system being developed with respect to the user interface, overall efficiency and acceptability of the application have to do with

knowledge representation,
   i.e. its conceptualization, organization and structure, as well as the

inference mechanisms,
   i.e. the strategies and procedures employed to apply, analyze and update the knowledge in the system.

Although Winston's rules for the development of AI-software, as cited in Section 4.2, require the establishment of the representation of knowledge as the second step and the choice of procedures for analysis as the fourth - distinct from the third step of looking for laws and constraints for reducing complexity - practice has shown that these three aspects, particularly in an environment as suitable for *prototyping* as a good Prolog system, should certainly be considered in the order mentioned, but always in an iterative and overlapping manner[4]. The respective decisions involved are generally interdependent. Let us look at a simple example. In principle, it is an algorithmic structure; yet it illustrates quite clearly how choosing a suitable, "knowledge-oriented" representation can produce a more efficient solution.

In the early 13th century *Leonardo Fibonacci* formulated a mathematical model for the reproductive behavior of rabbits, known today as the Fibonacci series. The *n*-th *Fibonacci number* can be calculated recursively from its predecessor, using the formula

$$F(0) = 0$$
$$F(1) = 1$$
$$F(n) = F(n-1) + F(n-2).$$

This allows one to implement the algorithm in a few lines of code, if the programming language permits recursion. Figure 4-3 shows a solution in Prolog together with a small procedure for timing the generation of a particular Fibonacci number.

---

[4] A *shell* typically provides one or two "prefabricated" knowledge representation structures which are supported by a suitable, built-in processing mechanism. This can save much effort, if the problem to be solved and the "prefab" solutions "fit" one another. Otherwise it can cause more problems than it solves.

```
fibonacci(0,0) :- !.
fibonacci(1,1) :- !.
fibonacci(N,F) :-
        N1 is N-1,
        N2 is N-2,
        fibonacci(N1,F1),
        fibonacci(N2,F2),
        F is F1 + F2,
        !.

time(N,F,T) :-                  /* Time in seconds */
        X is time,
        fibonacci(N,F),
        Y is time,
        T is Y - X.
```

Fig. 4-3. Recursive calculation of Fibonacci numbers

A test run on a Hewlett-Packard 9000 Model 500 – hardly a slow computer – yielded:

```
?- time(20,F,T).

F = 6765
T = 43
```

The (interpretative) Prolog system, then, took 43 seconds for the calculation! The reason for this is the quite simple, but impractical representation of the calculation as a doubly recursive rule, which, as one readily observes, calculates every Fibonacci number smaller than the one being sought anew – recursively – for each successive approximation. Furthermore, the demand on memory is considerable: the 21st Fibonacci number causes a stack overflow!

Since the rule shown in Fig. 4-3 is not an end recursion, the Prolog interpreter cannot automatically transform it into an iterative operation, which would dramatically improve performance. Thus, it becomes the responsibility of the programmer to optimize the program. In this case, representing the knowledge of Fibonacci numbers (already encountered) into an *automatically maintained, tabular* form radically reduces the inefficiency. Now each successive Fibonacci number need be calculated only once, later use involving mere "look-up" activity.

Figure 4-4 illustrates the improved version.

There is hardly another language which permits a comparably simple implementation; this derives from the fact that a Prolog knowledge base representing a given procedure, may contain facts and rules in arbitrary combination. In this

```
fibonacci(0,0) :- !.
fibonacci(1,1) :- !.
fibonacci(N,F) :-
        N1 is N-1,
        N2 is N-2,
        fibonacci(N1,F1),
        fibonacci(N2,F2),
        F is F1 + F2,
        asserta(fibonacci(N,F),!),
        !.
```

Fig.4-4. Calculating Fibonacci numbers using a table as knowledge base

specific case, the rule for calculation serves only as a "last resort", i.e. *default*, for deriving those *n*-values for which the corresponding Fibonacci numbers are not (yet) present in the table.

The difference between the two versions was such that the time for calculating *fibonacci(20,F)* with the new "method" fell to an immeasurable "less than a second". Indeed, even *a thousand* calls (whereby, of course, only the initial value required a true calculation, all others being found in the table) required no more than 1 second. And $n = 40$ no longer caused a stack overflow:

```
?- time(40,F,T).

F = 102334155
T = 0
```

Naturally, not every simple change to the knowledge representation will help you improve the efficiency of your programs by a factor of one thousand, but small modifications, especially in interactive systems, are often enough to make a package which was problematic on a big machine runnable on a PC.

The most important forms of knowledge representation and related inference mechanisms are the following:

Rules

were demonstrated in our simple MTA example. These are often referred to as *productions*, since they take "existing" knowledge (the *goals* in the rule body) to derive "new" knowledge, i.e. the statement validated by the resolution of these goals and the attendant unification of the variables involved. In the MTA example, for instance, we encountered the production "must_one_ride_without_paying". Rules are evaluated by an *inference mechanism*. There are two principal implementations of this mechanism, one using *forward chaining* and the other employing *backward chaining*. We shall be discussing these methods in greater detail below.

Frames

are more complex information structures, defining instances of an *object* or an *object type*. Frames often define individual instances of an object by invoking relationships to higher order object types. A "Prolog" frame, for example, may reference the frame "programming language", containing all characteristics which Prolog has in common with other programming languages (perhaps to be used for implementing an interpreter or compiler on some machine). These references constitute an essential aspect of the knowledge representation, as they build a logical *hierarchy* of concepts. The process of determining characteristics and capabilities of a specific object which are not directly documented in the object's own frame, is known as *inheritance*. It is an example of an inference mechanism dependent on a particular representation of knowledge. The procedures implementing the mechanism can be stored as rules in the respective frames. The "object-oriented" language *Smalltalk* calls such procedures *methods*. Lisp and Prolog programmers, taking a more "knowledge-oriented" view, tend to refer to these as *procedural attachments*. Aside from the differences in their practical implementation, however, the two concepts are fundamentally identical.

Semantic networks

are also complex structures built from frame-like data aggregates. The relationships between them, however, are not necessarily organized in a strict, tree-structured hierarchy and do not always have the same meaning (such as "X is a kind of Y"). Consequently, inheritance is not always meaningful, particularly as a linkage mechanism from the current object (type) to its respective "father frame". Hence, other mechanisms are used to guide the knowledge processing in such networks. One frequently employed method involves so-called *marker propagation*. Examples of this method and the corresponding techniques for implementing such systems can be found in literature about *Petri Nets* (e.g. see [REIS85]).

We prefer to focus our attention initially on rules and production systems because of their usefulness in implementing simpler expert systems. The implementation of frames will be dealt with specifically in Chapter 7.

4.5 Production Systems

Rules, as already mentioned, are often referred to as productions. Likewise, systems using this basic representation are called *production systems*.

Without regard to any special syntax, production rules are of the form

if *circumstance* → then *conclusion,*
if *constraint* → then *result*
  or
if *situation* → then *action.*

Examples of these various rule types are

if *age under 15* → then *status is child,*
if *liquidity is good* → then *exploit discount*
or

if *over 70 degrees F* → then *turn off heater.*

Thus, the same syntactic form can be interpreted as either a logical conclusion or an event-triggered action, depending on the semantic framework, i.e. the implementation of the elements *circumstance, conclusion, constraint, situation, result* and *action.* This is vital for the general applicability of production systems (and to Prolog as an implementation thereof) as a means of defining knowledge bases and building expert systems.

Not only can we describe the data and the applicable logical rules of inference with this method (as we have already seen in our ticket information system and shall see in examples in coming chapters), but we can also formulate any arbitrary calculation and describe any arbitrary processing strategies to be carried out by the Prolog interpreter with it.

Although the Prolog purists do not like to hear it and the detractors hate to admit it, this means we can use one and the same implementation of the language to do *procedural* as well as *logic* programming, indeed in a very compact and productive fashion.

This is the reason why not just the knowledge base, but all the components in the architectural model shown in Fig. 4-1 can be realized in Prolog. Thus, both the *programmer and* the *knowledge engineer* of an expert system can employ the same language!

We emphasize this because it is sometimes thought that since some production systems, e.g. *shells,* are often embedded in other language environments (such as Lisp) for the purpose of producing knowledge-based software, these are not viable independently of the supporting environment. Consequently, many people conclude that, although one can make a specification and perhaps even build a prototype of an inference engine in Prolog, the language is not practical for efficiently implementing a complete application or system[5]. One of this book's major objectives is to demonstrate that this is not the case and to show you not only how to program the various different representations of knowledge and inference mechanisms, but all the other components of a dialog system as well, be they "knowledge-based" or otherwise.

4.6   The Direction of Chaining

If the knowledge is represented as (logical) rules, as in our example for defect diagnosis for automobiles in Fig. 2-2, then there are two alternative methods of processing.

---

[5] If you ever wish proof of this: One of the functionally most powerful and fastest Prolog systems in the world is written almost entirely in Prolog itself!

Backward chaining,

or the so-called *top-down strategy*, proceeds from the rule head, i.e. the supposed *conclusion* or the expected *result*. The object then is limited to attempting to "prove" the conjecture by subsequently demonstrating ("proving") that *circumstances* or *constraints* in the rule body, the so-called goals, themselves hold. The recursion ends (we hope) when all goals have either been reduced to facts or any subordinate goal proves inconsistent with knowledge present in the knowledge base.

In contrast,

forward chaining,

or the so-called *bottom-up strategy*, attempts to derive new facts from existing ones in the knowledge base with the help of existing rules. Since this obviously must not occur indiscriminately, it is vital that a forward-chaining system be equipped with heuristics, constraints and similar *metaknowledge* to help keep the set of potentially relevant facts and rules manageably small. This is commonly referred to as the *set of support* of the inference mechanism. Occasionally it is referred to as the *conflict set* (for an example see [PUPP86]), implying that the problem which the inference engine must solve according to some strategy is precisely which of the rules contained in the conflict set is to be applied first and which are to be deferred.

Our ticket information system, if you recall, began with *hypotheses*, which it sought to either confirm or reject. This is typical for a *diagnostic system*. Medical systems of this sort proceed correspondingly from hypotheses about the patient's illness, an automobile repair system from hypotheses about the cause of a breakdown. Thus, such systems usually work *top down*, i.e. using backward chaining.

The advantage of this is that the query strategy driving the dialog corresponds to the typical user's way of thinking and thus seems "logical" to her. She tends to understand the "system's way of thinking" and is more likely to accept it, in sharp contrast to the oft seemingly confusing and incoherent line of questioning emerging from a forward-chained dialog, where the system, based on some arbitrary facts, tries to see if the questions might converge to the actual problem at hand.

The Prolog interpreter, as already mentioned, directly supports backward chaining. This permitted its immediate use as the inference engine in our MTA system, leaving us with the simple task of putting the individual clauses "in the right order". A forward chained solution would not be quite so simple. In addition, the procedures necessary for implementing a bottom-up inference engine fill no more than a standard alphanumeric screen.

Essentially, the clauses constituting the support set are placed in a *goal stack* or *goal queue* (see [SCHN87] for a simple example). The inference engine fetches and processes them one after the other using the *retract* predicate. The processing of one goal might lead to a consequently more interesting clause being "pushed" onto the stack or inserted into the queue. Various standard Prolog predicates, such as *asserta, assertz* and *asserto*, permit the realization of any number of processing strategies with a minimum of effort.

Here too, we encounter the strong relationship between knowledge representation and the inference strategy used. If we implement forward chaining in Prolog via such a goal stack, then just as the direction of processing changes so must the notational structure of the rules. The *head* contains the *constraint* (according to which the appropriate rule is selected) and the rule body (representing the action to be taken) indicates the conclusion(s) to be drawn. The rule

> if *Father diabetes_prone*
>
> → then *Patient diabetes_prone,*

would be formulated in Prolog, in the context of "normal" backward chaining, as the clause ·

```
diabetes_prone(Patient) :-
        diabetes_prone(father(Patient)).
```

Forward chaining, however, would be implemented such that a known fact

```
Fact = diabetes_prone(father(otto))
```

would be selected to be included in the support set and added to the goal stack via

```
   . . . .
clause(Fact,Conclusion),
asserta(goal(Fact :- Conclusion)),
   . . . .
```

This requires that the goal clause to be added be of the form

```
diabetes_prone(father(Patient)) :-
        asserta(diabetes_prone(Patient)).
```

The activation of the rule once it has been *fetched* from the goal stack by

```
   . . . .
retract(goal(Rule)),
Rule,
   . . . .
```

causes the *asserta* in the rule to write the "forwardly" derived conclusion diabetes_prone(otto).

to be added to the knowledge base as a *new* fact from which, naturally, other conclusions may then be drawn.

4.7 Inference Trees

There are many different possible representations for the hierarchy of levels of inference through which the *inference engine* moves, either *top down* or *bottom up*, depending on its basic processing strategy. Trees are a popular representation for such hierarchies. Figure 3-6, in the previous chapter, showed an *inference tree* for our MTA expert system. *Derivation tree* or *computational tree* are different names for essentially the same phenomenon.

If you examine the figure again, you will notice that we have constructed a pure *or tree*: each edge leaving a given node stands for an *alternative*. It may be of historical interest that this way of representing the logical derivation of a result from facts and rules, as well as the deduction of some result by building an *or tree* in preorder, is probably one of the oldest, non-numeric algorithms in the world. This method was already being taught in the schools of ancient Rome under the name of *arbor porphyriana*, or the "tree of Porphyrius".

Nowadays, however, we tend to use *and-or trees* rather than the *arbor porphyriana*. In *and-or trees* the edges leading from a given node to the next level down imply either *conjunction* or *disjunction*. We avoided the *and* connections, in our example, by merely *not* splitting the nodes at level 3.

In Fig. 4-5 we have an example of an *and-or tree*. Such trees are especially useful for representing a Prolog knowledge base, because they can be directly modeled in the syntax of facts and rules.

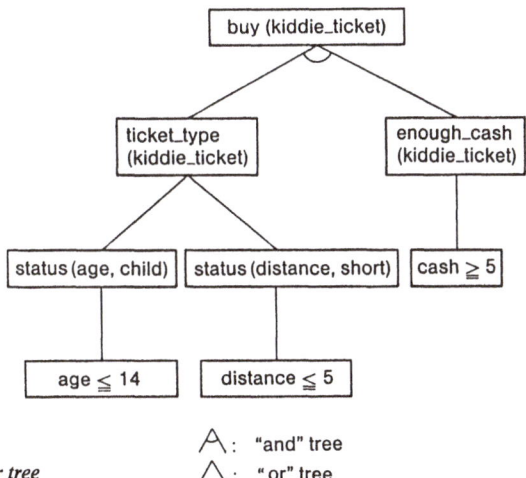

Fig. 4-5. An example of an *and-or tree*

$\bigwedge$: "and" tree

$\bigwedge$: " or" tree

- *Alternatives* (*or nodes*) represent different *clauses* for the same predicate[6].
- *Conjunctions* (*and nodes*) can be interpreted as *goals* of a *rule*.
- *Leaves* of a tree are either *facts* already in the knowledge base or *case data*.

A graphical representation of an inference tree provides the easiest means for understanding a problem which can occur during the process of resolution. The substitution of a goal in a rule by the rule body of another goal, whose rule head is unifiable with the original goal, can easily lead to a recursive loop. A simple example is the rule

```
diabetes_prone(Patient) :-
        diabetes_prone(father(Patient)).
```

The query

```
?- diabetes_prone(otto).
```

causes the endless loop

```
diabetes_prone(otto)
-> diabetes_prone(father(otto))
-> diabetes_prone(father(father(otto)))
->              . . . .
```

In a tree representation one recognizes the loop immediately: the edge leaving a node does not point to a lower level rule or fact, but rather leads back to the original rule node or indeed to a higher level node. If a system attempts to protect itself against such loops, this usually involves algorithms which rely on an internal protocol of the traversal activity with respect to the the inference tree maintained by the inference engine. An alternative method involves a more primitive, but more efficient *invocation count* to limit the depth of recursion.

Looking at the inference tree, one can also readily see that such a loop can occur only in backward chaining. If one employs a *bottom-up* strategy, starting, for example with the fact

```
diabetes_prone(father(father(otto)))
```

then no such problems arise:

```
diabetes_prone(father(father(otto)))
-> diabetes_prone(father(otto))
-> diabetes_prone(otto).
```

---

[6] *Or* can, naturally, also represent the connection of two clauses with the disjunctive operator, the semi-colon (;).

Thus the choice between different processing strategies can be a function of the structure of the respective knowledge base and not just the desired behavior of the user interface.

4.8 Rule Modification and Non-monotonic Logic

The knowledge base of an expert system is by no means static, as was illustrated in the architectural model in Fig. 4–1. On the contrary, it is updated quite frequently during a dialog with the user, be it to "adjust" flow of control or as a result of some activity on the part of the *modificatory or learning components*. The changes occur, primarily, in order to store *case data* entered or to register a particular *state*. One speaks here of *dynamic knowledge*, which accrues in the course of a particular consultation or session, and "temporarily" supplements the *static knowledge* that had been "permanently" built into the knowledge base by the area expert or the knowledge engineer.

In fact, however, the static part of the knowledge base is often not so unchanging. There may be good reason for modifying it during the processing of a user request. It can substantially increase efficiency, as we demonstrated in the example of calculating the Fibonacci numbers. There we wrote the derived results into the knowledge base and consequently changed the procedure being applied dynamically. Case data typically involves functors completely independent of the static rules.

Even the simplest form of *learning systems* usually involve some modification of the existing, static knowledge base. By recording the frequency with which different clauses of the same predicate were successfully applied, one can often improve the efficiency of the system by exploiting this "experience". This can be achieved by reorganizing the rules and facts in the knowledge base such that the more "probable", i.e. frequently successful rules and facts are encountered "earlier" by the selection strategy. A "re-sorting" of the contents of the knowledge base to this end can be implemented with the two predicates

```
         . . . .
 retract(SuccessfulPredicate),
 asserta(SuccessfulPredicate),
         . . . .
```

In Chapter 6 we shall be demonstrating an alternative implementation.

It cannot, however, always be assumed that the optimal arrangement of the rules is well understood and therefore should be made by the area expert. The probabilities governing this arrangement may indeed prove to be other than those assumed by the human expert. For example, the probabilities for different diagnoses experienced by a specialist at the Downstate Medical Center in New York may not even apply in Boston. And in Shanghai they are likely to be entirely inapplicable.

Changing the knowledge base "as you go" presents a fundamental problem. In the field of logic and, correspondingly, in logic programming one speaks of a *non-monotonic logic* if, during the derivation of a conclusion, the *axioms*, i.e. the rules and facts in our case, change so that it cannot be guaranteed that at some point an earlier, intermediate result is "suddenly rendered untrue".

It is especially critical if such changes were to occur during the course of a consultation. To deal with the problem one must construct a *truth maintenance* subsystem. In essence this is nothing more than an accounting system, which notes the origin of every new entry in the knowledge base, in the case of derived clauses for example, the predicates from which they were inferred. Should one such "predicate of origin" change, then all the clauses derived from it must be deleted and deduced anew. This sort of *truth maintenance* tends to be quite costly, since the clauses to be deleted may themselves be points of origin for other derivations, *ad nauseam*. Thus it is advisable to consider, as part of the problem identification phase, if a *monotonic* logic is applicable and, if not, to take measures to deal with the potential consequences from the very start. As in conventional programming, the most costly components in knowledge-based programming are those which were not foreseen, but rather "patched-in" from hindsight.

The inconsistencies which arise as a result of changes introduced by the knowledge engineer via the *knowledge gathering component* (see Fig. 4-1) are less difficult to master. Nonetheless, systems with large knowledge bases should provide for a verification procedure, which automatically checks new clauses for compatibility with the existing body of knowledge before permitting final storage.

4.9   Control of Flow

Let us just briefly examine the issue of dialog management, which, naturally, is highly dependent on the problem being dealt with, as well as on the form of knowledge representation involved. Many different approaches are possible, varying in both method and difficulty of implementation. We shall present several examples in the chapters following.

In general, one can assume that, in an expert system, a *consultation* or dialog session with the user goes through several *phases*. During the

problem recognition

phase the system determines just what the user's problem seems to be. It then initializes the subsequent dialog accordingly. We saw a primitive form of this in the ticket information system. The dialog varied, particularly with respect to the explanations, depending on whether the user initiated the exchange with a specific question, such as *is_a_Kiddie_Ticket-_possible*, or a request for general consultation, with *mta*. This is followed by a phase of *arbitrary knowledge processing*

  wherein the first hypotheses are made. This may be a random selection or a probabilistic one, the intention being that of chancing upon the first relevant fact or producing some rules. This is followed by a phase involving

targeted knowledge processing

  whereby a specific goal is pursued and, by virtue of the "proof" or "disproof" of a given assumption, a useful result for the user is derived. It is often necessary to perform some

algorithmic computations

  invoking conventional numeric or non-numeric programs to achieve this end and it may also be necessary to access existing data banks. We mentioned such a case in an earlier chapter, where the *coupling expert* utilizes a library of Fortran programs to make certain technical calculations. The developer of an expert system should always exploit such opportunities rather than (re)writing the programs. Such programs constitute an "attachment" to the "actual" expert system and therefore should be considered a separate phase of the consultation and planned accordingly.

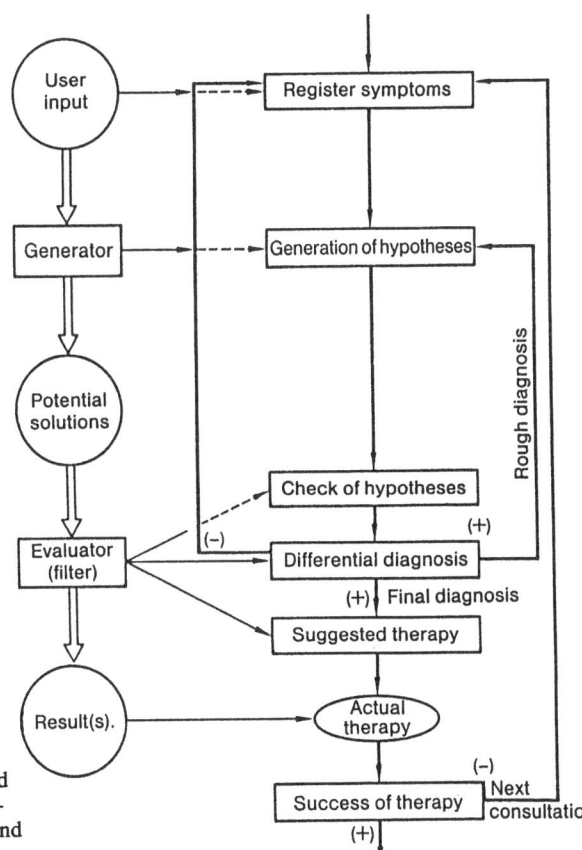

Fig. 4-6. *Generate and test* and its implementation in the diagnosis system *MED 2* (Puppe and associates)

These individual phases will, as a rule, overlap, causing additional design problems and making it all the more difficult to give hard and fast rules for planning a dialog.

In our experience, the *generate and test* strategy often provides a good basic structure around which the rough draft of the dialog strategy may be made (see for example [SCHN85]). Figure 4-6 represents it as a network of instances, on the left side of the illustration, with the comparable dialog components of the expert system *MED 2* [PUPP86] on the right side.

The scheme involves a *generator* which "somehow" generates a hypothesis or suggests a solution, e.g. by sequentially selecting clauses from a *support set* or by iterating through all possible permutations of some objects being observed. The latter, sometimes called the *exhaustive search* method, is usually practical only for simple problems due to the aforementioned problem of *combinatoric explosion.* The generator must foresee some suitable *constraints* or *heuristics* in order to minimize this effect.

The *testing component* consists of a set of rules which checks the viability of the hypotheses or solutions suggested by the generator. If acceptable, they are presented to the user as an answer or stored in the knowledge base as an intermediate solution for further processing. If unacceptable, the testing component will trigger the generator for another suggestion.

The generator and tester represent a *producer-consumer relationship.* If you have ever written systems software, you will recognize a basic structure of conventional software engineering here. Furthermore, you will find that your experience in building such sub-systems can be applied, with minor modifications, to designing your expert systems.

As you gain more experience with this approach, you will find that it is quite useful at many different levels, particularly when designing more complex systems. The generator does not randomly produce all possible solutions, but rather selects particular ones based on constraints and heuristic considerations. In a sense, then, it represents a "mini expert system" in its own right, its knowledge consisting of the rules for generating the most promising potential solutions or hypotheses. Indeed, it may prove to be practical to design and implement it around the same "generate and test" approach.

By doing so, one exploits a fundamental design principle valid in traditional and logic programming: the fewer mechanisms used in a design, the better, more robust and easily maintained the product will be!

5 Dialog and Explanatory Components

Our simple ticket information system included a primitive explanatory component, which could tell the user why some particular information was being requested by the system. A "serious" expert system, however, must be able to do more. It should be capable of explaining *why* it arrived at one result and not another. Based on a more complex example involving a portion of an actual expert system developed for diagnosing automotive defects, we shall be presenting a more professional method of conducting dialogs and providing explanations. The system's knowledge base has been reduced to dealing with problems relating to the heating system.

5.1 Implicit Dialog Texts

In our discussion about different inference strategies for production systems, we mentioned that for *diagnostic systems backward chaining* is advantageous, because it permits one to integrate the texts for the dialog into the particular rules involved, or at least to derive them from the rules. We now wish to show you that this is true not only for the questions posed by the system. The explanations which are given the user on demand can also be obtained in like manner from the same rules.

In contrast to the approach taken in our MTA system, involving *explicit texts*, we speak of *implicit dialog texts* and *explanations*, when the separation of rules and their associated texts is avoided.

This is an important design goal if the knowledge bases involved are large or the knowledge base is subject to frequent and significant modification[1]. In such cases, managing the rules and associated explanatory texts separately increases the chance of mistakenly introducing inconsistencies into the relationship between them and ultimately into the dialog itself.

Typical, large diagnostic systems are dialog-oriented systems for guiding a user in the diagnosis and repair of defective equipment, such as automobiles. Therefore, our next example is of an expert system for automotive repairs [GSCH85]. The knowledge base has been intentionally reduced to the aspects

---

[1] On the other hand, we must admit that the technique for implicit texts about to be demonstrated has the disadvantage that it makes adapting the system to another (foreign) language generally more difficult. In data processing too, nothing is "for free"!

relating to the heating system. Extending the system to cover other automotive problems, however, is essentially merely a matter of supplementing the stock of rules.

Before going into too great detail, let us get a sense of the dialog interface by examining a few sample interactions.

By entering the request *assistance*, the user receives a summary of possible commands she may issue to the system:

```
?- assistance.

Possible inputs :

start.               ==> Begin the diagnosis.
rule_of_thumb.       ==> Defect search with
                         preliminary testing.
reason.              ==> Display the line of reasoning.
why_not(N).          ==> Why does rule "N" not apply?
rule(N).             ==> Display rule "N".
facts.               ==> Display all currently
                         known facts.
restart.             ==> Delete accumulated facts.
statistics(N,Freq).  ==> How often has the cause "N"
                         already been diagnosed?
assistance.          ==> Display this list.
```

At any point in the dialog, the user can enter *reason* to see the line of reasoning followed up to that point in the dialog, or *why_not(N)* to get an explanation as to why a specific rule is not applicable to a given defect. With *rule(N)* she can cause a given rule to be displayed. Entering *facts* causes a report to be made on the current accumulated case data. To re-initialize, i.e. clear the fact basis to investigate another defect, one need only enter *restart*. Should this not be done, the case data accumulates in the knowledge base associated with the current session and is considered in subsequent diagnoses.

Lastly, the system collects statistics about causes of problems dealt with. These are then used to optimize the search for defects based on previous "experience", as well as to generate information about the activity in the shop and the quality control of the manufacturer. We shall discuss the details of this "ability to learn" in the next chapter.

Let us first look at a simple diagnostic dialog:

```
?- start.
Is the fuse defective? n
Is the switch defective? y
Is the cable defective? y
The heater is defective (Rule 1, Rule 12)

yes
```

```
?- reason.

The heater is defective
because the switch is defective
und because the cable is defective.

yes

?- reason.

It is the logical conclusion from the
facts given me.

yes
?- facts.

The heater is defective.
The heater blower is defective.
The cable is defective.
The switch is defective.
The fuse is not defective.

no
```

Note how the repeated request for a *reason* for a given response causes the system to display the path followed in reaching the conclusion. The text phrases constituting the explanation are the same ones as those used to formulate the questions posed. We shall be showing you how the proper grammatical sentence structure and capitalization of words is achieved.

If the user does not know how to answer a particular question, the system suggests that she check one thing or another to see if a specific problem exists. Let us examine an excerpt from such a dialog situation:

```
Is the Bowden cable broken? who knows

To see if
the Bowden cable is broken,
you can check if
the Bowden cable can be pulled out
toward the motor.

Please do the above and
respond to the following question.
```

```
Is the Bowden cable broken? n
Is the Bowden cable stuck? perhaps

Detach both ends of the Bowden cable.
To see if
the Bowden cable is stuck,
you can check if
the Bowden cable does not move freely.

Please do the above and
respond to the following question.

Is the Bowden cable stuck? why

If the Bowden cable is stuck
and the heater valve is stuck,
then the heating regulator is defective.

Is the Bowden cable stuck? do not know
Is the V-belt torn? n
Is the heat exchanger dirty on the outside? y
Is the heat exchanger clogged? n

The heater is defective (Rule 4, Rule 41).
```

This help dialog is put together from the implicit texts stored in the respective rules. As you can see, a "vague" answer on the part of the user causes the system to provide a means of making a more precise judgement. Only after this has been done, and the user again responds to the repeated question with another vague "do not know" or "perhaps", does the system truly consider the circumstance to be *uncertain.*

By asking *why* the user can find out which rule the system is presently verifying, perhaps because she does not want to get her hands all dirty pulling on the cable, if she can tell that the possible cause of the defect being checked by doing so is highly improbable.

And now another dialog excerpt illustrating the use of the *why_not* query and the displaying of rules.

```
?- rule(22).

If the Bowden cable is stuck
and the heater valve is stuck,
then the heating regulator is defective.

yes
```

```
?- why_not(22).
```

```
It is uncertain if
the Bowden cable is stuck.
It has not yet been clarified if
the heater valve is stuck.
```

```
yes
```

```
?- rule(13).
```

```
If the  blower is stuck,
and the jumper cable is defective,
and the blower motor is defective,
then the heater blower is defective.
```

```
yes
```

```
?- why_not(13).
```

```
The  blower is not stuck.
The blower motor is not defective.
It has not yet been clarified if
the jumper cable is defective.
```

If the system has not yet posed a question to the user, this is indicated in the response to *why_not* by formulating the possible cause as

```
It has not yet been clarified if ...
```

If, however, the user had answered the corresponding question with a response like "do not know", the system documents the fact as

```
It is uncertain if ... .
```

Thus the query *why_not* can also be used to determine that a particular diagnosis was not made because a specific cause was not *definitely* identified or some information which might alter the diagnosis, had not yet been requested. Up to now, in our example, apparently only the mechanical function of the heating regulator has been investigated and a defect has already been discovered. Nonetheless, it is conceivable that some electrical problems still remain. At this juncture, the user can decide whether the diagnosis should be pursued in this direction, or the mechanical defect repaired first and a further diagnosis attempted only if the heater continues to malfunction.

Having seen examples for the important elements of the dialog, let us turn our attention to its implementation. Of particular interest in this regard is the direct generation of the various texts from the rules.

5.2   The Structure and Processing of Rules

Figure 5-1 shows a number of rules for diagnosing defects in an automobile heating system. If the expert system is specialized in dealing with this field, then we find ourselves at the "highest level". The rules aim at making the first "rough" decision regarding the possible cause of a heating system problem. If the expert system were extended to cover all possible automotive problems, then there would be one or more levels above this one, whose task would be to localize a problem to the heating system (or some other sub-system of the auto involved).

```
defect(1,'the heater',is,defective) :-
        cause(1,'the heater blower',is,defective).

defect(2,'the heater',is,defective) :-
        cause(2,'the heating regulator',is,defective).

defect(3,'the heater',is,defective) :-
        cause(3,'the water pump',is,defective).

defect(4,'the heater',is,defective) :-
        cause(4,'the heat exchanger',is,defective).
```

Fig.5-1. Rules with implicit dialog texts for diagnosing automobile heating system defects (highest level)

A cursory examination of the rules in Fig. 5-1 should make evident, even to the uninitiated, just how the dialog texts are integrated into the rules. They are broken down into three "sentence" components, i.e. three *phrases*, which serve as the arguments of the rule headers *defect* and the goals *cause* in the rule body, respectively. If the phrases are not legal Prolog atoms, i.e. if they consist of more than one word or begin with an uppercase letter, then they are *quoted*, using single quotes, to convert them effectively into atoms.

In general, the syntax of these rules can be defined as follows:

```
defect(Rule_No, Subject, Verb, Attribute) :-
        cause(Rule_No, Subject_1, Verb_1, Attribute_1),
        .  .  .  .
        cause(Rule_No, Subject_2, Verb_2, Attribute_2).
```

The numbering of the rules via *Rule_No* serves as a simple reference, which can be used internally or by the user when requesting an explanation.

Thus, the rules associate a given defect, described verbally by the last three arguments of *defect*, with its possible causes. The different rules for the same defect can be seen as alternative sources of the same apparent problem. One could, of course, write several causes in *one* rule, separating them with the comma operator. This implies that the associated defect exists only if all the causes so described occur at the same time. We call this a *conjunction* of causes. The rules in Fig. 5-2 contain an example of this.

```
defect(11,'the heater blower',is,defective) :-
        cause(11,'the fuse',is,defective).

defect(12,'the heater blower',is,defective) :-
        cause(12,'the switch',is,defective),
        cause(12,'the cable',is,defective).

defect(13,'the heater blower',is,defective) :-
        cause(13,'the blower',is,stuck),
        cause(13,'the jumper cable',is,defective),
        cause(13,'the blower motor',is,defective).

defect(14,'the heater blower',is,defective) :-
        cause(14,'the blower motor',is,defective),
        cause(14,'the battery',is,empty).
```

Fig. 5-2. Some *defect* Rules for the *cause* Goals in Fig. 5-1.

As you may already have guessed, our inference engine derives its diagnosis from these rules by building an *inference tree* via backward chaining, i.e. *top-down*, as illustrated in an excerpt in Fig. 5-3. This involves matching the *cause* goals with their respective *defect* rule headers, based on the text arguments just discussed (we have intentionally omitted the rule numbers in Fig. 5-3).

In Fig. 5-2 one can see some further *defect* rules associated with the *cause* goals of Fig. 5-1 which can serve to build the inference tree.

It is possible to omit one of the phrases. This is done by defining the appropriate phrase argument as an "empty" or null atom, i.e. one whose name is an "empty string".

If the inference engine cannot find any further suitable, i.e. matching, *defect* rule, it asks the user about the corresponding *cause* using the implicit text stored in the rule, provided that no *fact* or facts stemming from answers to previous questions can be found in the knowledge base which eliminate or confirm the possible cause. In the latter case, the information is already part of the *case data*. We shall be discussing its internal representation in the next section.

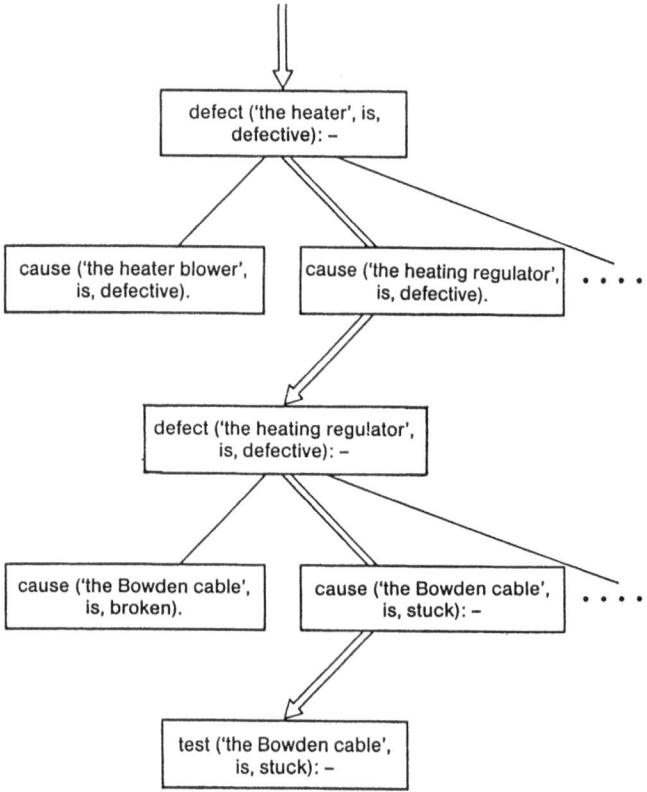

Fig. 5-3. Deriving an inference tree from the rules with implicit dialog texts

As indicated in Fig. 5-3, the user may be assisted in determining the proper response to such inquiries about the probable *cause* of a problem by some *test* rules. These rules constitute an important part of the explanatory component, as we shall see further on.

5.3   Facts and Degrees of Certainty

In our MTA-System we intentionally avoided a problem relating to the collection of case data which in the design and implementation of a professional expert system absolutely must be addressed. This involves the issue of the *degree of certainty of a fact.* What we mean by this is:

• Not only the applicability of a specific fact, for example a leak in the water pump, may be relevant for the finding, i.e. inferring the defect, but possibly its non-applicability as well.

• It is conceivable that the user cannot respond to a question, because she cannot, for instance, (physically) determine if the water pump is leaky or not.

Consequently, we must be able to attach a *truth value* to the facts derived from the case data gathered. At the very least, one should distinguish between facts which are *true, false* or *unknown*. In the MTA system we simply ignored those facts which remained unknown even after questioning the user, using the excuse that the user risked paying the fine of 40 German marks for errors based on such uncertainty regarding the ticket bought. Thus, if it was not 100 percent certain that the user wanted to travel a short route, we recommended a normal ticket to eliminate risking 40 marks in order to save a few pennies. This meant we only had to store *true* facts and could avoid the issue of certainty altogether.

In our new system this is no longer the case, hence we now store the *status* along with each fact added to the knowledge base. This is done as follows:

```
fact(Subject,Verb,Attribute,Status).
```

Thus we find entries like

```
fact('the V-belt',is,torn,false).
fact('the water pump',is,clogged,unknown).
fact('the water pump',is,leaky,true).
```

in the knowledge base. This convention is the first step towards dealing with *uncertain knowledge*. In fields in which neither the facts nor the conclusions can be unequivocally formulated, such as medical diagnosis or economic planning and forecasting, one often employs a *certainty factor* or a *probability factor* to describe the status. This is a numerical value which, depending on its interpretation and evaluation by the rules, can lie, for example, between -1 ("absolutely false") and +1 ("absolutely true") or between 0 and 100 ("percent probability").

Corresponding methods exist for processing these values in this context. The best known models are the *Bayesian probability* method [ADAM84], *certainty factors* of *MYCIN* [SHOR84] and *fuzzy logic* [SCHN85,ZADE83]. These are complex topics in their own right and we refer the interested reader to the literature in the bibliography for in-depth study.

The implementation of these algorithms is actually quite simple. The real problem lies in deciding which of the methods reflects the nature of the uncertainties involved in the logical derivation of conclusions for a specific area of expertise, and which model is most plausible, both for the expert supplying the knowledge incorporated in the system and the user of the final product.

We wish to limit ourselves to the aforementioned three-valued model for the time being. Thus, at the start of a dialog *all* facts are unknown. This is best implemented by initializing the knowledge base with a general

```
fact(_,_,_,unknown).
```

If the facts gathered in the course of a dialog are stored "before" this initial fact, using *asserta*, then this fact will automatically serve as a catch-all, i.e. *default* status for all as yet undetermined, potential case data.

5.4   The Inference Engine

The *Inference Engine* must

(1) initialize the inference tree structure shown in Fig. 5-3, and

(2) process each *cause* goal in a meaningful way.

This further processing of a particular *cause* depends on whether

• a fitting *defect* rule can be found which leads to further causes, or
• a *fact* confirmed to be *true* or *false* (based perhaps on a previous consultation or dialog phase) already exists in the knowledge base, or
• the system has a question for the user.

The simplest form of initialization is implemented via a *start* rule. This rule uses the predicate *examine* to work through a predefined list of numbers referencing the highest level *defect* rules, one after the other. Figure 5-4 illustrates the principle.

```
start :-
        examine([1,2,3,4]).

examine([Rule_No|_]) ;-
        defect(Rule_No,_,_,_).
examine([_|Rest_List]) :-
        examine(Rest_List).
examine([]) :-
        nl,
        write('I cannot find any defects.').
```

Fig. 5-4. The *start* rule for the inference engine

Since the *defect* rules, in turn, invoke their associated *cause* goals, these drive the second part of the inference engine. This is implemented as a general procedure for dealing with the three different ways in which *causes* propagate through the inference process, as described above. Figure 5-5 shows the implementation of the procedure.

```
cause(_,A,B,C) :-
        /* the cause already exists as a fact: */
        fact(A,B,C,true),
        !.
cause(_,A,B,C) :-
        /* the cause is definitely inapplicable: */
        fact(A,B,C,false),
        !, fail.
cause(_,A,B,C) :-
        /* the cause leads to further causes: */
        !, defect( ,A,B,C)
cause(N,A,B,C) :-
        /* the user must be questioned about the cause: */
        fact(A,B,C,unknown),
        ask(N,A,B,C).
```

Fig.5-5. The further processing of a *cause*

Note how the *cut* in Fig. 5-5 suppresses the attempt to find further causes, should a fact prove to be either true or false. Only an unknown fact will cause the system to pose a question to the user.

The predicate *ask* is used to query the user. It contains both the entire data gathering and explanatory components and will therefore be the focus of our attention.

5.5   Gathering Case Data

To acquire a fact from the user, *ask* must essentially carry out two actions. It must

(1) construct a question with the phrases it receives from *cause* and

(2) read and evaluate the user's response.

Figure 5-6 shows the predicate *ask*, along with the auxiliary procedure *write_this_sentence_uppercase*. These are responsible for the *formulation of an interrogative* from the "implicit" text arguments. The predicate *write_uppercase* converts a leading, lowercase letter into an uppercase one. All the other characters of a term are left unchanged, be they numerals or uppercase symbols.

```
ask(No,A,B,C) :-
        write_this_sentence_uppercase(B,A,C),
        write(' ? '),
        read_in(Answer),
        !, recognize(Answer,No,A,B,C).

write_this_sentence_uppercase(A,B,C) :-
        nl,
        write_this_term_uppercase(A),
        write(' '),
        write(B),
        write(' '),
        write(C).

write_this_term_uppercase(Term) :-
        name(Term,Word),
        write_uppercase(Word,Uppercase_Word),
        name(New_Term,Uppercase_Word),
        write(New_Term).

write_uppercase([Lowercase_Letter|Rest],
        [UC_Letter|Rest]) :-
        [LC_a,LC_z] = "az",
        LC_a =< Lowercase_Letter,
        Lowercase_Letter =< LC_z,
        !, UC_Letter is Lowercase_Letter - 32.

write_uppercase(Term,Term).
```

Fig. 5-6. The formulation of a question by the predicate *ask*

The standard procedure *read_in* is used to read the user's response *a word at a time* into a list of atoms and unary functions. Each atom is a "word" extracted from the line input by the user. "Whitespaces", i.e. blanks and tabs, are suppressed. Special characters are stored as the *skolem-function, char(A)*, of the respective numerical ASCII-code *A* [see SCHN87]. Figure 5-7 shows the implementation of this reading procedure. It is a somewhat "tricky" procedure borrowed from [SCHN87] with some minor changes. If you have difficulty understanding it, we suggest looking at this reference work.

Having once read in the user's *response*, the system must analyze its semantic content. This is done by the predicate *recognize*, which we shall be developing in a stepwise fashion, so as to illustrate the various aspects of the implementation of the explanatory and user guidance components. Figure 5-8 shows the first version.

```
recognize(Answer,_,A,B,C) :-
       meaning(Answer,yes),
       !, asserta(fact(A,B,C,true)).
recognize(Answer,_,A,B,C) :-
       meaning(Answer,no),
       !, asserta(fact(A,B,C,false)),
       fail.
/*
       Other "recognize" rules to deal with
       alternative responses must later be inserted
       here, "before" the final ("default") rule for
       erroneous, i.e. non-recognizable  user input!
*/
recognize(_,No,A,B,C) :-
       nl,
       write('I do not understand your response.'),
       nl,
       write('Please re-enter your answer.'),
       ask(No,A,B,C).

meaning([y|_],yes).
meaning([yes|_],yes).
meaning([yeah|_],yes).
meaning([n|_],no).
meaning([no|_],no).
meaning([nope|_],no).
```

Fig. 5-8. The procedure *recognize* for positive and negative user responses

5.6   Vague Knowledge

Regardless of how the user formulates a response, what should be done if the answer is neither an absolute "yes" nor an absolute "no"? We should begin by differentiating between the possible circumstances leading to such responses.

In the one instance, the system might foresee the use of such responses as "why" or "how_come", with which the user could demand an explanation relating to the question just posed. Such explanations could be implemented in much the same fashion as in the MTA system. This essentially involves generating the explanation from the implicit texts, in much the same way as the questions were constructed, based on a protocol of the inferential path followed up to the given point in the dialog.

Rather than going into repetitious detail with respect to the above, let us discuss a case that has not been previously dealt with at all. It is in one sense a far simpler problem, insofar as its solution requires no protocols (audit trails) or the like: How do we help a user who cannot answer a question, because she simply *does not know* what the answer is?

Using the same technique, we can implement behavior useful in two related situations, namely

(1) when the user explicitly requests *instructions* on how to acquire the information necessary to answering the question, for example by entering an "intermediate" response *test*, as well as

```
recognize(Answer,No,A,B,C) :-
        meaning(Answer,test),
        !, display_test(A,B,C),
        ask(No,A,B,C).
recognize(Answer,No,A,B,C) :-
        meaning(Answer,do_not_know),
        !, deal_with_vague_answers(No,A,B,C).

deal_with_vague_answers(No,A,B,C) :-
        /* as yet no help has been given : */
        do_not_know_entered(no),
        display_test(No,A,B,C),
        !, note_do_not_know_entered(yes),
        ask(No,A,B,C).
deal_with_vague_answers(_,A,B,C) :-
        /* the user has already received assistance : */
        asserta(fact(A,B,C,uncertain)),
        !,fail.

note_do_not_know_entered(X) :-
        retract(do_not_know_entered(_)),
        asserta(do_not_know_entered(X)).

meaning([test|_],test).
meaning(['Test'|_],test).
meaning([try|_],test).
meaning(['Try'|_],test).
meaning([do,not,know|_],do_not_know).
meaning(['I',do,not,know|_],do_not_know).
meaning([perhaps|_],do_not_know).
meaning([maybe|_],do_not_know).
meaning([],do_not_know).
meaning([char(C)|_],do_not_know) :-
        "?" = [C].
```

Fig.5-9. *recognize* vague answers and requests for instructions

(2) when the user, in fact, enters a *vague answer*, such as "do not know" or "perhaps", indicating the need for some guidance in determining whether or not the malfunction indeed involves the defect suggested by the question posed.

Thus, the predicate *recognize* must identify two additional classes of answers. Figure 5-9 illustrates the approach taken.

Please note how we interpret the entry of a lone question mark or merely a *carriage return* as meaning *do_not_know* via the last two clauses in Fig. 5-9.

In the event of a vague answer, the system can tell, based on the state indicator

```
do_not_know_entered(no),
```

if the user has already made a similarly vague response to the same question. If not, then the system behaves as if she had explicitly requested instructions, e.g. with *test*, as to what to do to be able to give a reasonable answer to the question just posed. This state indicator is always set to *yes* before the question posed is repeated and then back to *no* when the question has finally been (recursively) resolved.

We shall discuss, in the next section, the predicate *display_test*, which suggests an "experiment" the user can conduct to decide how the question should be answered. From a purely syntactic point of view, however, one can see, in Fig. 5-9, that it is written such that it *fails* whenever no test for the potential defect exists. In such cases, backtracking then moves to the second *deal_with-_vague_answers* rule, which immediately enters a fact into the knowledge base identifying the cause at issue as having the certainty factor *uncertain*.

Note that we have herewith introduced a *fourth* degree of certainty, namely *uncertain*. This is done to distinguish such potential causes from those whose certainty value by default, i.e. through the initial fact

```
fact(_,_,_,unknown).
```

are *unknown*, indicating that they have not yet been considered as potential sources of the overall malfunction.

5.7   Instructing the User to Perform a Test

Instructions for the user on how to find out the proper answer to a question, either in response to a vague answer or to an explicit request for guidance, should look something like:

```
Is there air in the coolant ? maybe

Loosen the bleeder screw on the heat
exchanger while the heater is switched on
and the motor is running.
```

```
To see if
there is air in the coolant,
you can check if
the heater runs now.

Please do the above and
respond to the following question.

Is there air in the coolant ?
```

Such instructions can be constructed, at least partially, from the implicit texts. As illustrated in Fig. 5–10, the components are drawn from three sources:

- the original question,
- a *test* predicate, containing the instructional text relevant to the specific cause, selected according to the phrases building the original question, and

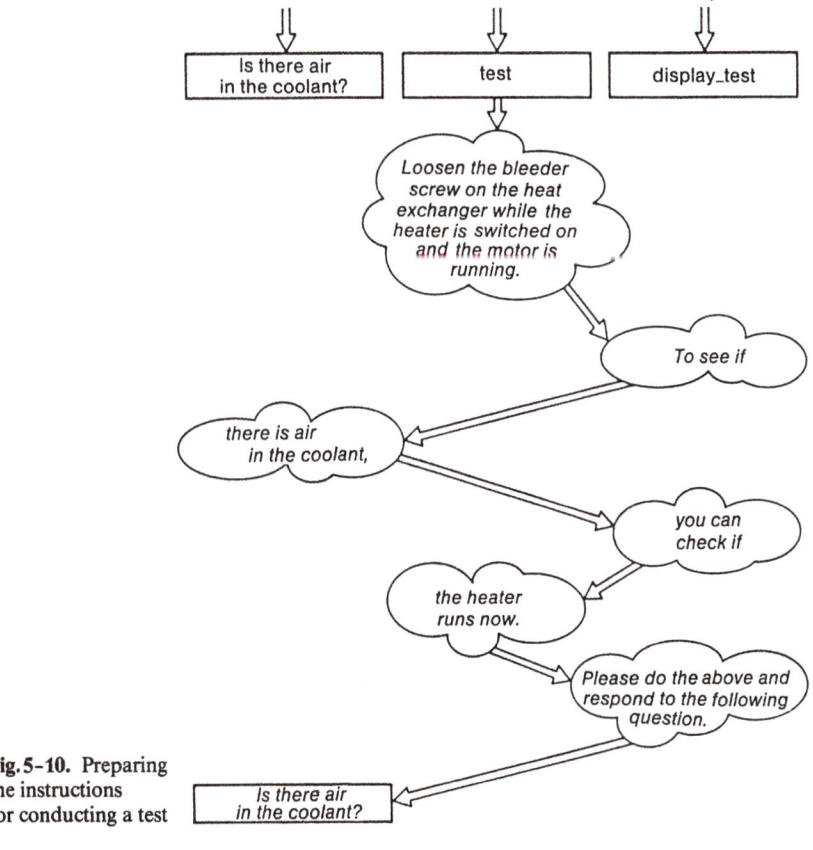

Fig. 5–10. Preparing the instructions for conducting a test

• standard text components, defined in the predicate *display_test*, which are used to introduce each such experiment.

The general structure for instructions on how to conduct a test is

```
test(A, B, C) :-
        try(LineList1, LineList2).
```

where *LineList1* and *LineList2* are two lists of lines of text. These lines of text are used to fill out the instructional outline defined in *display_test*, supplying the information specific to the potential cause being investigated, i.e. the question just posed. For the example in Fig. 5-10, the corresponding *test* clause would be:

```
test('air','there is','in the coolant') :-
        try([
                'loosen the bleeder screw on the heat',
                'exchanger while the heater is switched on',
                'and the motor is running.'
                ],
                [
                'the heater runs now.'
                ]).
```

Figure 5-11 shows the predicate *display_test*, which is used by *recognize* to prepare instructions for the user whenever they are needed, and as long as a *test* associated with the question, i.e. based on its constituent phrases, can be found in the knowledge base (see Fig. 5-9). The implicit text-phrase arguments of the question are exploited here.

```
display_test(A,B,C) :-
        note_do_not_know_entered(yes),
        clause(test(A,B,C),try(Part_1,Part_2)),
        /* : fail, if no "test(No)" exists! */ !,
        write_experiment(Part_1),
        write_text_module1,
        (
        /* Rearrange "there is" style tests */
        B == 'there is',
        write_this_sentence_lowercase(B,A,C);
        write_this_sentence_lowercase(A,B,C)
        )
        write(','), write_text_module2,
        write_experiment(Part_2),
        write_text_module3.
```

```
display_test(A,B,C) :-
        write_text_module4,
        (
        /* Rearrange "there is" style tests */
        B == 'there is',
        write_this_sentence_lowercase(B,A,C);
        write_this_sentence_lowercase(A,B,C)
        )
        write('.'), nl.

write_experiment([])
write_experiment([A|B]) :-
        nl, write(A), write_experiment(B).

write_text_module1 :-
        nl, nl, write('To see if'), nl.
write_text_module2 :-
        nl, write('you can check if').
write_text_module3 :-
        nl,nl,
        write('Please do the above and'),
        nl,
        write('respond to the following question.'),
        nl.
write_text_module4 :-
        nl,
        write('I know of no simple method '),
        write('for testing'),
        nl, write('if ').

write_this_sentence_lowercase(A,B,C) :-
        write(A), write(' '),
        write(B), write(' '),
        write(C).
```

Fig. 5-11. The predicate *display_test* for preparing instructions for the user

The procedure *display_test* and its auxiliary predicates are written such that *Part_1* of the explanation can be "omitted". This is represented in the goal *try* as an empty list, which is useful when the test requires no further preparation, as illustrated in the following dialog excerpt:

Is the Bowden cable broken ? **perhaps**

```
To see if
the Bowden cable is broken,
you can check if
the Bowden cable can be pulled out
toward the motor.

Please do the above and
respond to the following question.

Is the Bowden cable broken ?
```

The associated *test* predicate is

```
test('the Bowden cable',is,broken) :-
        try([],
                [
                'the Bowden cable can be pulled out',
                'toward the motor.'
                ])
```

Naturally, in addition to the instructions on how to find out the correct answer to the question, one also needs the usual, related explanation of *why* the system is posing it in the first place. After all, the test may be quite involved, as in the case

```
Is the heat exchanger dirty on the outside ? perhaps

Remove the heat exchanger casing.

To see if
the heat exchanger is dirty on the outside,
you can check if
any foreign bodies are visible.

Please do the above and
respond to the following question.

Is the heat exchanger dirty on the outside ? how_come
```

Clearly we cannot blame the mechanic for wishing to know, before going to all the trouble of unmounting the casing, why she should incur so much cost for herself and the customer by doing so. If this were a medical diagnosis system and the test involves a surgical procedure, then the question as to the purpose of the test is even more justified and urgent.

5.8   Explaining the Reason for a Question

We must now show how the "new" inference engine answers, i.e. explains itself, when the user responds to a question with *why* or *how come*. A typical explanation might be as follows:

```
Is the heat exchanger dirty on the outside ? how_come

If the heat exchanger is dirty on the outside,
and the heat exchanger is clogged,
then the heat exchanger is defective.

Is the heat exchanger dirty on the outside ?
```

The explanatory text can also be used to *display the contents of a rule*. Thus, we shall use the same mechanism for both tasks. In Fig. 5–12 we show the predicate *display_rule(Rule_No)*, used to prepare the rule, along with two synonyms for the task: *why(Rule_No)* defines the explanatory component for reasons of readability, and *rule(N)*, enables the user to request the display of a particular rule with minimal effort.

The figure also shows the embedding of *why(Rule_No)* in a *recognize* clause, which is responsible for explaining the system's reason for posing a given question.

```
display_rule(Rule_No) :-
        clause(rule(Rule_No,A,B,C),Causes),
        nl, write('if '),
        write_causes(Causes),
        write(','), nl,
        write('then '),
        (
        /* Re-arrange "there is" statements */
        B == 'there is',
        write_this_sentence_lowercase(B,A,C);
        write_this_sentence_lowercase(A,B,C)
        ),
        write('.').

write_causes(cause(_,A,B,C)) :-
        (
        /* Re-arrange "there is" statements */
        B == 'there is',
        write_this_sentence_lowercase(B,A,C);
        write_this_sentence_lowercase(A,B,C)
        ).
```

```
write_causes(cause(_,A,B,C),Causes) :-
        (
        /* Re-arrange "there is" statements */
        B == 'there is',
        write_this_sentence_lowercase(B,A,C);
        write_this_sentence_lowercase(A,B,C)
        ),
        write(','), nl, write('and '),
        write_causes(Causes).


/*
        Synonyms for "display_rule":
*/

why(Rule_No) :-
        display_rule(Rule_No).
rule(No) :-
        display_rule(Rule_No).


/*
        Embedded in "recognize" (must be added to
        the rules in Fig. 5-8) :
*/

recognize(Answer,No,A,B,C) :-
        meaning(Answer,why),
        !, why(No),
        ask(No,A,B,C).

meaning([why|_],why).
meaning([how_come|_],why).
```

Fig. 5-12. The predicate *display_rule(Rule_No)*, for preparing an explanatory text

Notice in Fig. 5-12 how several causes for the same problem (defect, malfunction) are handled: the predicate *write_causes* uses the same recursive mechanism with which you are familiar from list processing, the exception being that here the many *cause* goals in the *defect* rule connected by the *and*, i.e. the "," (comma) are the focus of recursion.

The *rule(No)* of Fig. 5-12 can also be employed independent of a dialog initiated by

```
?- start.
```

to invoke the display of an arbitrary rule:

```
?- rule(13).
```

```
If the  blower is stuck,
and the jumper cable is defective,
and the blower motor is defective,
then the heater blower is defective.
```

This is not only practical for "testing" the system; it also serves as a good basis for making a *training system* for auto mechanics.

5.9   Presenting and Explaining the Results

Now let us see how one goes about *presenting the results*. Naturally, one would like to not only output the results, but also present an explanation on how they were arrived at. As in the MTA example, we again need a *protocol of the dialog*. This requires a few small changes in the predicates *examine* (see Fig. 5-4) and cause (see Fig. 5-5). These are illustrated in Fig. 5-13.

print_result composes a statement from the implicit text-phrases of the defect (cause) highest in the hierarchic inference tree and outputs it to the user as a diagnosis. At the same time, it protocols the rules applied via the predicate *write_the_rules_applied*, which generates a list *L* of their respective numbers, based on protocol entries in the knowledge base. This list is used to control the output.

The predicate *findall* of arity three is used to collect the rules into the list. It is a built-in predicate of most Prolog systems[2]. Its first argument is a term containing one or more variables. The second argument is a predicate for the variables of the first. The third argument gets instantiated by *findall* with a list of all terms in the knowledge base which correspond to the first argument and match the predicate named as the second argument.

The protocol describing the path through the inference tree is kept by the predicate *store_this_step*. For each step taken it registers the rule applied in the form of a fact describing the current state of the process.

```
applied_rule(Step_Number, Rule_Number)).
```

Furthermore, the current step number is registered as

```
step(current_Step_Number).
```

---

[2] Should your Prolog system not provide *findall*, you can find an implementation described in [SCHN87].

```
examine([Rule_No|_]) :-
        defect(Rule_No,_,_,_),
        store_this_step(Rule_No),
        print_result(Rule_No,A,B,C).

cause(Cause_No,A,B,C) :-
        clause(defect(_,A,B,C),_),
        /* this cause leads to deeper causes : */
        !, defect(Rule_No,A,B,C),
        nl,
        store_this_step(Rule_No).

store_this_step(Rule_No) :-
        retract(step(Step_No)),
        New_Step_No is Step_No + 1,
        asserta(step(New_Step_No)),
        asserta(applied_rule(New_Step_No,Rule_No)).

print_result(Rule_No,A,B,C) :-
        write_this_sentence_uppercase(A,B,C),
        write_the_rules_applied, nl.

write_the_rules_applied :-
        findall(Rule,applied_rule(S,Rule),L),
        write_rules(L).

write_rules([A|B]) :-
        write(' (Rule '), write(A),
        write_additional_rule(B).

write_additional_rule([A|B]) :-
        write(','), write(' Rule '), write(A),
        write_additional_rule(B).
write_additional_rule([]) :-
        write(').').
```

Fig. 5-13. Presenting the explanation for a malfunction (extended version of the *examine* clause of Fig. 5-4 and the *cause* clause of Fig. 5-5)

The latter state variable is used in association with responses to repeated *reason* requests by the user as to the line of *reasoning* pursued by the system to reach the current conclusion. Since it reflects the current number of steps taken, when the user requests an explanation of the inferential process, the system works its way back along the derivation path, outputting the rules applied one at a time. It starts with the last *step* and decrements the *current_Step_Number* stored in the

```
reason :-
        step(0),
        nl,
        write('It is the logical conclusion from'),
        nl,
        write('the facts given me.').
reason :-
        retract(step(Step_No)),
        applied_rule(Step_No,Rule_No),
        clause(defect(Rule_No,A,B,C),Causes),
        nl, write_this_sentence_uppercase(A,B,C),
        nl, write('because '),
        write_causes(Causes),
        write('.'),
        New_Step_No is Step_No - 1,
        asserta(step(New_Step_No)).
```

Fig. 5-14. The predicate *reason* provides a stepwise explanation of the derived results

step state variable with each request for "more" reasons. Figure 5-14 illustrates the predicate reason which does the aforementioned.

The *reason* predicate is actually quite similar to the *display_rule* predicate used to prepare rules for presentation to the user. The primary difference is that the former selects the rule to be shown based on the information stored in the current state fact

```
step(Step_No)
```

and the corresponding protocol entry

```
applied_rule(Step_No,Rule_No).
```

In addition, it sees to it that the state fact *step* is always kept up-to-date.

5.10 "Why Not" Explanations

Sometimes the user is not only interested in why the system arrived at a particular diagnosis, but also why some other cause was not considered. A good explanatory component should provide for such "challenges" to the results. A first approximation to such a solution responds to the request as follows:

?- why_not(13).

The blower is not stuck.
It is uncertain if
the jumper cable is defective.
It has not yet been clarified if
the blower motor is defective .

```
why_not(Rule_No) :-
        clause(defect(Rule_No,_,_,_),Causes), !,
        separate(Causes,True,False,Uncertain,Unknown),
        something_is_false(False),
        something_is_uncertain(Uncertain),
        something_is_unknown(Unknown),
        (       check_if_still_applicable(
                        False,Uncertain,Unknown)
        ;       true
        ), nl.
why_not(_) :-
        nl,
        write('No such rule exists !').

something_is_false(False) :-
        write_the_false_facts(False).
something_is_false(_).

something_is_uncertain(Uncertain) :-
        write_the_uncertain_facts(Uncertain),
        write('.').
something_is_uncertain(_).

something_is_unknown(Unknown) :-
        write_the_unknown_facts(Unknown),
        write('.').
something_is_unknown(_).

check_if_still_applicable([],[],[]) :-
        nl,
        write('This rule could still be applied.'),
        nl.
```

Fig. 5-15. The predicate *why_not* for explaining why particular defects/causes were not diagnosed

We already had the system show us rule 13 for a defective heater blower and saw that all three defects must be present. Now when we ask *why_not(13)*, we discover that the blower is evidently not stuck and that therefore the system disregarded the associated diagnosis.

This example illustrates the essential problem in responding to *why_not* questions. A rule may involve many potential causes, for which, in turn, differing degrees of certainty may apply: *true, false, unknown* and *uncertain*. We introduced the last two in order to distinguish between causes for which the user had an ambiguous response and those causes which were never considered/investigated.

Thus, when explaining *why not* a particular diagnosis, the system must clearly differentiate between the false, the unknown and the uncertain. This gives the user the opportunity to decide if at least one of the characteristic causes of a problem definitely *does not* exist or if the system ignored a possible diagnosis only because the user had left one or more possibilities uncertain, i.e. perhaps she should (do you remember?) take the casing off the heat exchanger after all.

Figure 5-15 shows the implementation of the predicate *why_not*. It separates the causes of a *defect* rule into true, false, uncertain or unknown; the members of the last three groups are then prepared for output. If all the causes are "true", then it merely reports that the rule can be applied, i.e. the defect is "diagnosable".

The procedures for sorting the causes into different classes according to degree of certainty and composing the explanatory texts are not all too difficult, albeit somewhat long. We have shown them in Figs. 5-16 and 5-17.

The procedure in Fig. 5-16 is most easily understood when one notes that *separate*, like *write_causes* in Fig. 5-12, recursively processes a conjunction of causes, connected by the comma, i.e. *logical and* operator. At each level of recursion the first *cause* gets classified and the associated text-phrase triple

(A, B, C)

is added to the corresponding "certainty" list: *True, False, Uncertain* or *Unknown*.

It is probably a good idea to take a closer look at Fig. 5-17 to review how the implicit text-phrases, originating from the *ask* rules and *cause* goals, get deposited in the knowledge base, gathered into lists of facts and, finally, integrated into explanatory texts.

The example demonstrates how comparatively ambitious informational and explanatory text can be generated in Prolog, without necessarily having to resort to complicated, syntax- or semantic-driven techniques. This is because the Prolog programmer works much more closely with the input/output primitives of the language than someone using a shell or some similar tool. She can formulate the implicitly stored text-phrases and the predicates of composition very flexibly, readily facilitating an adaptation of the system to other languages (French, German, ...) or to customer suggestions with respect to dialog interaction, as well as to other areas of expertise.

```
/* True Facts : */

separate(cause(N,A,B,C),[(A,B,C)],[],[],[]) :-
        fact(A,B,C,true),
        !.
separate((cause(N,A,B,C),Causes),
        [(A,B,C)|True],False,Uncertain,Unknown) :-
        fact(A,B,C,true),
        !,
        separate(Causes,True,False,Uncertain,Unknown).

/* False Facts : */

separate(cause(N,A,B,C),[],[(A,B,C)],[],[]) :-
        fact(A,B,C,false),
        !.
separate((cause(N,A,B,C),Causes),
        True,[(A,B,C)|False],Uncertain,Unknown) :-
        fact(A,B,C,false),
        !,
        separate(Causes,True,False,Uncertain,Unknown).

/* Uncertain Facts : */

separate(cause(N,A,B,C),[[],[],(A,B,C)],[]) :-
        fact(A,B,C,uncertain),
        !
separate((cause(N,A,B,C),Causes),
        True,False,[(A,B,C)|Uncertain],Unknown) :-
        fact(A,B,C,uncertain),
        !,
        separate(Causes,True,False,Uncertain,Unknown).

/* Unknown Facts : */

separate(cause(N,A,B,C),[],[],[],[(A,B,C)]).
separate((cause(N,A,B,C),Causes),
        True,False,Uncertain,[(A,B,C)|Unknown]) :-
        separate(Causes,True,False,Uncertain,Unknown).
```

Fig.5–16. The procedure for separating true, false, uncertain and unknown facts

```
write_the_false_facts([(A,B,C)]) :-
        nl, write_this_sentence_uppercase(A,B,not),
        write(' '), write(C), write('.').
write_the_false_facts([(A,B,C)|Facts]) :-
        write_the_false_facts([(A,B,C)]),
        write_the_false_facts(Facts).

write_the_uncertain_facts([]) :-
        !, fail.
write_the_uncertain_facts(Facts) :-
        nl, write('It is uncertain if'),
        nl, write_an_uncertain_fact(Facts).

write_an_uncertain_fact([(A,B,C)]) :-
        write_this_sentence_lowercase(A,B,C).
write_an_uncertain_fact([Fact|Facts]) :-
        write_an_uncertain_fact([Fact]),
        write('and if'),
        nl, write_an_uncertain_fact(Facts).

write_the_unknown_facts([]) :-
        !, fail.
write_the_unknown_facts(Facts) :-
        nl, write('It has not yet been clarified if'),
        nl, write_an_unknown_fact(Facts).

write_an_unknown_fact([(A,B,C)]) :-
        write_this_sentence_lowercase(A,B,C).
write_an_unknown_fact([Fact|Facts]) :-
        write_an_unknown_fact([Fact]),
        write(' and if'),
        nl, write_an_unknown_fact(Facts).
```

Fig. 5-17. The procedures for outputting false, uncertain and unknown facts

5.11   Listing the Current Contents of the Fact Base

Our last example for the manipulation of implicit texts deals with a predicate for listing the contents of the fact base. When the user enters the request

```
?- facts.
```

the system should output a list of all the knowledge, i.e. *true*, *false* or *uncertain* facts currently at its disposal, in a readable, comprehensible form. Figure 5-18 shows our implementation.

```
facts :-
        fact(A,B,C,B_Degree),
        (       B_Degree == true,
                ( B == 'there is',
                  write_this_sentence_uppercase(B,A,C)
                ; write_this_sentence_uppercase(A,B,C)
                )
        ; `     B_Degree == false,
                ( B == 'there is',
                  write_this_sentence_uppercase(B,no,A)
                ; write_this_sentence_uppercase(A,B,not)
                ),
                write(' '), write(C)
        ;       B_Degree == uncertain,
                nl, write('It is uncertain, if '),
                ( B == 'there is',
                  write_this_sentence_lowercase(B,A,C)
                ; write_this_sentence_lowercase(A,B,C)
                )
        ;       B_Degree == unknown,
                !
        ),
        fail.
```

Fig.5-18. The predicate *facts* for listing the current contents of the fact base

The predicate is a typical loop, defined using a closing *fail*. It fetches the individual facts, of the form *fact(A,B,C,B_Degree)*, one at a time from the database
and after preparing them according to the respective degree of certainty, *B_De-
gree*, displays them. Note that we did *not* need to make the first goal,
fact(A,B,C,B_Degree), an argument to a *clause* predicate. This is because the system always initializes the knowledge base with

```
fact(_,_,_,unknown).
```

insuring that at least one *fact* will *always* be found. Thus, even a conscientious
Prolog interpreter will never complain that the predicate is *undefined* (most Prolog implementations do not even bother to check, leaving it up to the programmer to discover the potential problem)!

5.12   Shortcomings and Possible Improvements

This ends the discussion of the essential features of our system for finding defects in auto heaters. It performs a good deal more than our simple MTA expert but is still only a prototype. A commercial production system would require a number of improvements.

- Requiring the user to write *why_not* with a connecting underline symbol, and not providing synonyms for the request, is not particularly elegant. The user certainly will not understand why the system can handle blanks in requests for explanations as to why a particular question has been posed, but not when it is to explain its final results.
- The reason for this shortcoming is – as in the case of many other awkward aspects of the dialog – that the dialog is managed directly by the Prolog interpreter itself, i.e. the prompt " ?-" and the treatment of the user response as the primary goal serving as the basis for interaction. This makes it impossible to take the approach of using a more comfortable input procedure, such as *read_in* of Fig. 5-7 and a more flexible evaluation of the input, as per the *recognize* predicate, in all situations. The finished system should "hide" the Prolog interface entirely. Perhaps the simplest solution would be a *menu of the different services available* at the highest level (diagnosis, explanation of the final results, rule inspection). A simple *menu-shell* for such purposes is discussed in [SCHN87]. It originates from a design by S. Greenwood [GREE84] and is characterized by its compactnes, clarity of structure and ready adaptability to a variety of tasks.
- The instructions for conducting a test, which are presented either on demand or when the user gives a vague response to a question posed by the system, function only when a *test* predicate has been provided for the associated question. Since this is not always the case, the predicate *display_test* should construct a message explaining the situation and then, with *note_do_not_know_entered(yes)* insure that the same (!) message gets suppressed, should the user again enter an ambiguous answer.
- Another weakness is that the user must give an explicit *defect* rule number when invoking the predicates *why_not* and *rule.* One cannot always assume that the user knows the number of the rule in which she is interested. There should at least be a predicate with which one can get a listing of possible defects with their respective rule numbers. A more elegant solution would be a *retrieval procedure*, which would accept one or more keywords, such as "water pump" or "coolant", and would return a list of all *defect* rules and/or the associated *cause* goals in which the search key appears.
- A final shortcoming is the system's lack of knowledge with respect to possible correlations between individual causes of defects, leading to some awkward dialogs. For instance, it is conceivable that the user will be asked if the V-belt is loose after having already indicated that it is torn. The finished system should take measures to avoid such nonsense. A general mechanism for achieving this involves an additional *cause* clause

```
cause(_,A,B,C) :-
    excluded(A,B,C),
    !, fail.
```

which comes before the *ask* clause, preventing its invocation in the aforementioned cases. The exclusion of a potential *cause* can be formulated in the following fashion:

```
excluded(A,B,C) :-
    (    not_simultaneously([A,B,C],[A1,B1,C1])
    ;    not_simultaneously([A1,B1,C1],[A,B,C])
    ),
    fact(A1,B1,C1,true).

not_simultaneously(['the V-belt',is,torn],
                   ['the V-belt',is,loose]).
        . . . . .
```

Naturally this *excluded* predicate can be defined in such a way that the consideration of a potential cause is suppressed for other reasons as well.

These, in our estimation, are the major shortcomings. You may well feel that there are others. Regardless, we recommend that you consider possible solutions to these problems and take the time to implement as many as possible as a means of exercising the concepts discussed up to this point.

6 "Experience" and "Learning"

Our auto heater diagnosis system behaves rather inflexibly: it "obstinately" pursues the inference strategy determined by the structure and order of rules in the knowledge base. Furthermore, it only records the case data necessary for the diagnosis being currently performed. One should expect more from an "expert" system. If the user already suspects a particular defect, then she will usually want to steer the dialog actively in that direction. On the other hand, like an experienced mechanic, the system should be able "initiate" some preparatory tests ("do the headlights work?") to help quickly localize the probable general source of problems. A human expert is always learning how to make more efficient diagnoses. For instance, the relative frequency of particular diagnoses allows her to identify common defects of specific makes and models. This is useful knowledge for the manufacturer's quality control too! In any case, if the mechanic looks for the most probable defects first, she will in the long run work more effectively. In this chapter, we shall be demonstrating techniques for integrating such features into a system.

6.1 User Hunches

Studies have shown that *user acceptance* of an expert system depends largely on the naturalness, i.e. flexibility of the dialog conducted by it. This explains, for example, the far greater popularity of DENDRAL, a system for determining the structure of complex molecules, versus MYCIN, a medical diagnosis system. DENDRAL behaves more like an expert's assistant, whereas MYCIN acts as the expert herself (see the discussion of DENDRAL by [JACK86], Chap. 2, for more details).

It is certainly not just the user's feeling of being "patronized" which causes aversion to such computerized systems. Even the most patient and enthustiastic computer user will be frustrated, if she has a strong *suspicion* as to where the problem lies, but must go through a lengthy dialog with the system, waiting until it has searched its way to the general problem area where the actual "solution" is, in the eyes of the user, "obviously" to be found.

Consequently, the user should be given the opportunity to steer the diagnosis, from the start, in the direction where she expects the quickest results. In principle, this can be done quite simply by introducing a predicate

```
check(R_No) :-
        /* first approximation to a solution  */
        /* (to be expanded later):            */
        defect(R_No,_,_,_).
```

for a *partial diagnosis*, where the user can say, e.g.

```
?- check(3).
```

and request that the system begin searching for the cause starting with the water pump. And if the user says, alternatively,

```
?- check(44).
```

the system would begin with the defect rule number "44". As you recall, we can examine rule 44 with

```
?- rule(44).
```

```
If the system is low on coolant,
and there is air in the coolant,
then the heat exchanger is defective.
```

Such user directed starts have one disadvantage: what happens if the user's hunch was incorrect and the problem lies somewhere else? Well, in such cases, she can merely begin the dialog as usual with

```
?- start.
```

But we must be careful not to punish the user for her initiative by forcing her to re-enter all the information which she gave during her unsuccesssful attempt. Indeed, her responses may even prove sufficient to make a diagnosis other than the one she suspected.

6.2   Diagnostic Phases

Thus, one should see to it that when *start* is entered the "complete" diagnosis is conducted *in phases*. This also makes sense in other situations, besides when the user has made an unsuccessful attempt to shortcut the dialog using *check.*

For instance, it may often be the case that the auto still does not function properly even after one defect has been remedied, because another defect lurks undiscovered – or because during the repair some other part was unintentionally damaged. Regardless, the system should certainly see if, upon being *started* again, it cannot diagnose the subsequent problem using the information already acquired in remedying the previous defect.

Naturally this means that, just as in the case of an unsuccesful *check*, the system must preserve the information collected to date, even after a diagnosis has been made. Thus, the user must be provided with a

```
?- restart.
```

request, which retains the necessary information when *re-initializing the fact base*. Perhaps the simplest implementation involves *reconsulting an initialization file*:

```
restart :-
          [-init].
```

Figure 6-1 shows the contents of the initialization file.

```
fact(_,_,_,unknown).

do_not_know_entered(no).

phase(2).
```

Fig. 6-1. Initialization file for the auto heater diagnosis program

Phase determines if the inference engine,

• should question the user about every unknown fact (this is phase **2**, to which the system is initialized), or
• in the case of phase **1** (implying that a previous successful diagnosis, or a partial diagnosis based on some *check*, has already been made), that first an attempt should be made to find a diagnosis without requesting any further case data.

Thus, the command *start* must reset the state to *phase(1)*. Figure 6-2 shows the modifications which must be made to the predicates *start*, *examine* and *check* to achieve this.

Figure 6-3 shows how the predicate *cause* is modified with respect to the earlier version of Fig. 5-5.

The fourth clause of the *cause* predicate insures that all unknown facts in the first phase of the diagnosis are treated as being unknown. This, as you perhaps recall, causes all respective queries to the user to be suppressed. If the existing information suffices to make a diagnosis, then the second phase, i.e. the second *start* predicate never gets activated and no inquiries about unknown facts will be made. Only if the first phase proves unsuccessful will the inference engine enter the second phase, where more case data is requested.

```
start:-
        note_phase(1),
        hypotheses(Hypotheses_List),
        examine(Hypotheses_List).
start:-
        note_phase(2),
        new_priorities,
        hypotheses(Hypotheses_List),
        examine(Hypotheses_List).

examine([]) :-
        phase(2),
        nl,
        write('I cannot find any defects.').
examine([Alternative | Others]) :-
        (       check(Alternative)
        ;       examine(Others)
        ).

check(R_No) :-
        defect(R_No,A,B,C),
        store_this_step(R_No),
        print_result(A,B,C).

note_phase(P) :-
        retract(phase(_)),
        asserta(phase(P)).

/*
        The Hypotheses List here is a fact
        in its own right, so that it can
        be dynamically extended later on
*/

hypotheses([1,2,3,4]).
```

Fig. 6-2. Modifications to the *start* predicates needed for two-phased diagnoses

To allow the user to search for another defect, in addition to the one just found, we can modify the predicate *print_result* (Fig. 6-4) so that, after displaying the latest diagnosis, it asks her

```
Do you wish to look for other defects ?
```

and *fails*, if she responds positively, causing the system to backtrack for another session.

```
cause(_,A,B,C) :-
       clause(defect(_,A,B,C),_),
       !, defect(R_No,A,B,C),
       nl,
       store_this_step(R_No).
cause(_,A,B,C) :-
       fact(A,B,C,true),
       !.
cause(_,A,B,C) :-
       fact(A,B,C,false),
       !, fail.
cause(N,A,B,C) :-
       fact(A,B,C,unknown),
       /* in the first phase, unknown facts */
       /* are treated as being false :      */
       phase(1),
       !, fail.
cause(N,A,B,C) :-
       fact(A,B,C,unknown),
       note_do_not_know_entered(no),
       /* only in the second phase */
       /* are inquiries made :      */
       ask(N,A,B,C).
```

Fig.6-3. Modifications to the *cause* predicate for two-phased diagnoses

```
print_result(No,A,B,C) :-
     (
        B == 'there is',
        write_this_sentence_uppercase(B,A,C)
     ;  write_this_sentence_uppercase(A,B,C)
     ),
     write_the_rules_applied,
     nl, nl,
     note_phase(2),
     write('Do you wish to look for other defects ?'),
     read_in(Response),
     (      meaning(Response,yes),
            !, delete_previous_steps,
            fail
     ;      true
     ).
```

Fig.6-4. The modified predicate *print_result* (reloaded via reconsultation of the file *endless_search*)

The following dialog excerpt illustrates the method:

```
?- [-endless_search].

reconsult: file endless_search loaded in 0 sec.
yes

?- start.

Is the fuse defective? n
Is the switch defective? n
Is the blower stuck? y
Is the jumper cable defective? y
Is the blower motor defective? y
The heater is defective (Rule 1, Rule 13).

Do you wish to look for other defects ? y

Is the battery empty? n
Is the Bowden cable broken? y
The heater is defective (Rule 2, Rule 21).

Do you wish to look for other defects ? n

yes
```

If we accept a diagnosis, then a new *start* request leads back into phase 1:

```
?- start.
The heater is defective (Rule 1, Rule 13).

Do you wish to look for other defects ? y

The heater is defective (Rule 2, Rule 21).

Do you wish to look for other defects ? y

Is the Bowden cable stuck? n
Is the heater valve clogged? n
Is the water pump defective? maybe

To see if
the water pump is defective,
you can check if
the temperature gauge is in the red zone
after the motor is running for 5 minutes.
```

```
Please do the above and
respond to the following question.

Is the water pump defective? no
  . . . .
```

This makes sense, because the system should report all the diagnoses which can be made from the information already accumulated. Only after this is done should it proceed to search for other possible defects.

You should now better understand why the initialization file shown in Fig. 6-1 set the *phase(P)* state to *2*; if the user begins the session with a *check* request, then the questions should never be suppressed. On the contrary, the system must behave as if it were already in the second phase of the diagnosis, albeit with an inference tree "pruned" corresponding to the *Rule_No* at which the user decided to begin.

Thus, the introduction of the two diagnostic phases has contributed significantly to a more *flexible dialog*, adapting to the user's individual informational needs.

6.3 Heuristics

An auto mechanic, naturally, does not always have an idea as to what might be causing a problem. Even so, she does not, like the system just described, "mechanically" run through some forever fixed solution search algorithm to solve the problem. Instead, the mechanic typically applies a few *rules of thumb* and *preparatory initial tests* to try to determine approximately where the defect might lie.

She may see if the headlights function or if the motor can be started. The results of the initial test(s) will influence the order in which subsequent problems are investigated in a - presumably -optimal way. The developer of expert systems refers to these "intuitive" approaches as *heuristics*. They are as important a part of the expert's special knowledge as the systematic, formal rule-structured knowledge.

As mentioned in Chap. 4, heuristics are vital to preventing the "combinatoric explosion" of potential solutions when the knowledge base reaches a "useful" size: in our specific case, when we wish to avoid tiresome, and ultimately unnecessary dialog and defect testing. How can we achieve this?

The second part of the task, i.e. varying the procedure depending on specific criteria, is not very difficult. We merely remove the *Hypotheses_List* from the *start* procedure, where it originally served to steer the investigation of the various potential defects from the highest level. We must now administer it separately, in the manner illustrated in Fig. 6-2, as the independent fact

```
hypotheses(List_of_Defects).
```

Then we can, at any time, fetch the *List_of_Defects* from the knowledge base with *retract*, re-sort it as necessary and restore it with *asserta.*

We need only decide what the sort criterion should be. This is, naturally, dependent upon the *symptoms* to be checked in the preparatory tests, such as

(1) "The headlights work",

(2) "The motor starts",

(3) "....".

The expert mechanic can define a *network of relationships* between the afore-mentioned symptoms and the potential defects: the presence or absence of each such symptom increases or decreases the probability of a specific defect, or per-haps even eliminates the possibility entirely. Figure 6-5 is an example of such a network of relationships[1].

In order to avoid the problem of normalizing the probabilities, we treat the positive or negative values entered into the network merely as *points* which

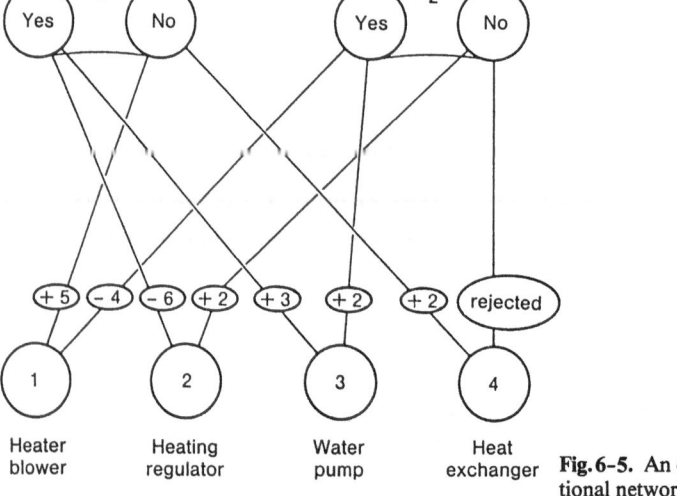

Fig. 6-5. An example of a relational network between symptoms and defects

---

[1] Should the reader happen to be an automotive engineer, and should our network of relation-ships appear somewhat improbable, we beg your pardon: we are merely "knowledge engineers" and are dependent upon our "area experts" for such data. We could, of course, claim that the whole thing was planned as the basis for the exercise "improve this outlandish relational net-work".

"speak" for the particular defect. Also, our experience shows that when initially defining such a relational network with an expert mechanic, it is usually easier to talk about "points" than "probabilities". People seem more familiar with point systems from sports or games, whereas typically only mathematicians really know what a *probability* is (even though many persons talk as if they knew too).

Therefore, we store the result of a symptom query as *points* facts for the alternative defects as

```
points(Hypothesis,Points,Possibility).
```

Here *Hypothesis* is the defect number, *Points* a counter for the positive or negative weight attached to it by the network of relationships and *Possibility* an indicator, initialized to *possible*, which gets changed to *impossible* when a symptom excludes this hypothesis entirely.

The initialization of the *points* facts and the hypotheses list is as follows:

```
points(1,0,possible).
points(2,0,possible).
points(3,0,possible).
points(4,0,possible).

hypotheses([1,2,3,4]).
```

The initialization file *init* (see Fig.6-1) must be modified accordingly, as well as the predicates starting the user dialog. In order to cleanly separate the various modifications to the basic dialog structure, as discussed in the previous chapter, we dispense with the two-phased aspect for taking existing information into account (as was demonstrated in Fig.6-2). We leave it to the reader to combine the two improvements suggested. When doing so, recall that you must register the fact that a given query about symptoms and the re-sorting of the hypotheses list has been made in a status variable. Otherwise the user will wonder why, after the diagnosis has been restarted to find other defects, she is asked if the headlights work!

For this reason, we introduce a new start instruction into our prototype with which the symptom queries are temporarily implemented and tested:

```
?- rule_of_thumb.

Do the headlights work ? yes
Does the motor start ? yes
Is the V-belt torn ? why
If the V-belt is torn
and the water pump is stuck,
then the water pump is defective.
Is the V-belt torn ? yes
The heater is defective (Rule 3, Rule 31).
```

According to our network of relationships, if the two symptom queries are answered positively, then most probably the water pump is defective. Consequently, the dialog will begin with defect rule 3, which ended up at the top of the hypotheses list after it was re-sorted with respect to points per hypothesis. Figure 6-6 shows the corresponding predicates for starting a dialog with symptom queries.

```
rule_of_thumb :-
        make_hypothesis(List),
        !, test_hypotheses(List).

make_hypothesis((Hypolist) :-
        /* Ask about symptoms : */
        nl, write('Do the headlights work ? '),
        read_in(Answer_1),
        test_questions1(Answer_1),
        nl, write('Does the motor start ? '),
        read_in(Answer_2),
        test_questions2(Answer_2),
        /* Sort the hypotheses according to points : */
        points(1,P1,_), points(2,P2,_),
        points(3,P3,_), points(4,P4,_),
        sort([P1,P2,P3,P4],_,[1,2,3,4],Hypolist),
        retract(hypotheses(_)),
        asserta(hypotheses(Hypolist)).

test_hypothoooo([]) :
        nl,
        write('I cannot find any defects.').
test_hypotheses([Alternative|Remainder]) :-
        (       points(Alternative,_,possible),
                check(Alternative)
        ;       test_hypotheses(Remainder)
        ).
```

Fig. 6-6. The start predicates for producing a resorting of the hypotheses list according to symptoms queried

Ignoring the *sort* predicate for the time being, the other predicates in Fig. 6-6 are essentially self-explanatory. *test_hypotheses* processes the hypotheses list as usual, using the predicate *check*, which we have already discussed. Based on the third argument of the corresponding *points* fact, it is decided whether the associated hypothesis is at all possible given the result of the investigation of the symptoms.

Figure 6-7 shows the predicate *test_questionsN* used for *evaluating the symptoms*. We have allowed here for user responses other than *yes* or *no*, e.g. *maybe*. In such cases, the *points* value for the particular defect remains unchanged. If, based on the network of relationships in Fig. 6-5, the evaluation of a symptom

```
test_questions1(Answer) :-
        meaning(Answer,yes),
        increase_probability(3,3),
        decrease_probability(2,6).
test_questions1(Answer) :-
        meaning(Answer,no),
        increase_probability(1,5),
        increase_probability(4,2).
test_questions1(_).

test_questions2(Answer) :-
        meaning(Answer,yes),
        decrease_probability(1,4),
        increase_probability(3,2).
test_questions2(Answer) :-
        meaning(Answer,no),
        impossible(4),
        increase_probability(2,2).
test_questions2(_).

increase_probability(Hypo,Points) :-
        retract(points(Hypo,Old_State,possible)),
        Newer_State is Old_State + Points,
        asserta(points(Hypo,Newer_State,possible)),
        !.
increase_probability(_,_).

decrease_probability(Hypo,Points) :-
        retract(points(Hypo,Old_State,possible)),
        Newer_State is Old_State - Points,
        asserta(points(Hypo,Newer_State,possible)),
        !.
decrease_probability(_,_).

impossible(Hypo) :-
        retract(points(Hypo,_,possible)),
        asserta(points(Hypo,0,impossible)), !.
impossible(_).
```

Fig. 6-7. The test predicates for evaluating symptoms

indicates that a hypothesis is impossible, then the associated *points* fact is modified accordingly. The predicate *impossible* sets the *Points* value for the hypotheses back to zero, for the sake of orderliness, since the hypothesis itself is no longer of consequence for the diagnosis.

Let us now examine the *sort* predicate of arity 4 in Fig. 6-6. The syntax of the *sort predicate* call is

```
sort(Points,New_Points,Hypos,New_Hypos).
```

Hypos is the old hypotheses list (the input parameter) and *New_Hypos* the re-sorted one (the output parameter, i.e. a variable argument at the time of invocation). *Points* is a list of the points accumulated for the corrresponding hypotheses in the *Hypos* list. *New_Points* is an auxiliary variable in which the points from the *Points* list are stored after being re-sorted (highest to lowest) in conjunction with the hypotheses. This occurs parallel to the generation of the *New_Hypos* list. Figure 6-8 shows the predicate *sort*.

```
sort([],[],[],[]).
sort([P|Points],New_Points,[H|Hypos],New_Hypos) :-
        split(P,Points,UP1,UP2,H,Hypos,UH1,UH2),
        sort(UP1,VP1,UH1,VH1),
        sort(UP2,VP2,UH2,VH2),
        append(VP1,[P|VP2],New_Points),
        append(VH1,[H|VH2],New_Hypos).

split(_,[],[],[],_,[],[],[]).
split(H,[H1|T1],[H1|U1],U2,
           HA,[HA1|TA1],[HA1|UA1],UA2) :-
        H1 > H,
        split(H,T1,U1,U2,HA,TA1,UA1,UA2).
split(H,[H1|T1],[U1],[H1|U2],
           HA,[HA1|TA1],UA1,[HA1|UA2]) :-
        H1 =< H,
        split(H,T1,U1,U2,HA,TA1,UA1,UA2).
```

Fig. 6-8. The predicate for sorting the hypotheses according to accumulated points

It is a somewhat more complex variation of a *quicksort* (see for example [SCHN87]). The basic difference lies in the last two variables, which represent the old arrangement of the hypothesesis list and the new arrangement, respectively. The latter is generated from the former, based on the results of the re-sorting of the old *Points* list. To understand the "algorithmic process" it is certainly useful to observe the activity of the *sort* predicate interactively via the Box-debugger (provided your system has one) with *debug_mode* turned off for the *split* predicate.

6.4 Diagnostic Statistics

In the previous sections we illustrated how one can exploit the user's experience to supplement the formal, causal rule-knowledge and optimize the man-machine dialog. We discussed techniques for steering the inference process via user hunches, as well as the implementation of heuristics through networks of relationships between symptoms and defects, incorporating an expert's know-how when developing the initial knowledge base.

Both the mechanic and the automotive engineer accumulate their knowledge and expertise mostly through their daily experience repairing and designing cars. It would make sense to provide our expert system with a *learning component* with which it too could gather experience from its successful diagnoses. In its most primitive form this implies collecting statistics about each defect discovered and its related causes.

One can use this data to let the system "learn" in which order the hypotheses list should be sorted and the diagnosis should be pursued. We will postpone a detailed discussion of the implementation of the learning component to the next section, however, since the *statistics* gathered are, in and of themselves, quite valuable even without their being directly employed to optimize the diagnosis. Naturally, they can be used to increase the knowledge of the expert, as well as of the user. Furthermore, they can help a manufacturer improve its quality control and design processes. There are cases where the collection of *product defect data* – via world-wide automatic querying of the locally employed diagnosis systems – was the primary motive for introducing such defect diagnosis systems into commercial operations.

The defect statistics use *statistic* facts which are initialized when the system itself is initialized. This is best done from a special initialization file *statistics*:

```
statistic(1, Defect_Frequency_1).
statistic(2, Defect_Frequency_2).
statistic(3, Defect_Frequency_3).
statistic(4, Defect_Frequency_4).
```

The values for *Defect_Frequency_N* are equal to zero, as long as the cause of a defect N has not yet been encountered. With each successful diagnosis the predicate *increment* increases each of the corresponding frequencies by one.

```
increment(Rule_Number) :-
        retract(statistic(Rule_Number,N)),
        N_new is N + 1,
        asserta(statistic(Rule_Number,N_new)).
```

If the statistics are only to be collected at the highest level, as in our example here, then this predicate should be inserted into the *check* rule.

```
check(R_No) :-
        defect(R_No,A,B,C),
        increment(R_No),
        store_this_step(R_No),
        print_result(R_No,A,B,C).
```

The statistics thus gathered can be directly output, on demand, with

```
?- statistic(Defect,Frequency).

Defect = 3
Frequency = 4;

Defect = 2
Frequency = 20;

Defect = 1
Frequency = 13;

Defect = 4
Frequency = 1;

no
```

Since we stored the *statistic* facts using *asserta* and fetched them successively by repeatedly inputting a semi-colon, i.e. exploiting Prolog's backtracking mechanism, the information is displayed automatically with the more recent defects preceding the older ones. Thus, in our example, the waterpump (3) was the last defect diagnosed, whereas the heat exchanger (4) was the defect which had not occurred the longest.

In order to preserve this information between sessions, a commercial system would always store the *statistic* facts collected during the current session as so-called *system statistics* by updating the file *statistics* as follows:

```
telling(Output),
tell(statistics),
listing(statistic),
told, tell(Output).
```

Then, as part of the system initialization, we always load the *statistic file*, containing the cumulative values, with the command

```
consult(statistics)
```

And now we shall show you how one can use the statistical data to effect an automatic optimization of the defect search strategy according to the system's "experience".

6.5 Learning from Experience

In Chapter 4 we had already indicated that it is not always sensible to allow the expert from whom one acquired the information about the various defect-cause relationships, tests for determining the presence of certain "causes" for defects and the measures to be taken to repair the defects, to (pre-)define the probability of different diagnoses. The main reason for this is that the frequency of particular defects or breakdowns in machines - and similarly for diseases affecting humans or animals - often heavily depends upon where the particular diagnostic system is being used.

Let us assume, for example, that our system for finding defects in a particular make of automobile has been developed in Hawaii. If it is then employed in a repair station on the edge of the Sahara or somewhere in Siberia, it is extremely unlikely that the probabilities of various defects and, therewith, the "reasonable" order for checking certain hypotheses, as defined based on the experience of an expert mechanic in Honolulu, will be of any practical use.

Consequently, it would certainly pay if every system installed could optimize its own diagnosis strategy based on the "statistical" experience accumulated locally. This is an essential advantage of potentially *non-deterministic flow of control* in an expert system, as opposed to the strict, *deterministic flow of control* in conventional algorithms. In the latter, the flow of control is fixed in static control structures and can only be modified by re-writing the program itself[2].

In many cases involving the probability of events, such as the occurrence of a particular defect, the well-known *20/80 % rule of thumb* applies: 20 % of the possible defects are the reason for 80 % of all necessary repairs (and those 20 % are presumably very different ones at the edge of the Sahara than in Hawaii). After sorting the diagnostic steps corresponding to their statistical frequency, one will, on the average, have to investigate only $20/2 = 10$ % of the possible defects in 80 % of the cases. On the other hand, in the remaining 20 % of the cases one will be successful only after having investigated approximately 60 % of the possible causes.

A rough estimate indicates that, using an optimal search strategy, a defect should be discovered after having checked about $(80*10 + 20*60)/100 = 20$ % of the alternatives. That is less than half of the steps needed when using an unsorted rule base, which would average 50 % of all the possibilities. Thus the exploitation of the diagnostic statistics to increase performance certainly pays; particu-

---

[2] This also applies, as a rule, to decision table generators, which are often - with good reason - considered to be an alternative means for implementing systems which are primarily controlled via selection of alternative cases.

larly when it not only saves "computer time", but – as in our case – also avoids time-consuming and therefore expensive testing of the object being investigated.

We base our example on the start predicates for two-phased searches (without queries regarding symptoms) illustrated in Fig. 6-2. Figure 6-9 shows the modifications needed when the predicate *new_priorities* is introduced to sort the hypotheses list according to the frequencies "learned".

```
start:-
        note_phase(1),
        hypotheses(Hypotheses_List),
        examine(Hypotheses_List).
start:-
        note_phase(2),
        new_priorities,
        hypotheses(New_Hypotheses_List),
        examine(New_Hypotheses_List).

new_priorities :-
        statistic(1,A), statistic(2,B),
        statistic(3,C), statistic(4,D),
        sort([A,B,C,D],_,[1,2,3,4],New_List),
        retract(hypotheses(_)),
        asserta(hypotheses(New_List)).

examine([]) :-
        phase(2),
        nl,
        write('I cannot find any defects.').
examine([Alternative | Others]) :-
        (       check(Alternative)
        ;       examine(Others)
        ).

check(R_No) :-
        defect(R_No,A,B,C),
        increment(R_No),
        store_this_step(R_No),
        print_result(R_No,A,B,C).

note_phase(P) :-
        retract(phase(_)),
        asserta(phase(P)).
```

Fig. 6-9. Accounting for the frequency of diagnostic success and adaptation of the hypotheses list (modifications with respect to Fig. 6-2)

The predicate *new_priorities* provides for a re-sorting of the hypotheses list corresponding to the current *statistic* values. We can borrow unchanged the *sort* predicate from Fig. 6-8, which we had used for optimization according to symptoms.

Obviously, one would, in practice, extend the gathering of statistics to the lower levels of potential causes, and not restrict it to the uppermost, as we did for simplicity's sake. This requires the inclusion of the *increment* predicate in the successful *cause* rules too. This modification is itself quite trivial, in contrast to the problem of having the additional statistical information considered automatically as part of the diagnostic strategy.

At the deeper levels one can no longer merely re-sort the hypotheses list. Instead, one must change the order of the various clauses for each possible defect, and, in the case of clauses containing a conjunction of *causes*, the order of the *cause* goals *within* each clause, according to the frequency of given *cause*. Such a *re-structuring of the knowledge base* is not particulary difficult to implement, but would significantly affect run-time performance. In such a case, it is preferable to provide a *utility program for system optimization*, which one runs at regular intervals, perhaps daily after business hours. After all, the relative frequencies of defects cannot change so radically in the typical daily routine, that it would pay to re-optimize before each diagnosis made.

6.6   Shortcomings and Possible Improvements

The problems discussed in this chapter, particularly the "self-teaching" facility of a system, are among the most difficult tasks in the design and implementation of expert systems. We shall therefore limit ourselves here to a few, especially significant shortcomings of the solutions presented.

- It is not necessarily a good idea to merely ignore a particular hypothesis, as we did after evaluating a symptom and deciding to "exclude" certain hypotheses, by changing the attribute in the associated *points* fact to *impossible*. Heeding the notion that "nothing is impossible", it may be wiser (and make the implementation easier) to instead just radically decrease the points count of such "impossible" alternatives by some large amount, e.g. 1000. This should move them to the end of the re-sorted hypotheses list allowing them still to be considered, should all the "possible" ones prove fruitless.
- Treating all "uncertain" facts as being "false" is similarly problematic. Those defects for which these facts are symptomatic cannot be excluded with certainty. Therefore, it would probably be a good idea to add a third phase to the diagnosis, in which such facts are then considered as being relevant. This would, however, necessitate some changes in the presentation of the results of the diagnosis, since we would then have to indicate to the user that the defects discovered on that basis are themselves merely "a possibility":

```
Perhaps the heater is defective
because it is uncertain
if the heater blower is defective.
```

The modifications required to achieve this are not so great and would be good practice in manipulating implicit texts.

- It is not a good idea to require the user to enter a rule number as argument to the *check* command, to select a particular defect area. Allowing for the use of mnemonics for this is preferable. This can be achieved in many ways. For example, the highest rule in the hierarchy could be identified by a symbolic name instead of a number. The fact that the argument to *defect* is a number is merely suggested by the variable name *Rule_No*, but as such used *nowhere* else. And if the rule were called "heating_regulator" instead of "2", then the user could simply write *check(heating_regulator)*. If one wishes to keep the rule numbers, one could achieve the above effect anyway, by introducing a new predicate like

```
start_with(heating_regulator) :-
        check(2).
```

- Alternatively, as suggested in the previous chapter, a menu could also be used as an aid to the user who wishes to inquire about rules whose numbers are unknown to her. As a general solution, one could present a *help menu*, whenever the user enters an illegal response or argument – be it a non-existent rule number or merely some input like

```
?  check(heater_thingamajig).
```

Depending on the predicate involved – and maybe even according to the context derived from the protocol of the dialog path to date – the system can then present the appropriate menu.

In general, the implementation of a good user interface is especially difficult when the system must exhibit a high degree of "intelligence" in its autonomous search for solutions and self-optimization, and, at the same time, be very adaptive to the varying approaches taken to a problem by the different users of the system. This area of endeavor is more the subject of research than the *state of the art*. As such, we consider the techniques presented here more as contributions to the exploration of these and related approaches. It should not prove difficult for the reader to find other shortcomings in the system discussed in this chapter. Unfortunately, correcting the weaknesses is usually more difficult than recognizing them. On the other hand, this makes it all the more worthwhile to think about how they might be improved!

7   Object-Oriented Knowledge Management

The "one dimensional" representation of knowledge using facts and procedures gets very involved when one tries to manage more complex knowledge structures. In a number of procedural languages, as well as certain extensions to LISP, object-oriented techniques have been adopted to remedy this. This approach enables one to define objects such that facts and procedural knowledge are packaged into single units. Furthermore, specialized object classes can be constructed in a manner which allows the more specific objects to "inherit" knowledge from more generally defined object classes. This yields a great saving in cost with respect to the gathering and representation of information. A particularly suitable organizational form for object-oriented knowledge involves so-called *frames*. We shall illustrate how easily one can implement an object-oriented knowledge base in Prolog, on the basis of a system for managing software licenses.

7.1   Objects, Instances and Classes

"Knowledge" is often "knowledge about objects". In our previous examples these *objects* were "tickets" or "auto heaters". They were not very highly refined. Indeed, there were four different types of tickets, but the knowledge stored about them consisted merely of their price and a few rules regarding their validity. The auto heater was somewhat more complex in structure, but we intentionally limited ourselves to a particular type – in the (unspoken) assumption that the mechanic would always consult the knowledge base for the particular model to be repaired.

In practice, however, the knowledge to be manipulated is more comprehensive and diverse. Thus, a medical diagnosis system like MYCIN [BUCH84] must administer data and knowledge about many different objects of many different *types* or *classes*: patients, operations, bacteria cultures, organisms, medications, ...

Or imagine an investment consulting system for banks. There we have different classes of customers (private individuals, companies, organizations, foundations) and investments (securities, real estate, precious metals, insurance policies, ...). And each form of investment can be broken down into sub-classes: securities, for example, into stocks, various bonds, mining shares, etc.

The complexity of the knowledge for each individual object (i.e. each individual customer or each individual security) increases naturally in another "dimension". This involves the practical organization of the multitude of objects and object classes overall: which knowledge components – e.g. rules – and which case data are valid independent of the type of a special security, which are valid only for particular classes thereof (e.g. only for stocks) and which apply only to a single specific object (e.g. the daily price of IBM stock)?

Consequently, we need a method for dealing with this second dimension of complexity, the multitude of objects to be manipulated. This is precisely the goal of *object-oriented knowledge management* and *software development.*

Let us begin by talking about the concepts of *object class* and *instance of an object.* Taking a pragmatic approach, let us say that an *instance* implies an *end node* or "leaf" in the *hierarchy of objects* (tree) defined by the relation "is a kind of". On the other hand, the higher-order, non-leaf nodes are referred to as *classes.* There may be many of these, each of which potentially contains a set of different instances or sub-classes. The distinction between instances and classes amounts to the consideration of the level at which we possibly wish to manage "different" knowledge. An example should clear up any misunderstanding.

In a medical diagnosis system, the individual patient will certainly be represented as an instance of an object of the class "patient". On the other hand, an organism, i.e. a pathogenic agent, is also an instance but not a class, although there may exist millions of individuals of this type. The reason for this is that we have no desire to gather information specific to each individual bacterium, while we do in the case of the individual patient.

Since the distinction can be somewhat arbitrary, and is merely a function of the degree (or depth) of the knowledge structure involved, we generally speak of "objects" when we talk about nodes in the tree and do not especially wish to differentiate between a "leaf", i.e. an "instance" of an object, and an intermediate node, i.e. a "class" of objects.

7.2   Representing Objects with Frames

The next concept which we must introduce is that of the so-called *frame.* It is the data structure used to represent an object, regardless of its level in the hierarchy, and store all the knowledge relevant to it.

One of the best and most intuitive explanations of a frame was made by *Puppe* (see [PUPP86], p. 6). In his description, a frame is a *"framework of expectations* for accepting and storing knowledge." This tersely captures the fundamental idea of the programming method: the formal structure of the knowledge being processed should be pre-defined to the greatest extent possible, so that the knowledge engineer and the user need only "fill out" the given, fixed "frame" or outline with the problem- and case-specific knowledge content. This approach should ease the gathering of knowledge, ensure the consistency of the knowledge base and simplify the implementation of the procedures for accessing and processing the knowledge represented in this manner.

In the following system, we will avoid making any structural distinction between frames, regardless of whether they are employed as object classes or instances of objects. This is important, because it is quite conceivable that an instance later becomes a class, when we are unexpectedly forced to distinguish between individuals or sub-classes in the given category. Recall our investment consulting system: it may occasionally become necessary to upgrade the instance "IBM stock" to a class if, after an increase of capital, we must differentiate "young" and "old" IBM stock, until the next payment of dividends has been made.

A frame has a unique *(object) name*, identifying the object it represents. In a medical diagnosis system the names *patient* and *bacteria_culture* could be names of object classes, and *miller_anna_071234* or *pseudomonas* the names of specific instances.

A frame may contain an arbitrary number of *entries* for the characteristics of an object; they are often referred to as the *arguments* or -more commonly - the *slots* of the frame. Slots might be *symptoms*, *dietary_restrictions* or *allergies*. In addition, it is conceivable that slots of the same name occur in different frames, even in ones at higher hierarchical levels.

If, for example, the slot *dietary_restrictions* occurs in (the instance) *miller_anna_071234* as well as in (the class) *patient*, then this merely indicates that the patient Anna Miller has her own special diet, whereas the slot in *patient* contains the *dietary_restrictions* valid for all those patients who do not have an entry for the corresponding slot in their individual frame.

The strategy for accessing knowledge thus defined, with implicit access to higher-order frames, is called *inheritance*:

- if a slot for the data sought exists in the current object being processed, then the information contained therein is applied,
- otherwise, the information in the corresponding slot in the frame at the preceding (higher) level, i.e. the definition of the next higher class, is accessed and thus "bequeathed from the father object to its sons",
- and, if necessary, this inheritance can be pursued up to the very highest object frame in the hierarchy.

Only if a slot cannot be found at all, even in the highest order frame, is the information considered to be not available.

In order to be able to determine which frame is the nearest ancestor ("father") of a given object, i.e. to which class of objects an object directly belongs, each frame, except the uppermost, contains a so-called *ako* slot with this information; "ako" is an abbreviation for "a kind of", i.e. "of the class"[1]. The

---

[1] In principle, one can define far more complex inheritance mechanisms, where an object may have several *ako* values or references. We shall define our inheritance "primitives" in such a manner that they will function for the more complex cases too, but will, nevertheless, limit ourselves to the simple tree hierarchies in our examples.

highest level frame represents "objects in general" and we therefore give it the name *general*.

Figure 7-1 illustrates such an object hierarchy based on our example of a medical diagnosis system. According to it, the patient "Anna Miller" must observe a diet designed for her specifically, whereas Maria Huber follows the diet applicable for patients in her class. On the other hand, allergy information exists for Maria Huber, while none can be found for Anna Miller, not even via inheritance.

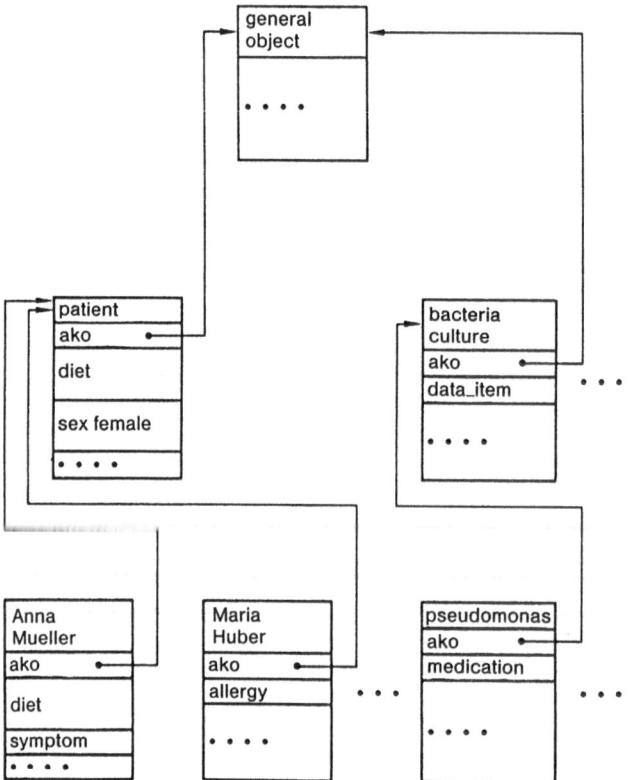

Fig. 7-1. Object and frame hierarchy in a medical diagnostic system (highly simplified)

The fact that both Anna Miller and Maria Huber are female is "inherited" from the slot "sex" in the frame for patient. If our system is installed in a gynecological institute this could be a legitimate arrangement. And should a man – perhaps in a dire emergency – be treated, one can always record his sex by entering a corresponding slot in his individual frame. Thus, the inheritance mechanism is an especially practical means of economically managing *default* information.

An entry in a frame can be interpreted in various ways. For example, it is possible that in some cases the corresponding data gets stored directly in the frame, while in other cases only the name of a procedure is stored there, which, when activated, can produce the desired information. Another possibility is that either before or after the modification of some specific data certain actions are to be automatically taken, for example making a protocol of the pending change of state. The associated, interpretative attributes of the entry in a slot are referred to as its *facet*.

We shall be discussing concrete example of facets shortly. For the time being, let us simply note that facets control the interpretation or evaluation of data in a slot.

In summary, an informational unit in an object-oriented system consists of four components:

- the object name, identifying the frame,
- the slot in this frame,
- the facet, defining how to interpret the slot,
- and finally the actual data stored in the slot.

We shall refer to a knowledge base built from such informational units as an *object-oriented knowledge base*, or simply, an *object base*.

7.3   The Organization of an Object Base

Since Prolog is designed to deal with knowledge bases composed of arbitrarily complex data structures, it is especially easy to implement expert systems based on frames and procedures for their manipulation in any number of ways. An example of a practical application can be found in [KEMP86]. There the authors used a single, relatively deeply embedded relation as the frame for an object.

We want to present just the other extreme here: for each facet of each slot we will be storing a separate relation of arity 4,

    frame(*ObjectName, Slot, Facet, ValueList*)

so that a frame, in general, consists of a set of such *frame* facts. They are identified via the unique name *ObjectName* associated with the object class or instance, as well as the *Slot* and *Facet*. The fourth argument is always a *ValueList*, even if it only contains a single element [*Value*]. This makes it possible to store multiple values for a facet.

Empty value lists are not stored. If there is no value for a slot or facet – perhaps because it is to be inherited from a higher-level frame – then no entry exists for it.

Instead of the *frame* relation defined above, one might consider using a tertiary relation of the form

    object_name(*Slot, Facet, ValueList*)

where all entries for an object would be identified via the respective functor name (represented here by *object_name*). This is certainly a conceivable alternative; indeed, it would also lead to faster access times in most implementations of Prolog, since fetching a clause with a particular functor is typically done more quickly than fetching one with the same first argument. Particularly in very large knowledge bases such a storage representation would be seriously worth considering.

Nonetheless, we chose the arity 4 *frame* solution because it offers three essential advantages:

(1) We can choose our object names more freely. For example, if we want to call an instance of an object or a class of objects *functor*, we can do so. The alternative approach would cause a name conflict with the corresponding built-in predicate *functor*.

(2) We can, with no further ado, also use the arguments *Slot* or *Facet* as search criteria and, for example, fetch all the instances of an object from a particular class of objects. They would all have the same value in the *ako* slot.

(3) We can write the quaternary *frame* relations directly into our clauses. The tertiary *object_name* relations, on the other hand, would always have to be constructed, as needed, using the *univ operator* (= ..).

The reader will have to decide whether these advantages outweigh the probable reduction in access speed on a case-by-case basis.

In those situations, as in our case, where one is not sure from the very start that one has found the optimal storage structure, or perhaps decides to change things around later, this *data abstraction* has proven to be quite practical. In the same vein, the respective data is never accessed directly, but rather always fetched via *primitive operations*. These will (we hope) remain unchanged, even if we should sometime decide to organize our data differently.

This is the fundamental idea behind *abstract data types*, which we wish to exploit here to avoid eventual problems arising from later modifications. Thus, in the following section, we shall formulate a set of access predicates which we will be using exclusively to manage our objects and the frames representing them.

7.4   Primitive Operations for Managing Objects

The basic set of operations for accessing and manipulating frames need not be all that large. We must be able to find facets of slots (and thus, naturally, per backtracking, frames too), delete and modify them. Furthermore, we want to be able to insert entries, as well as display instances and frames. At the end of a session, we would like to save the current state of the system in an external file, which we can later consult when we wish to continue where we had left off.

be variable and, furthermore, is treated as a single data value, even if it is a list or a structure.

If there is as yet no entry for the *Facet* named, then it will be created, the given data value becoming the sole element of the new value list [*Data_Item*] for that *Facet*.

If, on the other hand, an entry already exists, then *Data_Item* is merely added to the end of the list. No check is made to see whether the data just added already occurs in the list.

If *Facet= value*, and the system has an *if_added* procedure for the respective *Slot*, then it will be activated with the data value just passed in.

The predicate is not backtrackable.

delete(*Frame,Slot,Facet***)**

Frame, *Slot* und *Facet* must be instantiated with valid names at the time of invocation. If a matching entry exists, it is deleted.

If *Facet= value*, and the system has an *if_removed* procedure for the particular *Slot*, the primitive will activate it with the data list of the deleted slot. The predicate is successful, even if the associated entry did not exist in the first place.

delete(*Frame,Slot***)**

Both arguments must be instantiated with appropriate names at the time of invocation. All *Facet* entries of the respective *Slot* will be deleted. The tertiary *delete* primitive is used to carry this out, which means that, whenever possible, an *if_removed* procedure will be activated. This primitive also terminates successfully, even if there was no entry for the given slot

delete(*Frame***)**

The sole argument must be instantiated with a *Frame* name. All slots of the corresponding frame are deleted, with possible activation of *if_removed* procedures, as above. The primitive is successful even when the frame named does not exist.

If one or more frames make reference to the frame to be deleted via their *ako* slot, then the frame will not be deleted and a corresponding message will be issued.

modify(*Frame,Slot,Facet,Data***)**

Frame, *Slot* and *Facet* must be instantiated with the corresponding names and *Data* with a single data value, or a list of data, at the time of invocation. The primitive modifies the entry identified by the information above by applying the *delete* and *add* predicates. If *Data* is a list, then its individual elements will be added one at a time. In the process of doing so, *if_removed* and *if_added* procedures will be activated as required.

display_frame(*Frame*)

> This predicate displays the data stored in the entries where *Facet= value* for the slots of the *Frame* addressed. The output is made on the current output stream (typically the user's terminal).
> If the argument is a variable or the atom *all*, then the predicate is invoked with the name of the first (highest) frame of the object base. This causes the system to display every frame in the object base, one after the other, using backtracking. In this case, each slot will be preceded by the name of the *Frame* currently being displayed.
> This predicate never *fails*.

display_object(*Object*)

> Similar to *display_frame*, this predicate displays all slots for the given *Object*. In the process, however, inheritance and the associated *if_needed* procedural attachments are applied.

display_instances(*Frame*)

> This predicate recursively displays the sub-classes and instances of the *Frame* named, on the current output stream, indenting the list to indicate the hierarchical levels. If the argument is variable, or if it has the value *all*, then the list begins with the first (highest) frame of the hierarchy, which by convention has the name *general*.

store

> This predicate outputs the current state of the system into a file which is consulted at the beginning of the next session. The very first session on the system is an exception to this rule: the initialization of a new knowledge base is done by *consulting* the individual modules, which effectively links them together into a problem-oriented object management component.

This concludes our representation-independent specification of our object management component. The actual implementation thereof, with respect to our internal representation of the frames as a quaternary relation, is shown in the following section.

7.5   The Knowledge Base for Software License Administration

In order to illustrate the implementation on the basis of a concrete data structure, our example will deal with the *administration of software licenses*. We will be showing you the significant portions of a system which is being used commercially to store and process the licenses for IF/Prolog, a software product distributed world-wide in numerous different versions [HUKE86].

In this system, each individual license is an instance of an object. The different types of possible licenses build the higher-order classes of objects. The definition of the object classes was done rather pragmatically: *no* attempt was made to establish a, let us say "logical", *a priori* structure, e.g. with separate classes for each type of computer or operating system for which the product is available. This would likely lead to the situation where, for some of these classes of objects, very few or, perhaps, no instances existed, simply because the particular computer or operating system proves –for whatever reasons – to be "unpopular" for users of Prolog[2].

Since the primary reason for a hierarchical structure is the exploitation of the "inheritance" principal and since inheritance is only advantageous when there is something to "bequeath" and a sufficient number of beneficiaries or "heirs", the essential *criteria for establishing a class of objects* are

(1) the (expected) existence of enough members (instances or sub-classes) and

(2) an *abstraction of object characteristics* being conceivable, where as many object attributes as possible are administered in common via the slots of higher-order classes and inherited from them.

If the criteria are satisfied, this speaks clearly for a design approach involving hierarchies of objects, which views the higher-order object classes as *generalizations* abstracted from their individual instances or sub-classes. In the opposite direction, one derives the subordinate objects as *specializations* or refinements of the directly preceding (higher-order) object classes.

In the concrete case of the aforementioned software product, this kind of class definition via appropriate specialization leads to the hierarchy shown in Fig. 7–2.

The root of the object hierarchy, by convention a frame named *general*, represents all types of licenses for all versions of the product. Most of the licenses are *normal* ones, i.e. they are object code licenses, which are not transferable. Software houses, hardware manufacturers and distributors can purchase *OEM* licenses, which permit them to sell the software as part of their own products or directly market it as distributor. Other categories consist of so-called *special* licenses, which are issued in exceptional cases (e.g. when another company is working on a project in co-operation with the owners of IF/Prolog), and *on_loan* licenses, e.g. when the software is being used in the context of an "in-house" instructional seminar by some manufacturer. Since the contractual obligations among these different types of licenses and, consequently, the necessary slots and their associated default, as well as acceptable values, vary, it makes sense to define a separate class of object for each.

Among the *normal* licenses, on the other hand, more are issued for IBM/PC and compatibles than for all other manufacturers together. Therefore, it seemed

---

[2] This is not necessarily an indictment of the respective hardware: the fact that there are fewer Prologs installed on Amdahl machines than on PCs is probably because fewer individuals can afford an Amdahl.

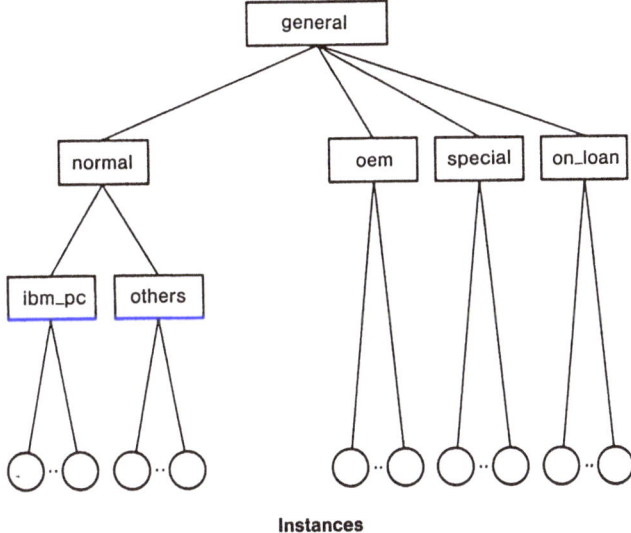

Instances

Fig. 7-2. The object hierarchy for managing software licenses

reasonable to divide this class of licenses into two sub-classes, *ibm_pc* and *others*.
As soon as enough licenses have been issued for other computer systems, e.g. *vax*
or *sinix*, one can then create separate sub-classes for them by defining corresponding frames and modifying the member licenses, which had been administered as *general* ones, so that the values in their specific *ako* slots now reflect
their new class membership.

The same thing can be done if other circumstamces dictate that these objects
should be newly (sub)-classified: in the next chapter we shall be extending this
license management system into a documentation system for memoranda and
reports. If we then wish to administer documents which, for example, refer
strictly to *hewlett_packard* licenses (and no others), then it would be practical to
represent these via a frame for such objects.

Figure 7-3 shows an excerpt from the internal representation of a frame as a
quaternary *frame* entry for each facet of a slot.

In this example all the entries are for the facet *value*, i.e. they directly build a
list of the respective values; other possible facet "types" will be discussed later.
The list usually consists of single data values. The *computer* entry for *ibm_pc*
shows, however, that this need not always be the case: since the models XT and
AT are equivalent with respect to the software, the licenser makes no distinction
between them. Thus, they both are included in the value list.

The frame for the customer *artificial_intuition* demonstrates the inheritance
mechanism. Its *ako* entry indicates that it has a license for the *ibm_pc* software.
They are running it, however, on a PC-D computer from Siemens; this is docu-

```
frame(general,quantity,value,[1]).
frame(general,language,value,[german]).
frame(general,uni,value,[no]).
frame(general,discount,value,[0]).
frame(general,currency,value,[dm]).

frame(normal,ako,value,[general]).
frame(normal,time_limit,value,[unlimited]).

frame(special,ako,value,[general]).
        . . . .

frame(ibm_pc,ako,value,[normal]).
frame(ibm_pc,gross_price,value,[1500]).
frame(ibm_pc,operating_system,value,[msdos]).
frame(ibm_pc,computer,value,[ibm_xt,ibm_at]).
frame(ibm_pc,medium,value,[diskette]).
frame(ibm_pc,storage,value,[256]).

frame(others,ako,value,[normal]).
        . . . .

frame(artificial_intuition,ako,value,[ibm_pc]).
frame(artificial_intuition,computer,value,
                              [siemens_pcd]).
frame(artificial_intuition,storage,value,[512]).
frame(artificial_intuition,uni,value,[yes]).
frame(artificial_intuition,discount,value,[30]).
        . . . .
```

Fig. 7-3. Some frames from the license knowledge base

mented by the "local" *computer* entry, which suppresses inheritance for this slot for this customer. The values for *gross_price, operating_system, time_limit* for the validity of the license issued, as well as the *quantity* of licenses granted or the *currency* of payment, on the other hand, are all inherited from some "ancestor" object. The customer has an entry indicating it is indeed a *uni*, i.e. a university or research institute, which automatically entitles it to a 30 percent *discount*. Consequently, we find a corresponding slot directly in its frame.

7.6   The Primitives for Accessing Objects

We are now going to implement the primitive operations, specified in Sect. 7-4, for a knowledge base of the kind shown in Fig. 7-3. This should be done, however, in a general form, so that the primitives can manipulate an arbitrary, frame-oriented knowledge base. In the next section we shall then see how one can describe the concrete application system using a "generic frame", which defines the structure of objects in the current knowledge base. Using this "generic frame", we shall then create the actual, application-specific frames for our system.

Let us begin with the – generalized – *search_for* primitive. It does not exploit the inheritance mechanism and, thus, we will not make it (directly) available to

```
search_for(Frame,Slot,Facet,Data_Item) :-
        (       var(Data_Item)
        ;       is_list(Data_Item)
        ),
        clause(frame(Frame,Slot,Facet,Data_Item),_).
search_for(Frame,Slot,Facet,Values_from_List) :-
        nonvar(Values_from_List),
        Values_from_List = evaluate([Data_Item|Rest]),
        search_for_x(Frame,Slot,Facet,
                                [Data_Item|Rest]).
search_for(Frame,Slot,Facet,Data_Item) :-
        nonvar(Data_Item),
        Data_Item = evaluate([_|_]),
        not is_list(Data_Item),
        search_for_x(Frame,Slot,Facet,[Data_Item]).

search_for_x(Frame,Slot,Facet,[Data_Item|Rest]) :-
        nonvar(Data_Item),
        clause(frame(Frame,Slot,Facet,DataList),_),
        (       member(Data_Item,DataList)
        ;       search_for_x(Frame,Slot,Facet,Rest)
        ).
search_for_x(Frame,Slot,Facet,[Data_Item|Rest]) :-
        var(Data_Item),
        search_for_x(Frame,Slot,Facet,Rest).

is_list(X) :- var(X), !, fail.
is_list([_|_]) :- !.
is_list([]).
```

Fig. 7-4. The basic *search_for* primitive for accessing a facet entry

the enduser. Nonetheless, it is, for us, the most important predicate for implementing the remaining access primitives for frames. Figure 7-4 shows the implementation.

As described in the specification, the three clauses distinguish between three possible applications:

- If the fourth argument, *Data_Item*, is a variable or a list, then these will – if possible – be instantiated with the data item from the entry found; this entry is always a list of values. To test if the argument is a list, we use the predicate *is_list(X)*, which can also be found in the figure. We shall be applying it frequently in the following.
- If the fourth argument is a structure of the form *evaluate(SearchList)*, then entries will be sought, where, in turn, their fourth argument, i.e. their data list contains *all* the elements contained in the *SearchList*. Those arguments among the first three parameters which are not yet instantiated at the time of invocation will be instantiated with the values from the corresponding facet entries found.
- If the fourth argument is neither a variable nor a list nor an *evaluate* structure, than it is transformed into a list containing a single element, and this is then used, internally, as the search argument.

We can now use the basic *search_for* primitive to implement *ask*, our first "genuine" access primitive. This primitive takes inheritance into account when accessing the *Data* of a slot. It is a primitive which can actually be placed directly at the user's disposal. Figure 7-5 shows the implementation.

The predicate inquires about the *Data* in the *Slot*, named in the second argument, of a given *Frame*. The value for *Data* comes either directly from a *value* facet or, alternatively, may be established by an *if_needed* procedure associated

```
ask(Object,Slot,Data) :-
       nonvar(Object), nonvar(Slot),
       (       var(Data)
       ;       is_list(Data)
       ),
       (       search_for(Object,Slot,value,Data),
               !
       ;       procedure_call(if_needed,Object,
                              Slot,Data),
               !
       ;       search_for(Object,ako,value,Fathers),
               member(Father,Fathers),
               ask(Father,Slot,Data),!
       ).
```

Fig. 7-5. The predicate *ask* for ascertaining the value of a slot

with the *Slot*. The predicate *procedure_call* activates a *procedural attachment* for the slot, if one has been provided.

If the direct access to the slot, as well as the procedure call, fails, then the inheritance mechanism is applied to find a "father" and, if he exists, *ask* him. It is possible that a *list* of fathers appears in an *ako* slot, in which case, they get processed one after the the other. As soon as one has been found which can "bequeath" the desired data, the *cut* ends the search immediately. Thus, our primitives are also suitable for *multiple inheritances* from different ancestors; nonetheless, we shall be limiting ourselves here to a simple, tree-structured hierarchy.

If the third argument, *Data*, is not a variable, then we assume that the user is searching for a frame or a slot. In this case, we treat *ask* as a synonym for "*search_for* a corresponding entry with the facet *value*".

The next primitive needed is *add*, which adds a single data item to the value list of an existing facet entry or, if the respective entry does not yet exist, creates it. Figure. 7-6 illustrates its implementation. If an *if_added* procedure is defined for the corresponding slot, *add* sees to it that it gets invoked once the new facet *value* has been added.

As already explained in the specification, this predicate only makes sense when all its arguments are instantiated at the time of invocation. Note that the

```
add(Frame,Slot,Facet,Data_Item) :-
        nonvar(Frame), nonvar(Slot),
        nonvar(Facet), nonvar(Data_Item),
        (    retract(frame(Frame,Slot,
                            Facet,Previously)),
             (      member(Data_Item,Previously),
                    !, Afterwards = Previously
             ;      append([Data_Item],
                            Previously,Afterwards)
             )
        ;    Afterwards = [Data_Item]
        ),
        assertz(frame(Frame,Slot,Facet,Data_Item)),
        % activate "if_added"-Procedure, if
        % "value" slot and "Afterwards" do not equal
        % "Previously" (i.e., a new value was
        % actually added) :
        (    Facet == value, Afterwards == Previously,
             procedure_call(if_added,Frame,
                            Slot,Data_Item), !
        ;    true
        ).
```

Fig.7-6. The access primitive *add* for entering a facet value into a slot

```
delete(Frame,Slot,Facet) :-
        nonvar(Frame), nonvar(Slot), nonvar(Facet),
        (    delete_x(Frame,Slot,Facet)
        ;    true
        ).

delete(Frame,Slot) :-
        nonvar(Frame), nonvar(Slot),
        (    search_for(Frame,Slot,Facet,_),
             delete_x(Frame,Slot,Facet)
        ;    true
        ).

delete(Frame) :-
        nonvar(Frame),
      . findall(Dependent,
              search_for(Dependent,ako,value,Frame),
              List),
        List \= [],
        nl, write('The frame "'), write(Frame),
        write('" cannot be deleted.'), nl,
        write('The following frames depend on it:'),
        nl, write_list(List), nl,
        !, fail.
delete(Frame) :-
        /* no dependent frames via "ako" : */
        nonvar(Frame),
        (    search_for(Frame,Slot,Facet,_),
             delete_x(Frame,Slot,Facet)
        ;    !
        ).

delete_x(Frame,Slot,Facet) :-
        retract(frame(Frame,Slot,Facet,Data)),
        /* invoke "if_removed" proc, if "value": */
        Facet == value,
        procedure_call(if_removed,Frame,Slot,Data),
        fail.

write_list([]).
write_list([Element|Rest]) :-
        tab(1), write(Element),
        write_list(Rest).
```

Fig. 7-7. The primitives for deleting frames, slots and facet entries

Data_Item passed in is treated as a single value and thus is *inserted into the value list* of the entry. Even if the argument is itself a list, it is considered a single element (or unit). Consequently, if one wishes to put a set of new individual data, which has been presented in the form of a list, into the value list, then each individual element of the list passed in must be added via a separate call to *add.*

We have implemented the predicate such that the set of values always remains a "genuine" set: if one attempts to *add* a particular value repeatedly, it only gets added to the list of values the first time, and an associated *if_added* procedure is also only invoked on that one occasion. It may, of course, be debatable whether this truly reflects the user's intention. Should your application have good reason to allow identical elements in the value list, you need only drop the corresponding check from the predicate.

What now follows is a family of predicates for deleting single facets from slots and, ultimately, from entire frames. As can be seen in Fig. 7-7, they are all based on an auxiliary predicate *delete_x*, which deletes a single entry. It gets called repeatedly until no more facts for the structure concerned exist. The repetition is implemented by simply letting *delete_x* always *fail.*

Here too we activate an *if_removed* procedure automatically, as soon as a *value* facet has been deleted.

Note how the unary primitive *delete(Frame)* checks whether there are any dependent frames, i.e. frames containing an *ako* slot referring to the one to be deleted. It uses *find- all* to collect the names of all such frames into a list. If the list is *not* empty, the deletion is aborted and a message is issued informing the user that the very frames named in the list are the reason for doing so.

The primitive *modify* for changing a single entry is, in principle, simply a sequence of *delete* and *add.* But since we permit the fourth argument to be a list of *Data* whose individual elements are to become the individual elements of the modified (i.e. new) value list (as opposed to the entire list as a single element therein), we use the auxiliary procedure *new_data* to process such lists of data an

```
modify(Frame,Slot,Facet,Data) :-
        nonvar(Frame), nonvar(Slot),
        nonvar(Facet), nonvar(Data),
        delete(Frame,Slot,Facet),
        new_data(Frame,Slot,Facet,Data).

new_data(_,_,_,[]) :- !.
new_data(Frame,Slot,Facet,[Data_Item|Rest]) :-
        !, add(Frame,Slot,Facet,Data_Item),
        new_data(Frame,Slot,Facet,Rest).
new_data(Frame,Slot,Facet,Data_Item) :-
        add(Frame,Slot,Facet,Data_Item).
```

Fig. 7-8. The predicate *modify* for facet entries

element at a time. By using the primitives *delete* and *add* we can be sure that any *if_removed* and *if_added* procedures defined for the slot will be applied correctly when *modify* is invoked.

7.7   Displaying Complex Structures

With the help of the predicates *search_for* and *ask* we can, of course, interactively inquire about individual slots in our object base. On the other hand, we typically wish to see more complex structures, such as the individual instances or sub-classes of an object, or perhaps the complete set of current values for a frame or an object. And, when displaying an object, inherited characteristics and *if_needed* values should naturally be taken into account.

To this end, we provide the output procedures *display_instances, display_frame* and *display_object*. The following example demonstrates these predicates with respect to the excerpts of the license administration object base shown in Fig. 7-3.

```
?- display_instances(all).
general
   normal
      ibm_pc
         artificial_intuition
         . . . .
      others
         ' ' ' '
   special
      . . . .
   . . . .
yes
?- display_frame(artificial_intuition).
ako: ibm_pc
computer: siemens_pcd
storage: 512
uni: yes
discount: 30
yes
?- search_for(artificial_intuition,price,value,P).
no
?- ask(artificial_intuition,price,P).
P = 1050
yes
?- search_for(artificial_intuition,gross_price,value,P).
no
```

```
?- ask(artificial_intuition,gross_price,P).
P = 1500
yes
?- search_for(ibm_pc,gross_price,value,P).
P = 1500
yes
?- display_object(artificial_intuition).
ako: ibm_pc
computer: siemens_pcd
storage: 512
uni: yes
discount: 30
price: 1050
operating_system: msdos
medium: diskette
time_limit: unlimited
quantity: 1
language: german
currency: dm
yes
```

It would pay to compare the dialog with the information from the license knowledge base in Fig. 7-3. You will probably notice that neither a direct inquiry about the *price* charged to *artificial_intuition* using the predicate *ask* nor an examination of its instantiation using the procedure *display_object* returns the value *1500*, which it inherits from its class frame, *ibm_pc*, but *1050* instead. Apparently the gross price has already been reduced by the 30% *discount* registered in the object.

Here the *procedural attachment* provided is the predicate shown in Fig. 7-9. Based on the tree-structured hierarchy of Fig. 7-2, we assume that only one "father" is registered in the *ako* slot.

```
calculate_price(Frame,Slot,[Price]) :-
        ask(Frame,discount,[Discount]),
        ask(Frame,gross_price,[Gross]),
        Price is (100-Discount)*Gross/100.
```

Fig. 7-9. The procedural attachment for calculating prices

We shall be discussing the invocation mechanism for procedural attachments in greater detail in the next chapter. For the time being it suffices to note the following points:

- In our primitive predicates, as in all procedures which we define ourselves, we can request a (conditional) activation of the procedural attachment named in the first argument for a slot by using *procedure_call.*

• This invocation must occur, however, *before* the inheritance mechanism is triggered, because (like a value entry stored directly in the object frame) the *if_needed* procedure overwrites the inherited value.
• On the other hand, a *value* entry stored directly in a frame has priority over a procedural attachment for the respective slot. If we had stored an explicit *price* for *artificial_intuition* -perhaps based on some special agreement – then the *if_needed* procedure would never have been activated.

Note also that the *gross_price* used to calculate the actual price charged did not come from the *artificial_intuition* frame itself, but rather was bequeathed to the procedure *calculate_price* by the ancestor *ibm_pc.*

In the following figures you see the three new output predicates introduced in our sample dialog. The first, Fig. 7-10, is *display_instances.* Starting with the object *Frame* named, it displays the sub-tree of the hierarchy in indented format. If one requests *all,* as we did in our example, then the listing begins from the highest-order frame, *general,* and effectively yields a *table of contents* of our *object base.*

```
display_instances(Frame) :-
        display_instances(Frame,0).

display_instances(all,I) :-
        !, display_instances(general,I).
display_instances(Frame,I) :-
        search_for_instance(Frame,I),
        !, indent(I),
        write(Frame),
        J is I+1,
        search_for(Instance,ako,value,Frame),
        display_instances(Instance,J),
        fail.
display_instances(_,_).

search_for_instance(Frame,I) :-
        (       search_for(Frame,_,_,_),
                !
        ;       indent(I),
                write(Frame),
                write(' does not exist'),
                fail
        ).

indent(I) :-
        nl, T is I*3, tab(T).
```

Fig. 7-10. The predicate for listing the instance in an object hierarchy

To enable the use of the procedure *display_instances* for listing all defined object classes and object instances in a file (and thus also on a printer), it instantiates a variable argument initially with *general* and – after backtracking – with all the other defined frame names. This is simply achieved by fetching the particular *ako* entry, of which every frame, except the very highest, must have at least one.

Perhaps you should briefly consider why calling the binary predicate *display-_instances* from the unary predicate guarantees that a variable argument, as well as the argument *all*, will cause the listing to begin with the root of the hierarchy tree, i.e. the frame *general*.

Figure 7-11 shows the predicate *display_frame*. It displays all the *value* entries in the *Frame* named.

```
display_frame(Frame) :-
        var(Frame),
        (        Frame = general
        ;        search_for(Frame,ako,value,_)
        ),
        nl, nl, write(Frame), nl,
        display_frame(Frame),
        fail.
display_frame(Frame) :-
        nonvar(Frame),
        search_for(Frame,Slot,value,Data),
        write_slot(Slot,Data),
        fail.
display_frame(_) :- nl.

write_slot(Slot,Data) :-
        nl, write(Slot), write(' :'),
        write_list(Data).
```

Fig. 7-11. Displaying a frame without activation of *if_needed* procedures and inheritance

If invoked with a variable argument, *display_frame* outputs all frames except the first one, i.e. *general*. This is achieved by backtracking through all the respective *ako* value entries of which there is exactly one in each of the subordinate frames.

The procedure *write_list*, used by *write_slot*, is familiar to us from Fig. 7-7.

display_frame disregards inheritance and procedural attachments. The procedure *display_object*, shown in Fig. 7-12, takes both into account. On the other hand, in contrast to *display_frame*, *display_object* cannot be called with a variable argument, since the user would only invoke it to examine a specific object of interest.

```
display_object(Object) :-
      nonvar(Object),
      display_values(Object,[],SlotsShown),
      findall(Slot,
              search_for(_,Slot,if_needed,_),
              IfNeededSlots),
      display_if_needed_slots(IfNeededSlots,Object,
              SlotsShown, AllSlots),
      display_father_slot(Object,AllSlots,_).

display_values(Object,Shown,Afterwards) :-
      search_for(Object,Slot,value,Data),
      not member(Slot,Shown),
      write_slot(Slot,Data),
      display_values(Object,[Slot|Shown],Afterwards).
display_values(_,Shown,Shown).

display_if_needed_slots([Slot|Slots],Object,
                        Shown,Afterwards) :-
      member(Slot,Shown),
      display_if_needed_slots(Slots,Object,
                              Shown,Afterwards).
display_if_needed_slots([Slot|Slots],Object,
                        Shown,Afterwards) :-
      not member(Slot,Shown),
      (       procedure_call(if_needed,Object,
                              Slot,Data),
              nonvar(Data),
              write_slot(Slot,Data)
      ;       true
      ),
      display_if_needed_slots(Slots,Object,
                              [Slot|Shown],Afterwards).
display_if_needed_slots([],_,Shown,Shown).

display_father_slot(Object,Shown,Afterwards) :-
      search_for(Object,ako,value,Fathers),
      display_fathers_slot(Fathers,Shown,Afterwards).
display_father_slot(_,Shown,Shown).

display_fathers_slot([Father|Fathers],Shown,After) :-
      display_values(Father,Shown,Now_Shown),
      display_father_slot(Father,Now_Shown,
                          To_Be_Shown),
      display_fathers_slot(Fathers,To_Be_Shown,
                          After).
display_fathers_slot([],Shown,Shown).
```

Fig. 7-12. Displaying an object taking *if_needed* procedures and inheritance into account

Note how the predicate *display_object* ensures the proper ordering of the object's "own" slots, with both the values inherited and those generated by procedural attachments, by applying three special auxiliary predicates. The predicates use the procedure *write_slot*, shown in Fig.7-12, to output the individual slot values.

The predicate *findall* is used to determine when the predicate *display_if_needed_slots* should be applied to have *procedure_call* generate the value and display it.

Since the *if_needed* procedures or inheritance should only be applied for those values which have *not already* been established, the procedure must keep track of all the slots already displayed. This is achieved with the help of the last two list arguments of the auxiliary predicates *display_values*, *display_if_needed_slots*, *display_fathers_slot* and *display_father_slot*. The first list contains all the slots which have already been displayed at the time of invocation and the second is uninstantiated. The procedure then passes the former back out via the latter, extended by those slots which it has meanwhile displayed.

Here too, multiple inheritance from more than one "father", i.e. ancestor is "algorithmically" supported. In such a case, the list of fathers stored in the *ako* slot would be processed from left to right. Entering the slots just displayed into the corresponding list ensures that the correct "order" of inheritance is guaranteed, even in the event of identically named slots among the ancestors.

7.8   The "System" as an Object

Should you attempt to build an object base with the access predicates provided up to now, in order to try out the output predicates, you will quickly realize that it is an extremely difficult and error-prone enterprise, using *add* and *modify*. Being true "primitives", they operate at the level of individual entries or values and do not bother testing if your input yields valid frame structures – indeed they could not do so, because they are supposed to be "generally applicable", i.e. independent of any semantics.

Furthermore, you have probably noticed that, up to now, with the exception of the small sample excerpt from the knowledge base, no mention has been made of the promised, concrete application, i.e. the license administration. Thus, it is difficult to write comfortable, higher-level input procedures for the instances, e.g. a new customer. To provide the user with the kind of support for such actions which one can rightfully demand from a knowledge-based system, one must first establish "what the system is actually supposed to do". Or, in other words, we must know/decide what the precise, syntactic structure of the frames for the instances, the hierarchy of the object classes and the procedural attachments are. Since the procedures guide the system and process the knowledge, they define, in essence, the *semantics* of our system. Once we have the primitives for building and manipulating an (arbitrary) object base, then implementing a specific, concrete application consists, primarily, of developing the object-type frames and the necessary procedural attachments.

The actual structure of an application system is described via a *generic frame*. It stands "above" the "normal" object hierarchy and defines a *generic object*, which one can conceive of as being the schemata of a concrete, object-oriented knowledge base.

This generic frame can thus be considered the representative for the *system as an object*. Consequently, we define this *metaobject*'s name as a fact stored in the database at system initialization:

```
system_ident(Gen_Object).
```

All other objects are created from the generic frame and obtain "knowledge" from it as needed. The generic frame contains, among other things, entries for facets like *if_needed* and *if_removed* for those slots for which predicates are to be defined as procedural attachments.

The interpretation of the generic frame is also different from that of the "normal" ones. It depends entirely on the current reason for its being accessed. This is how the generic frame, for example, controls the creation of a new, "normal" object – the exact details, however, are the subject of the next chapter. Consequently, we shall forego our full implementation of the license administration system until then.

Instead, let us close this chapter with a discussion of the problem of system initialization and maintenance. Regardless of the degree of comfort with which we create and modify the different instances of licenses, we naturally wish to store them at the end of a session in such a fashion that we can resume our work in another, later session, with the system in precisely the same state as when we last stopped.

The procedure *store*, shown in Fig. 7-13, is used for just this purpose. It writes the complete, current state of the system into a file, which can be consulted in the next session with the system. The name of the file is, at the same time, the name of the system.

```
store :-
        system_ident(SystemName),
        telling(Whom), tell(SystemName),
        listing,
        told, tell(Whom).
```

Fig. 7-13. The procedure *store* for saving the current state of the system

The individual system components only get consulted as separate modules, i.e. the primitives, the generic frame and the object classes, as well as the procedural attachments, when the system is used to build an entirely new, object-oriented knowledge base.

Thereafter, the system starts each time by loading the last current state saved via *store*. This is best initiated simultaneously with the invocation of the Prolog interpreter per

```
ifprolog -c SystemName .
```

If you have no experience with Lisp, where storing and fetching the complete system is common practice and has been a tradition for decades, it will probably strike you as being odd to manage "programs" and "data" as a single, large object. You should get accustomed to it, however, since that is the fundamental characteristic of *knowledge-based programming* – making no distinction between these two components of a software system. The sooner you accepts the idea that procedures constitute knowledge just as much as facts, the easier a time you will have with this new approach to software.

7.9   Shortcomings and Possible Improvements

The primitives presented here for administering objects on the basis of a hierarchy of frames is merely a prototype system, as are all the systems presented in this book. Thus, they do not satisfy typical, professional standards of quality. Nonetheless, they should provide a sound basis for an object-oriented expert system if one does not merely treat them as a *frame* for the knowledge needed, but also goes on to embed them in an appropriate "shell-like" user interface.

Let us point out a few problems which one should solve in the process of refining the systems along those lines.

- Maintenance of the *integrity of the object base* is a major weakness of our primitives. We do not, for example, check if a frame with the name given even exists, when we create a new *ako* slot, and we (still) have no protection against mispelling of object or class names. This will be improved in the next chapter, when we introduce the *generic frame* and a predicate *new* for defining new instances, but this will not alleviate all such problems. Thus, a warning in advance: we suggest that the reader always consider, during our discussions of these concepts, how one could make the object base robuster with respect to such possible errors, and how the individual predicates could be refined for a professional system.
- The procedure *store* in Fig. 7-13 has the disadvantage that the user must remember to explicitly call it before leaving the system, otherwise she will lose all the changes made during the session. A primitive but neither particularly safe nor elegant remedy would be the definition of a predicate

```
end :- store, bye.
```

to terminate the session.

- When embedding the Prolog dialog in a user interface one should provide a command to end the session, which always asks the user if she wishes to save the current state of the system before terminating. It would be useful to modify those procedures which change the state of the system, i.e. *add, delete, modify* and *read_value_entered*, such that they always make a corresponding entry in the data base indicating the current system state, which *store* then removes (before calling *listing*!). The system would then only remind the user if she had indeed presumably forgotten to consider saving the state of the system.

- The predicate *store* has one other weakness. Such a system should probably do something about backing up its particular "former" state; perhaps by not updating the last version of the file *SystemName*, but rather moving (renaming) it as a *backup copy*. Just how this can be done most efficiently depends on the quality of the embedding of the operating system in your Prolog system. The ideal situation is when you can pass an operating system command directly to it from within Prolog. Thus, under a Unix system, you could then say

```
mv SystemName SystemName.bak
```

which would then be translated into the corresponding system call,

```
sh(UnixCommand)
```

to be executed before *tell* in the *store* predicate.

- A more subtle problem arises in the procedure *modify* in Fig. 7-8. What happens if all, or perhaps just some of the entries in the new *Data* list match the existing ones exactly? Perhaps the user merely wishes to employ the predicate to change or remove a few values of a longer list, while leaving the rest unchanged? As long as no *if_added* or *if_removed* procedures have been defined for the corresponding slot, the total deletion or re-insertion of values is inelegant and inefficient, but we could leave the correction of this shortcoming to a later optimization. If such procedures exist, however, then it is no longer certain that one should activate them, since the corresponding data has not actually been deleted or newly added. After all, the purpose of the *procedural attachments* in the rule is to deliberately provide for specific *side effects*, and any unnecessary invocation of them is not guaranteed to be harmless. Perhaps the side effects for *if_added* and *if_removed* end up cancelling one another out. In any case, a good implementation should take appropriate measures to avoid this (even if this turns out to be no more then an unmistakeable, boldfaced entry in the handbook or a message to the user pointing out the problem).

This list of shortcomings is certainly not complete, but will, we hope, help orient you in your own search for possible improvements to the basic approach.

8 Frames and Procedures

The frames approach to knowledge management presented in the previous chapter is nothing more than a simple, object-oriented extension to Prolog. In and of itself, it represents no more an "expert system" than a Prolog interpreter without the knowledge base implemented in Prolog. Frames become a form of knowledge organization, as opposed to a mere data structure, through the procedures embedded in them, which assume an active role in the collection and processing of information. In this chapter we illustrate the necessary techniques for achieving this, based on the recording of new objects via generic frames, as well as the "intelligent" administration of memoranda. The latter serves as an extension to our license administration system and is a typical example for knowledge-based programming techniques on a frame-oriented basis. You will see that it heavily exploits the processing possibilities permitted by the embedding of procedural attachments in the *facet* entries of frames.

8.1 Interactive Definition of New Objects

Building new frames with the primitive predicate *add* was not terribly convenient. Furthermore the process is very much subject to error. Since the primitive operations do not really check the input with regard to syntactic or semantic correctness, it is almost impossible to guarantee the long-term integrity and consistency of the object base.

For instance, when entering an *ako* slot, no check is made if the frame to which the given value refers even exists. If we should ever happen to misspell the frame name parameter, then the slot defined in the process ends up belonging to some other frame – either to one which already exists or to some non-existent one –depending on the nature of the typographical error. Furthermore, absolutely no plausibility tests are made with respect to the input values, which in itself is completely unacceptable in any system of practical use.

The concept of *generic frames* will help eliminate this problem. We can consider it as the introduction of a *metaobject*, which exists "outside" the normal object base and embodies the essential knowledge about the *structure of the object base* and the instance frames. Figure 8-1 illustrates the generic frame for the license administration system *license*[1]. In essence, the generic frame describes each slot of a typical instance of an object, e.g. those of the frame for the customer *artificial_intuition* shown in Fig. 7-3, with the help of a few standardized facets.

```
system_ident(license).

frame(license,ako,default,[ibm_pc]).
frame(license,ako,prefer,[in_list([ibm_pc,others])]).
frame(license,ako,require,
      [in_list([ibm_pc,others,oem,special,on_loan])]).

frame(license,computer,default,[ibm_pc]).
frame(license,computer,prefer,
        [in_list([ibm_pc,vax,cadmus])]).
frame(license,computer,require,[]).

frame(license,operating_system,default,[msdos]).
frame(license,operating_system,prefer,
        [in_list([msdos,unix,vms])]).
frame(license,operating_system,require,[]).

frame(license,storage,default,[256]).
frame(license,storage,prefer,[in_list([256,5000])]).
frame(license,storage,require,[larger(0)]).

frame(license,gross_price,default,[1500]).
frame(license,gross_price,prefer,
                        [in_list([1500,8100])]).
frame(license,gross_price,require,
                        [between(1050,22600)]).

frame(license,currency,default,[dm]).
frame(license,currency,prefer,[in_list([dm,dollar])]).
frame(license,currency,require,[]).

frame(license,language,default,[german]).
frame(license,language,prefer,
        [in_list([german,english])]).
frame(license,language,require,[]).
```

---

[1] We omit the higher-order structures, such as *general* or *normal*, as shown in the excerpts in Fig. 7-3, from the object class frames here. Nonetheless, these should be considered part of the generic frame and should be defined along with it in the same module.

```
frame(license,uni,default,[no]).
frame(license,uni,prefer,[in_list([yes,no])]).
frame(license,uni,require,
          [in_list([yes,no,unknown])]).

frame(license,discount,default,[0]).
frame(license,discount,prefer,[in_list([0,30,40,70])]).
frame(license,discount,require,[less_than(100)]).

frame(license,time_limit,default,[unlimited]).
frame(license,time_limit,prefer,
                         [in_list([unlimited,3])]).
frame(license,time_limit,require,[]).

/* Procedural attachments : */

frame(license,uni,if_added,[store_discount]).
frame(license,price,if_needed,[calculate_preis]).
```

Fig. 8-1. The generic frame for license administration

The following facets play a role in our example.

default provides a *default value* if the user enters none and there is no procedural attachment (see below) available for calculating it automatically.

prefer   suggests *typical values* for the entry when requested by the user.

require specifies a list of *constraints for slot values*. In our example we employ the constraints *in_list([...,...])*, *between(‹Value1›,‹Value2›)*, *larger(‹Value›)* and *less_than(‹Value›)*. These can be used as predicates for checking the *plausibility of slot values*. Their names indicate their respective function. In Fig. 8-5 we shall see how the predicate *recognize* uses these entries to check user input and reject incorrect information.

A *default* and a *prefer* facet should be provided for every slot of an instance. If any arbitrary input is permitted for a particular slot, then one need only omit the corresponding *require* facet. Alternatively, one could merely provide an empty list of values; examples of this approach are the corresponding entries for the slots *computer*, *operating_system* or *time_limit*.

Procedural attachments may also be defined and used as "values" for slot entries of the generic frame. These procedures are invoked automatically when the constraints specified by the correspondingly named *facet* are satisfied. We shall be discussing this in detail a bit further on.

For the time being, the generic frame in Fig. 8-1 contains only two such facets, *if_added* and *if_needed*, for the slots *uni* and *price*. As we shall see shortly, the *if_added* attachment is used to automatically generate the correctly discounted value for university or research institutes – as in the case of our sample customer *artificial_intuition* – as soon as the value *yes* is registered in the *uni* slot. As shown in Fig. 8-2, the procedure for making the necessary entry is merely a call to the *add* primitive. It gets activated when the slot is *uni* and its value is *yes*.

```
store_discount(Frame,uni,yes) :-
        add(Frame,discount,value,30).
```

Fig. 8-2. The procedure for automatically storing the discount

The generic frame is essentially employed to manipulate the knowledge base. For example, the predicate *new*, illustrated in Fig. 8-3, can be used to create a new instance of an object.

The implementation employs the predicate *read_in* and the following primitive operation to read in the user's response as an atom or integer:

read_value_entered(*Gen_Object, Slot, Frame* **)**

> A value for a slot in a frame is read in interactively, checked and stored in the knowledge base under the control of a generic object called *Gen_Object*.

We shall discuss this primitive predicate in greater detail after we have finished examining the predicate *new*.

Figure 8-3 shows the *two* predicates involved, a unary one, which is called by the user with the name of the new object instance to be created, and a binary one, which is called by the former with the name *Gen_Name* of the generic object as an additional parameter. The latter predicate's task is to actually create the new object frame in a dialog with the user.

The first rule of the unary predicate *new* checks if a frame with the name suggested by the user already exists. If so, it asks the user if she wants to delete the existing frame. As you recall, the *delete* primitive used to do so guarantees that no frames get deleted if they are referred to via the *ako* slots of other frames; thus, the predicate *new* itself need not take any measures to prevent this.

The predicate *read_in* reads the user's response up to the next ‹return› transforming the answer into an atom or, if it contains only numerals, an integer. We shall be using *read_in* frequently in the remainder of the book. Once transformed, the predicate *meaning* checks if the answer may be interpreted as meaning "yes", using a technique discussed in earlier chapters.

The binary version of the predicate *new*, which actually creates the new objects, consists of two clauses which get invoked one after the other. Both are quite trivial:

• The first one iterates between the goal *search_for*, which fetches the slots of the generic frame, i.e. the respective *default* facet, one at a time, and the closing

```
new(ObjectName) :-
        search_for(ObjectName,_,_,_),
        nl, write('There already is an object "'),
        write(ObjectName),
        write('". Should it be modified? '),
        read_in(Input),
        (       meaning(yes,Input),
                delete(ObjectName),
                !, new(ObjectName)
        ;       !, fail
        ).
new(ObjectName) :-
        system_ident(Gen_Frame),
        new(Gen_Frame,ObjectName).

new(Gen_Frame,ObjectName) :-
        nonvar(Gen_Frame),
        search_for(Gen_Frame,Slot,default,_),
        read_value_entered(Gen_Frame,Slot,ObjectName),
        fail.
new(Gen_Frame,ObjectName) :-
        nonvar(Gen_Frame),
        nl, write('New Object: '),
        write(ObjectName),
        display_frame(ObjectName).

read_in(Input) :-
        read_till_return(List),
        (       is_a_number(List),
                !, number(Input,List)
        ;       name(Input,List)
        ).

read_till_return([A|B]) :-
        get0(A),
        A \= 10,        /* no "return": */
        !, read_till_return(B).
read_till_return([]).

is_a_number([Element]) :-
        Element >= 48, Element =< 57.
is_a_number([Element|Rest]) :-
        is_a_number([Element]), is_a_number(Rest).
```

Fig. 8-3. The procedure *new* for creating an instance of an object

fail. In between, the predicate *read_value_entered* supplies the information necessary for constructing the slots of the new instance of the object, according to instructions acquired interactively from the user. This predicate shall be explicated in the next section.

- Once all the slots have been defined, the second *new* clause then displays the frame just created with the help of the now familiar predicate *display_frame.* This gives the user an opportunity to correct possible entry errors immediately, using the *modify* or *delete* primitives.

8.2   The Dialog for Constructing a New Object

Before we go on to discuss the techniques of inquiry and the interpretation of user inputs, as embodied in the aforementioned primitive *read_value_entered,* let us examine a sample dialog. With the initial input, *assistance,* we have the system show us the various possible responses in this context. This should make the dialog relatively self-explanatory.

```
?- new('Institute of Linguistics').
ako: assistance

Possible responses are :
assistance,help        ==> display this list.
?                      ==> display some possible values.
??                     ==> display limits on values.
.                      ==> take the default value.
<return>               ==> omit this slot.
<other input>          ==> will be interpreted as a value.

ako: .
computer: ?

Some possible responses are :
ibm_pc vax cadmus

computer: olivetti
operating_system: ??

Arbitrary values are permitted.

operating_system: ms_dos
storage: ??

The value must be greater than 0.
```

```
storage: .
gross_price: .
currency:
language:
uni: sure

The possible responses are :
yes no unknown

uni: yes
discount: .
time_limit:

Slot: Institute of Linguistics
ako: ibm_pc
computer: olivetti
operating_system: ms_dos
storage: 256
gross_price: 1500
uni: yes
discount: 30
```

As illustrated in the example, if the user makes a response which is contrary to prerequisites of the *require* facet, then the system informs the user as to the acceptable values. This is the same output given as when the user explicitly demands the limits on values for a given slot by responding to a system inquiry with "??".

If the slot exhibits no such *require*ments, then a user input of "??" yields a message indicating that an arbitrary value is permitted.

Slots for which neither an explicit value nor a period (selecting the default value) has been given are simply omitted.

Notice that the generic object's *default* value of "0" (zero) for the *discount* slot was not bequeathed on the new object. The fact that the user indicated that the *uni* slot was to be assigned the value "yes" caused the *if_added* procedure *store-_discount* to place the value "30" into the *discount* slot. Had the user made an explicit entry for *discount*, however, then it would have overwritten the automatic value.

Let us now turn our attention to the implementation of the dialog component.

8.3 Acquiring and Evaluating User Input

As we have just seen, the predicate *read_value_entered* bears the essential responsibility for constructing a new object. Its implementation is shown in Fig. 8-4. This entails reading and interpreting the user's response to the system's

```
read_value_entered(Gen_Frame,Slot,Frame) :-
      write(Slot), write(': '),
      read_in(Input),
      recognize(Input,Gen_Frame,Slot,Frame),
      !.
```

Fig. 8-4. The predicate *read_value_entered*

request for the value of a slot, as dictated by the information in the generic frame. To this end, it employs the *read_in* predicate, which we saw in Fig. 8-3.

The predicate *recognize* is used to interpret and check the user response, typically with the help of the generic frame. This relatively complex procedure is shown in Fig. 8-5. Synonym detection is done, as already explained in previous chapters, via the application of a *meaning* clause.

The various *recognize* clauses deal with different possible user inputs. Should the user make the corresponding request, the clause labeled /*1*/ displays, with the help of *explain_input*, a summary of the inputs recognized, as we saw in the sample dialog above. We shall forego further discussion of this procedure as it is quite straightforward.

If a period is entered to select the default value for a given slot, the two clauses labeled /*2*/ assume control. The first one tests if the slot already has a value, in which case nothing more is done. And that is precisely the function of the second clause - to do nothing more! This is how the 30 percent discount value, installed as a consequence of the *yes* response for the *uni* slot, was preserved despite the presence of a default value in the generic frame.

However, if the corresponding slot has no value, then a search of the generic frame is made for the *Data* of the slot's *default* facet. The *add* primitive places the data found into the appropriate slot of the new object.

Clause /*3*/ (Fig. 8-5) deals with the question mark response, where the user is interested in seeing some typical responses for the given question. These are extracted from the *prefer* facet of the current slot in the generic frame and displayed to the user. This is done by the predicate *write_constraint*, shown in Fig. 8-6.

This predicate is really quite simple: essentially it displays the contents of the list of constraints passed to it, whereby the procedure *write_this_constraint* helps "translate" the information in the *prefer* slot into a "readable" form. We shall restrict ourselves here to an explanation as to why, in clause /*3*/ (Fig. 8-5), we also pass the atom *prefer*, i.e. the name of the facet just interpreted, as a second argument. We do so because we wish to write different headers depending on the facet involved. The default for *write_this_constraint* is, based on the unary invocation of *write_constraint*, just that for the alternative facet, *require*.

Clause /*4*/ (Fig. 8-5) responds to the double question mark input with which the user can inquire about limitations on possible input values. This information is stored in the *require* facet of the generic object. If the facet contains an

```
recognize(Input,Gen_Frame,Slot,Frame) :-          /*1*/
      meaning(Input,assistance),
      explain_input,
      read_value_entered(Gen_Frame,Slot,Frame), !.
recognize('.',Gen_Frame,Slot,Frame) :-            /*2*/
      not search_for(Frame,Slot,value,_),
      search_for(Gen_Frame,Slot,default,Data),
      add(Frame,Slot,value,Data), !.
recognize('.',_,_,_) :- !.
recognize('?',Gen_Frame,Slot,Frame) :-            /*3*/
      !, search_for(Gen_Frame,Slot,prefer,Data),
      nl, write_constraint(Data,prefer),
      read_value_entered(Gen_Frame,Slot,Frame), !.
recognize('??',Gen_Frame,Slot,Frame) :-           /*4*/
      !, search_for(Gen_Frame,Slot,require,Data),
      nl,
      ( Data == [],
         write('Arbitrary values are permitted.'),
         nl, nl
      ; write_constraint(Data)
      ),
      read_value_entered(Gen_Frame,Slot,Frame), !.
recognize('',Gen_Frame,Slot,Frame) :-             /*5*/
      ( search_for(Gen_Frame,Slot,
                require,in_list(_)),
         nl, write('Obligatory entry'),
         recognize('??',Gen_Frame,Slot,Frame)
      ; true
      ), !.
recognize(Input,Gen_Frame,Slot,Frame) :-          /*6*/
      ( search_for(Gen_Frame,Slot,require,Constr),
         !
      ; Constr = []
      ),
      ( check_these_constraints(Input,Constr), !,
         add(Frame,Slot,value,Input)
      ; nl, write_constraint(Constr),
         read_value_entered(Gen_Frame,Slot,Frame)
      ).
```

Fig. 8-5. The procedure *recognize* for interpreting user responses

```
write_constraint(L) :-
        write_constraint(L,require).

write_constraint([],_).
write_constraint([Constr|Rest],Which) :-
        write_this_constraint(Constr,Which),
        write_constraint(Rest,Which).

write_this_constraint(in_list(L),Which) :-
        (       Which = require,
                !, write('The possible')
        ;       write('Some possible')
        ),
        write(' responses are: '), nl,
        write_list(L), nl.
write_this_constraint(between(A,B),_) :-
        write('The value must lie between '),
        write(A), write(' and '),
        write(B), nl.
write_this_constraint(larger(A),_) :-
        write('The value must be greater than '),
        write(A), nl.
write_this_constraint(less_than(A),_) :-
        write('The value must be less than '),
        write(A), nl.
```

Fig. 8 6. Predicates for displaying the constraints

empty list, then there are no limitations and the user is informed accordingly. Otherwise, the *require* option of the *write_constraint* predicate (Fig. 8-6) is invoked and the limitations are displayed in readable form.

Clause /*5*/ (Fig. 8-5) deals with the case where the user merely responds by hitting the *carriage return* key, indicating the desire to omit the current slot from the new frame. Should, however, a *require* value exist in the generic frame for the slot affected, then this means that the entry is obligatory[2]. In this case, we inform the user of the situation and proceed to list all the acceptable values by calling clause /*4*/. If, however, one is permitted to omit the value, then the predicate simply ends with *true*.

Finally, we have clause /*6*/ for processing actual values for the given slot. If a *require* facet exists, the constraints which the value must satisfy are extracted from it; otherwise, the variable *Constr* is instantiated as an empty list. The user

---

[2] If this is not the implication, then one should foresee another facet in the generic frame to handle this situation.

```
check_these_constraints(_,[]).
check_these_constraints(Input,[Constr|Rest]) :-
        not is_list(Input),
        check_this_constraint(Input,Constr),
        check_these_constraints(Input,Rest).
check_these_constraints(Input,[Constr|Rest]) :-
        is_list(Input),
        nl, write('List ('), write(Input),
        write(') for "check constraints" '),
        write('not provided'),nl.

check_this_constraint(Input,in_list(L)) :-
        member(Input,L).
check_this_constraint(Input,between(A,B)) :-
        integer(Input),
        Input >= A,
        Input =< B.
check_this_constraint(Input,larger(A)) :-
        integer(Input),
        Input > A.
check_this_constraint(Input,less_than(A)) :-
        integer(Input),
        Input < A.
```

Fig. 8-7. Predicate for checking constraints

input is, in any case, then checked for acceptability by the predicate *check_the-se_constraints* based on the information in the list, as illustrated in Fig. 8-7.

If the value entered by the user satisfies the given limitations, it is added to the new instance by the primitive *add.* If not, then the predicate *write_constraint* informs the user of the constraints to be satisfied and *read_value_entered* is reactivated to process the user's subsequent response.

The predicate *add* will automatically invoke an *if_added* procedure if the generic frame provides one for the current slot. This is true, in our case, for the *uni* slot and so, when *yes* is entered there, the *discount* slot will be assigned an appropriate value. We shall examine this mechanism more closely in the next section.

8.4   Procedural Components

As could be seen in the sample dialog at the end of Sect. 8.2, we only record a single *gross_price* in the frame of the instance of an object. And yet, we can interactively inquire about the actual price –discount included:

```
?- ask('Institute of Linguistics',price,P).

P = [1050]
yes
```

The price is determined as needed using the procedural attachment *calculate-
_price,* illustrated in Fig. 7-9. Its activation, as we saw in Fig. 8-1, is provided by
the corresponding *if_needed* facet of the generic frame:

```
frame(license,price,if_needed,[calculate_price]).
```

Procedural attachments are special facets of the attribute represented by a particular slot. They are invoked whenever, as in the example above, a value is needed,
but not explicitly provided by the frame (*if_needed*) or a value is added
(*if_added*) or one is removed (*if_removed*). They are usually defined *globally* for a
specific slot, i.e. for the attribute represented by it. They are then valid independent of the current frame. That is why we always define them here as facets of
the generic frame.

This is, however, a somewhat arbitrary convention. We choose to take this
approach only because, in most applications, such procedures are in fact seldom
class-specific, not to mention instance-specific. Thus, assigning them to special
frames, at least in this case, would unnecessarily complicate things without offer-
ing any advantages for the implementation.

Should this not be the case for your application, you can, of course, take any
number of different approaches. The implementation of the predicate *ask*
(Fig. 7-5) is entirely independent of them. Where the procedural attachments are
actually to be found is a "secret" known only to the access predicate *procedure-
_call* activated in *ask.* Let us take a closer look at it. It is a particularly important
predicate, insofar as it is the one to be modified if you decide to take a frame-
specific, rather than a global, approach to the *management of the procedural
attachments.*

As such, we do not consider *procedure_call* to be a primitive predicate. It
would be better to implement it via a more generalized predicate for executing
procedures. We shall supplement the set of primitive operations for managing
objects illustrated in Sect. 7.4 with:

execute(*Procedures, Frame, Slot, Data)*

> *Procedures* is a procedure name or a list of procedures, *Data* a list of data
> values, *Frame* and *Slot* are the respective names of same. *All* the given
> *Procedures* will be activated individually for *all* the given *Data*; the indi-
> vidual invocation is of the syntactic form

```
Procedure(Frame, Slot, Data_Item).
```

The *Procedures* to be executed must, consequently, always be defined as a tertiary predicate. If they do not have any need for the arguments *Frame* and *Slot*, then (anonymous) variables may be specified. If *Data_Item* is uninstantiated at the time of invocation, then the procedure can "calculate" a value for it.

Please note, however, that we not only foresee a list of procedures, but *also* a list of data, both of whose members are to be "processed" one at a time. The idea is to enable one to write the individual procedures in the simplest form possible. Figure 8-8 presents the primitive predicate *execute*, as well as the predicate *procedure_call* implemented with it.

```
procedure_call(Facet,Frame,Slot,Data) :-
        system_ident(SystemName),
        search_for(SystemName,Slot,Facet,Proc),
        execute(Proc,Frame,Slot,Data).

execute([],_,_,_) :- !.
execute(Proc,Frame,Slot,Data) :-
        Data == [], !.
execute(Proc,Frame,Slot,Data_Item) :-
        not is_list(Data_Item), !,
        execute(Proc,Frame,Slot,[Data_Item]).
execute([Proc|Rest],Frame,Slot,Data) :-
        !,
        execute(Proc,Frame,Slot,Data).
        execute(Rest,Frame,Slot,Data).
execute(Proc,Frame,Slot,[Data_Item|Rest]) :-
        nonvar(Proc), !,
        Procedure =.. [Proc,Frame,Slot,Data_Item],
        clause(Procedure,_), !,
        activate(Procedure),         % never fails !
        execute(Proc,Frame,Slot,Rest).
execute(_,_,_,_).

activate(Procedure) :-
        Procedure, !.
activate(_).
```

Fig. 8-8. The predicates *procedure_call* and *execute*

If the fourth argument to *execute*, the data item for the procedure, is not a list, then it is converted into one, as illustrated in Fig. 8-8. This protects the user against forgotten list-brackets in the case of a single data element, assuming, of course, that the element itself is not supposed to be a list. The last clause guarantees that the predicate *execute* always terminates successfully and the procedures all get processed, even if one of them is not executable, e.g. because of a variable element in the list of procedures or a functor *Proc* for which no tertiary predicate has been defined. The goal *clause(Procedure,_)* is inserted to calm conscientious Prolog interpreters, which often treat the absence of a clause as an exception condition and abort the process altogether.

Notice, too, that the first argument of the *procedure_call* predicate, also shown in Fig. 8-8, is designated as *Facet.* This should remind the programmer employing the predicate that she must supply *procedure_call* with the corresponding facet identifier for which the procedure is to be run, e.g. *if_needed.* As mentioned earlier, the predicate "fetches" the associated procedure, as a data value, from the entry in the generic frame for the slot and facet. This is, as a rule – like every data value in our system – a list of one or more procedures. But *execute* is constructed such that it digests procedure lists, as well as individual procedure names as its first argument.

We invite the reader to "walk through" this mechanism, beginning with the primitive predicate *ask,* shown in Fig. 7-5. It is the basis for incorporating *procedural knowledge* into the frames used to represent objects. Without this possibility, one could hardly characterize the method as "knowledge-based", but, at best, a clear and – due to inheritance – economical means for structuring data.

To emphasize its significance, we shall now present a more demanding application of procedural attachments, in the form of an automated system for managing and indexing memoranda.

8.5   Managing Free Format Text in External Memory

In our product administration system, however, we would like to manage *free format text,* such as *memoranda* or the like.

In databanks it is not particularly good organizational technique to attach such "unstructured" text material directly to the formatted data base. This is is even more unadvisable in the case of our knowledge base: to be sure, one can embed arbitrarily long character strings in Prolog structures, either as lists or as atoms, but the demands on main memory are sufficiently great to make such solutions highly impractical.

Thus, in expert systems too, one is inclined to store *texts,* which are primarily to be administered and occasionally printed or perhaps displayed to the user, in the *operating system's filesystem.* One then need merely store a reference to the particular text, e.g. the name of the file in which the text is actually stored, in the corresponding frame entry. In our specific case, in the Unix environment, the reference will take the form of

    MEMOS/*SystemName*⟨*n*⟩.

SystemName will be the name identifying the application system, in our case *licenses.* The identifying name is used to distinguish memos from one application

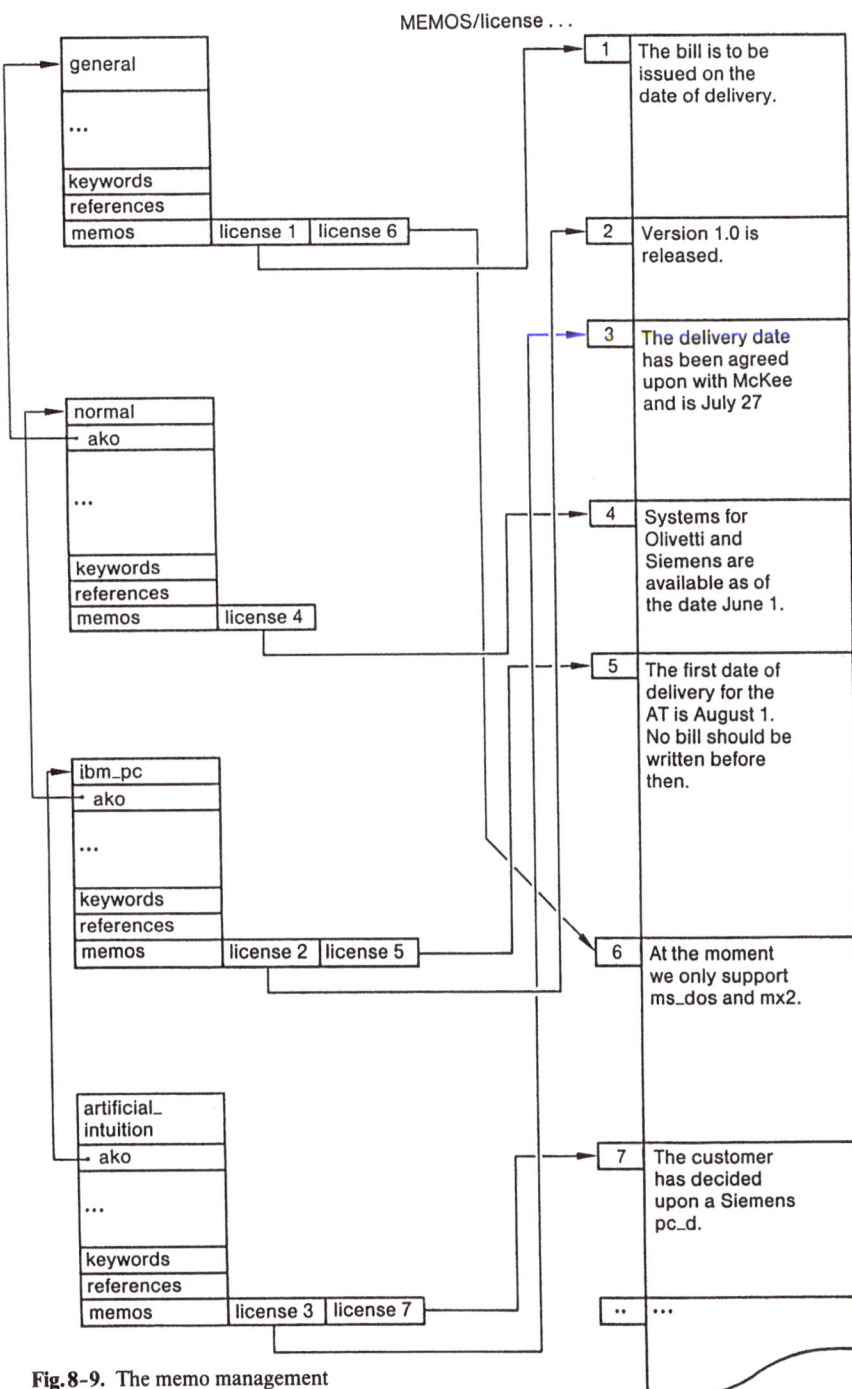

Fig. 8-9. The memo management

from those of another, i.e. the directory *MEMOS* can be used as a store for memos from all over. The ‹*n*› is the serial number of the text; it begins at 1 and is simply incremented.

Figure 8-9 shows a schematic of a simplified version of such a memo management. It should be noted that we have limited ourselves here to a single "branch" of the object tree. The references to the actual files containing the memo texts will be kept, as illustrated in the figure, as a value in the *memos* slots of each frame. In anticipation of some other functions related to the memo management we have also foreseen two other slots, *keywords* and *references*, which we shall be using later on to generate an index of memo topics.

To implement the *text management on external memory* we shall be needing a few auxiliary predicates. Figure 8-10 illustrates the ones used for a Unix environment and a screen editor named *tiptop*. If you are operating in a different environment, then you will have to make adaptations accordingly.

This is why *memo_prefix* and *editorname* contain the Unix pathname of the memo directory and the name of our preferred editor, respectively. Note that they are strings, i.e. lists, and *not* atoms. They are used in *next_memo_name* to construct a unique, serialized filename and in *compose_memo* to put together the system command line to activate the editor. This is done using standard Prolog techniques. Should you have difficulty following what is done here, we recommend a review in one of the books in the bibliography (e.g. [SCHN87]).

Once *compose_memo* has formulated the necessary *Command*, it calls upon the Unix system with *sh(Command)*, which activates the editor in a *subshell* and returns to Prolog as soon as the user has written her memo and leaves the editor.

The predicate *output_file* writes the contents of a file, whose name is passed in via the argument *FileName*, into the current output stream[3]. It is employed by the predicate *output_memo*, which prints/displays the given text enclosed in a header and footer consisting of a horizontal line, produced by the predicate *write_line*. Should your Prolog system not provide the *for* predicate shown, you can just as easily produce the separator by defining *Text_Separator* as an atom and printing it with *write*.

The last procedure shown in Fig. 8-10, *words_from_file*, is used to read "words" from a *File* into a *WordList*. It uses a subprocedure *read_file*, which corresponds, with the exception of minimal changes in the terminating conditions, to the procedure *read_in* (Fig. 5-7), used for reading an input line. The adaptation of *read_in* for this purpose is left as an exercise for the reader. This procedure also represents the non-printable (special) characters in the word list produced via the logical function *char(ASCII)* for the equivalent ASCII symbol.

Using the auxiliary procedures shown in Fig. 8-10, we first define two predicates *memo(Frame)* and *write_memos(Object)*. The first one permits the inclusion

---

[3] We have defined the end-of-file (EOF) symbol as being either the ASCII value 4 or 26, which covers all the Unix implementations we are familiar with, as well as MS-DOS. Should your system observe a different convention, then you will have to modify the predicate *is_EOF* accordingly.

```prolog
memo_prefix("MEMOS/").
editorname("tiptop ").

is_EOF(4).          /* <control>D */
is_EOF(26).         /* <control>Z */

next_memo_name(Memo) :-
        memo_prefix(NP), system_ident(System),
        name(System,SS), append(NP,SS,NPS),
        next_memo_number(N), number(N,NA),
        append(NPS,NA,Name), name(Memo,Name).

next_memo_number(N) :-
        ( retract(memo_number(N)) ; N = 1 ),
        N1 is N + 1,
        asserta(memo_number(N1)).

compose_memo(Memo) :-
        editorname(EditorCall),
        name(Memo,FileName),
        append(EditorCall,FileName,CommString),
        name(Command,CommString), sh(Command).

output_memo(Memo) :-
        write_line,
        output_file(Memo),
        write_line.

output_file(FileName) :-
        seeing(Was), see(FileName),
        repeat,
        get0(C),
        ( is_EOF(C) ; put(C), fail ),
        seen, see(Was).

write_line :-
        [Text_Separator] = "-",
        for(1,I,80), put(Text_Separator), fail.
write_line :-
        nl.

words_from_file(File,WordList) :-
        seeing(Was), see(File),
        read_file(WordList),
        seen(File), see(Was).
```

Fig. 8-10. Auxiliary predicates for managing texts in external memory

of a new memo in a specific *Frame*. The second one outputs the memos associated with a given *Object* in reverse chronological order, i.e. the most recent
first, paying regard, naturally, to the hierarchy of objects.

The predicate used to do this is *show_memos(MemoList)*, which can be found
in Fig. 8-11. It, in turn, employs the predicate *conditional_output_memo*, which
determines if the output is intended for the user terminal or a file. In the former
case, it asks the user if the corresponding memo should be displayed or not. If
the output is to a file, however, it unconditionally writes the memo to the file.

```
show_memos([]).
show_memos([MemoEntry|Rest]) :-
        conditional_output_memo(MemoEntry),
        show_memos(Rest).

conditional_output_memo([Memo,Frame]) :-
        not telling(user),
        !, show_memo_name(Memo,Frame),
        output_memo(Memo).
conditional_output_memo([Memo,Frame]) :-
        show_memo_name(Memo,Frame),
        write('------- display (y/n) ? '),
        get0(C),
        skip(10),    % Fetch input till end of line
        (       [C] = "y",
                output_memo(Memo)
        ;       true
        ).

show_memo_name(Memo,Frame) :-
        write('Frame: '), write(Frame),
        write('  Memo: '), write(Memo), nl.
```

Fig. 8-11. The predicate *show_memos* for outputting memos

The *MemoList*, which the predicate *show_memos* expects as an argument, is a
list of entries, each of which is a list itself of the form

```
[Memo_name, associated_Frame]
```

An example of a memo list for the two frames in Fig. 8-9 would be

```
[ [MEMOS/license6,general],
  [MEMOS/license4,normal],
  [MEMOS/license1,general] ]
```

The following dialog excerpt illustrates the input and output of memos, based on the set of memos shown in Fig. 8.9. Due to space limits, we refrain from a complete display of the full-screen editor typically employed by the user to compose the memorandum. As mentioned above, the actual Prolog dialog is only resumed when the user leaves the editor.

```
?- memo(normal).

<<<<<<<<<<< Invocation of Full-Screen Editor >>>>>>>>>>

From now on, customers are to receive a separate
description of the C-interface in addition to the
standard manual.

<<<<<<<<<<< End of Full-Screen Editor  >>>>>>>>>>

yes
?- write_memos(normal).

Frame: normal  Memo: MEMOS/license8
-------- display (y/n) ? n
Frame: general  Memo: MEMOS/license6
-------- display (y/n) ? y
----------------------------------------------------
At the moment we only support ms-dos and mx2.
----------------------------------------------------
Frame: normal  Memo: MEMOS/license4
-------- display (y/n) ? y
----------------------------------------------------
Systems for Olivetti and Siemens are deliverable
beginning June 1.
----------------------------------------------------
Frame: general  Memo: MEMOS/license1
-------- display (y/n) ? n

yes
?-
```

Note, when comparing the dialog output with the contents of Fig. 8-9, that the request to *write_memos(normal)* only displays the memos of the two highest frames, *general* and *normal,* starting with the most recent one. Figure 8-12 illustrates the implementation of the unary predicates *memo* and *write_memos.*

The predicate *memo* stores the name of the *Memo* just compiled in the specified *Frame.* The use of our primitive predicate *add* for this purpose facilitates the implementation of certain post-processing, such as the production of an index,

```
memo(Frame) :-
        (   clause(frame(Frame,_,_,_),_),
            !, next_memo_name(Memo),
            compose_memo(Memo),
            add(Frame,memos,value,Memo)
        ;   nl, write('Unknown object'), nl
        ).

write_memos(Object) :-
        findall(Ancestor,
                ancestor(Object,Ancestor),
                FrameList),
        search_for_memo_list(FrameList,MemoList),
        show_memos(MemoList).

ancestor(Object,Object).
ancestor(Object,Ancestor) :-
        search_for(Object,ako,value,Fathers),
        member(Father,Fathers),
        ancestor(Father,Ancestor).

search_for_memo_list([],[]).
search_for_memo_list([Frame|Rest],MemoList) :-
        search_for_memo_list(Rest,RestMemos),
        (   search_for(Frame,memos,value,NewMemos),
            !, n_insert(Frame,NewMemos,
                                RestMemos,MemoList)
        ;   MemoList = RestMemos
        ).

n_insert(_,[],List,List).
n_insert(Frame,[NewMemo|RestNew],[],
            [[NewMemo,Frame]|RestList]) :-
        n_insert(Frame,RestNew,[],RestList).
n_insert(Frame,[NewMemo|RestNew],
            [[OldMemo,OldFrame]|OldRestList],
            [[NewMemo,Frame]|RestList]) :-
        compare(>,NewMemo,OldMemo),
        n_insert(Frame,RestNew,
                    [[OldMemo,OldFrame]|OldRestList],
                    RestList).
n_insert(Frame,NewMemos,
            [X|OldRestList],[X|RestList]) :-
        n_insert(Frame,NewMemos,
                    OldRestList,RestList).
```

Fig. 8-12. Recording and outputting memos

via *if_added* attachments, without having to modify the memo compilation process at all.

The predicate *write_memos* first applies *findall* to generate a *FrameList* of all the ancestors of the given target object. The predicate *search_for_memo_list* then proceeds to construct the *MemoList* needed to select the memos for output, consisting of the list elements

[*Memo_name, associated_Frame*]

from the information in the *FrameList*.

The procedure *n_insert*, used to prepare the memo list might, at first glance, appear somewhat complex. It is, however, really a very simple, recursive processing of the list of new memos passed in through the second argument. The third argument is a sorted list of the preprocessed memo-frame pairs. For each memo in the second·argument a new memo-frame pair is produced, referring to the *Frame* named in the first argument. The different *n_insert* clauses implement the correct insertion of each new pair into the emerging list, consisting of the pairs-to-date and the newest pair. It is this list which is returned via the fourth argument.

It is safe to assume that the user will, typically, only be interested in a particular memo regarding some specific topic, i.e. she would like to select a memo containing some keyword(s). In order to make this possible, we shall introduce an index of memos, as a content-oriented post-processing feature. If we are indeed prepared to engage in such post-processing of a memo entered, we should at least make it "knowledge-oriented": it should not only provide a keyword mechanism for producing indexes but also permit arbitrary, text-dependent manipulative services. This is best achieved through the use of procedural attachments which insert the references automatically into the corresponding *memos* slot.

8.6   Assistance Systems for Information Preparation

Such processing and analysis of a document which has just been composed or modified can play a central role in the *collection of case data* and, thus, in the *flow of control in an expert system*. It is, indeed, far more important than our simple little example might suggest at first glance.

As we mentioned earlier, the rather tedious dialogs for collecting data are often a major cause of user dissatisfaction with typical expert systems. This is one reason why we tried to vary the dialogs somewhat in Chap. 6, as well as to provide a means for "shortcutting" them. We must, however, admit that these are all cures for the symptoms: the pedantic requests for facts by the system are not fundamentally eliminated.

The trend in modern expert systems is to attempt to replace the dialog-oriented approach to gathering case data by completely different ones. One of these is the approach first taken in the expert system for cancer diagnosis, *Oncocin*, and referred to as an *assistant system*[4].

The basic idea behind its user interface is to present the system as an "intelligent" *documentation assistant*, whose primary task is to manage forms, reports, correspondence or memoranda. In contrast to traditional text processing or documentation systems, such a system merely takes "another look" at the texts, before they are filed away. This analysis of the contents is used to extract data for

```
/* extension to the generic object : */

frame(license,memos,if_added,memo_trigger).

/* trigger procedure : */

memo_trigger(Frame,_,Memo) :-
        /* Read memo word-at-a-time into a list : */
        words_from_file(Memo,List_of_all_words),
        unique_word(List_of_all_words,WordList),
        word_trigger(Frame,Memo,WordList).

unique_word([],[]).
unique_word([Word|Rest],UniqueRest) :-
        (       /* eliminate special characters : */
                Word = char(_)
        ;       member(Word,Rest)
        ), !,
        unique_word(Rest,UniqueRest).
unique_word([Word|Rest],[Word|UniqueRest]) :-
        unique_word(Rest,UniqueRest).

word_trigger(_,_,[]).
word_trigger(Frame,Memo,[Word|Words]) :-
        trigger(Frame,Frame,Memo,Word),
        word_trigger(Frame,Memo,Words).

trigger(InFrame,FromFrame,Memo,Word) :-
        exec_trigger(InFrame,FromFrame,Memo,Word),
        search_for(InFrame,ako,value,Fathers), !,
        member(Father,Fathers),
        trigger(Father,FromFrame,Memo,Word), !.
trigger(_,_,_,_).
```

Fig. 8-13. Trigger mechanism associated with new memo entries

---

[4] See the insert *Using assistant, not executive, systems* in [SHEI85], p. 135.

the knowledge base and to *trigger events* or, in more crass terms, to *invoke procedures*, which either provide the user with immediately useful information or dispatch some (routine) task for her.

Naturally, there is no reason why the event may not involve a dialog along the lines previously illustrated. The advantage is that these may now be briefer and more to the point and, thus, less tiresome. Imagine an analysis of the lending policy of a specific branch of a national bank, which is only activated when certain routinely collected index values deviate significantly from those of comparable branch offices.

The core of such an assistant system is a procedural attachment for the adding of new information, in our specific case, for the slot *memos*. Figure 8-13 illustrates the corresponding *if_added* facet of the generic object, as well as the procedure itself.

The procedure *memo_trigger* reads the words in the newly created memo file into a list for some post-processing. The predicate *unique_word* converts this into a list containing only unique occurrences of a word, whereby special characters are culled in the process. Other *lexical pre-processing* could also be included in this predicate, e.g. the elimination of *lexical noise*, i.e. the words "and", "or", "etc." and the like, or even some form of *normalization*, such as transforming all words into lower case representation.

The predicate *word_trigger* then activates a *trigger* procedure for each word in the list finally produced. It respects the inheritance factor, by climbing the hierarchy via the *ako* slots, up to the highest, general frame, invoking itself recursively for each respective "father" frame. Before each such recursion, however, it activates the procedure *exec_trigger* associated with the given frame, triggering an action specific to the given word. The first two arguments of the predicate are *InFrame* and *FromFrame*. *InFrame* is the frame in the hierarchy in which the procedure was activated. *FromFrame* is the frame from which the original memo originates, i.e. the one which triggered the recursive processing of the hierarchy of frames in the first place. In addition, the name of the *Memo* and the *Word* originating from it are passed into *exec_trigger* for processing.

We shall be employing this trigger mechanism to add an automatic indexing feature to our license administration system, extending it along the lines of an "intelligent" assistant system.

8.7   Building an "Intelligent" Index Manager

As shown in Fig. 8-9, the modified objects now contain slots for *keywords* and *references* in addition to the slots for *memos*. The user can, with the help of *add*, put new values, in the form of arbitrary Prolog atoms, into the *keyword* slots. These will be used by the trigger mechanism to produce an index of memos. Whenever a frame or hierarchically lower-order, i.e. more specific object contains one of the given *keywords* of the memo entry, then an entry should be made in the memo's *references* slot "pointing" at the respective frame or object. Figure 8–14 illustrates such entries for the example shown in Fig. 8–9.

The recording of these references is the job of the procedure *exec_trigger* invoked via the trigger mechanism (see Fig. 8–13).

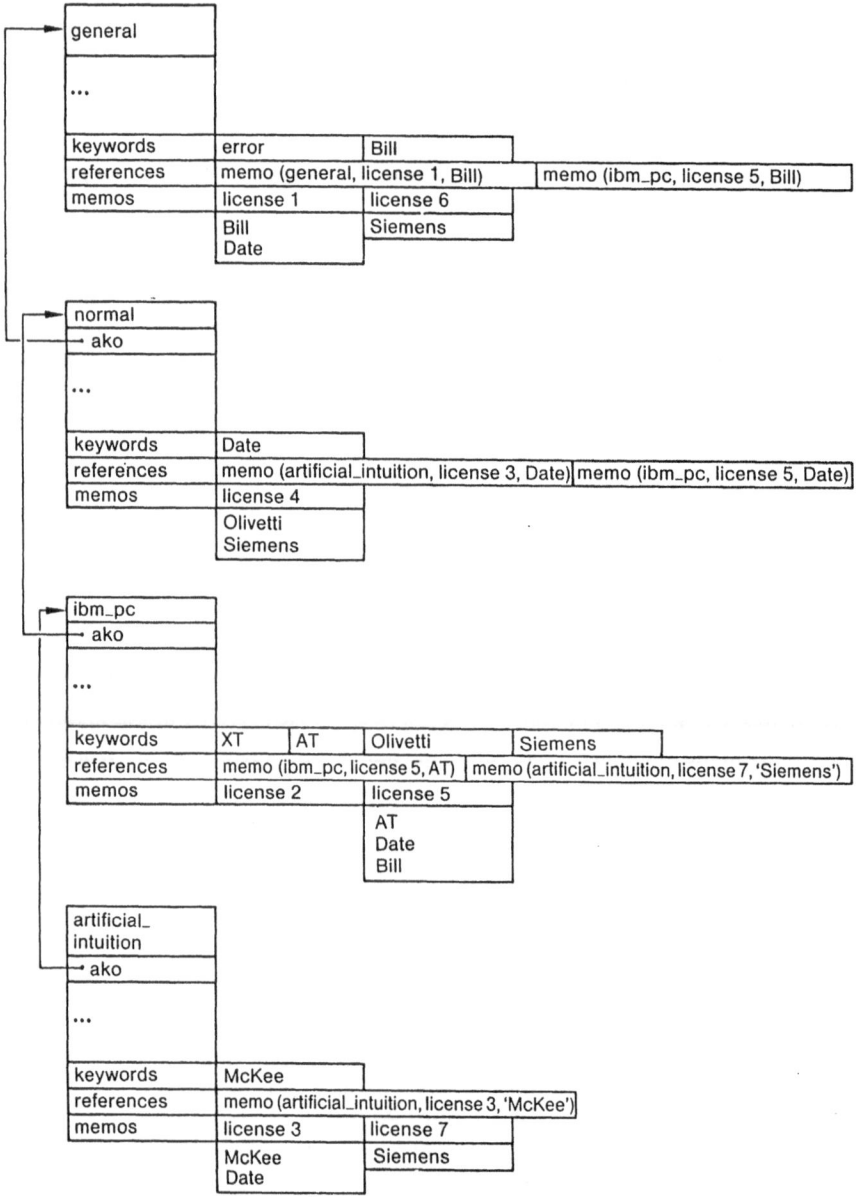

Fig. 8-14. Memos, keywords and references

Figure 8-15 shows the implementation of *exec_trigger*. As indicated by the comments, it can invoke an arbitrary set of actions. In this specific case it contains but a single one, i.e. the recording of a *keyword_reference* in the *references* slot of the current *InFrame*, should it happen to contain the particular *Word* in its *keyword* frame.

```
exec_trigger(InFrame,FromFrame,Memo,Word) :-
    keyword_reference(InFrame,FromFrame,Memo,Word),
    % One could insert any arbitrary procedures
    % here to realize other actions
    !.
exec_trigger(_,_,_,_).

keyword_reference(InFrame,FromFrame,Memo,Word) :-
    search_for(InFrame,keywords,value,Word),
    !, add(InFrame,references,value,
                    memo(FromFrame,Memo,Word)).
keyword_reference(_,_,_,_).
```

Fig. 8-15. The procedure *exec_trigger* and the recording of keyword references

As already indicated in Fig. 8-14, a *keyword_reference* is of the form

```
memo(FromFrame,Memo,Word)
```

and thus contains all the information needed to find and output memos.

The binary version of the *write_memos* predicate designed for this purpose can be found in Fig. 8-16.

The predicate *memo_list* collects, for a given *Object* (taking all hierarchically higher-order frames into consideration), all the *Memos* which contain *references* to at least one of the words in *KeywordList* into a list.

The procedure *unique* then takes the list of memos and, like *unique_word* in Fig. 8-13, produces, as its second argument, a list containing only unique memo references.

The actual displaying/printing of the memos found is done by the now familiar predicate *show_memo*.

Before we close this chapter, let us take a look at a sample dialog for the features just discussed. The dialog is based, once again, on the store of memomoranda shown in Fig. 8-9.

```
write_memos(Object,KeywordList) :-
        is_list(KeywordList),
        memo_list(Object,KeywordList,Memos),
        unique(Memos,MemoList),
        show_memos(MemoList).
write_memos(Object,Keyword) :-
        not is_list(Keyword),
        write_memos(Object,[Keyword]).

memo_list(_,[],[]).
memo_list(Object,[Keyword|Rest],MemoList) :-
        findall([Memo,Frame],
                fetch_memo(Object,Keyword,
                                Memo,Frame),
                List),
        memo_list(Object,Rest,RestList),
        append(List,RestList,MemoList).

fetch_memo(Object,Keyword,Memo,Frame) :-
        search_for(Object,references,value,
                memo(Frame,Memo,Keyword)).
fetch_memo(Object,Keyword,Memo,Frame) :-
        search_for(Object,ako,value,Fathers),
        member(Father,Fathers),
        fetch_memo(Father,Keyword,Memo,Frame).

uniquo([],[]).
unique([Element|Rest],UniqueRest) :-
        member(Element,Rest),
        !, unique(Rest,UniqueRest).
unique([Element|Rest],[Element|UniqueRest]) :-
        unique(Rest,UniqueRest).
```

Fig.8-16. Printing memomoranda according to keywords

```
?- write_memos(ibm_pc,['AT',bill]).

Frame: ibm_pc  Memo: MEMOS/license5
-------- display (y/n) ? y
-----------------------------------------------------
The first date of delivery for the AT is August 1.
No bill should be written before then.
-----------------------------------------------------
Frame: general  Memo: MEMOS/license1
-------- display (y/n) ? y
-----------------------------------------------------
The bill is to be issued on the date of delivery.
-----------------------------------------------------


yes
?-
```

As can be seen in Fig. 8-14, two frames make a reference to *license5*: *ibm_pc*, due to the keyword *AT* and *general*, because of the word *bill*. Despite the multiple references the memo is shown to the user only once. This is achieved by the application of the predicate *unique* prior to *show_memos*, as illustrated in Fig. 8-14.

The automated indexing is a very simple example of "knowledge-based" post-processing of written texts, but we hope that it will inspire one or the other reader to tackle more complex tasks in text processing and document management, exploiting the underlying principles and techniques presented here.

8.8   Shortcomings and Possible Improvements

Once again we would like to discuss a few problems we see in our implementation.

- The use of the complete file name as a reference value is simple but wastes memory. A more practical solution would record the running number of the text in the frame and only generate the full name as needed. Writing the necessary Prolog procedures to implement this is a good exercise in string handling!
- Another shortcoming is that we do not automatically timestamp the memos and record the author's name. Such information should also be displayed when the user is being asked if she would like to see the contents of a given memo, since the memo's internal name does not in any way indicate what the memo might be about. This additional feature is rather easily implemented if your Prolog provides a good operating system query predicate or has a good interface to Unix.
- In the last chapter, we indicated that we would be using the concepts discussed here to, among other things, insure the integrity and consistency of the object

base against incorrect usage by the user. This has been partially achieved: the automatic construction of instances by the predicate *new* helps remedy the problems involving mispelling of the object name or the entry of incorrect values for slots with a *require* facet. This guarantees that only "legal" *ako* values are stored in the knowledge base. Protection against the deletion of frames for classes of objects for which some member instances still exist is easily implemented; one must merely check, using *search_for*, if any objects still exist with the given frame name as an *ako* value, before one actually deletes the frame.

• What happens if we eliminate a higher-order frame *before* a first instance of that object has been entered? The generic frame will still "know" of it and will not try and stop the instance from being created. The simplest and most general method of avoiding such inconsistencies is to not let the end user have direct access to the primitive operations. Instead, every manipulation of the object base should be controlled by the "knowledge" in the generic object and executed by predicates associated directly with it, such as the predicate *new*. Professional systems for object-oriented management of knowledge bases generally take this approach. Such systems treat all elements of the system as *objects*, the I/O streams, windows, frames and so on, and implement them via corresponding frames and inheritance mechanisms. Examples of this approach are the popular, object-oriented extensions to Lisp, *Flavors* and *Loops*. Naturally, one could implement such a package for Prolog too, but it is a task of far greater complexity than we can reasonably deal with here.

• A far less critical, but nonetheless desirable feature for a commercial system with respect to consistency involves the interdependence of *default* and *require* entries in different slots of the generic frame. For example, the *default* values for the *operating_system*, *memory* and *gross_price* are only relevant when *default* value was selected for *computer*, i.e. *ibm_pc*. Taking *interdependence between slots* into account is not a trivial task. The use of an *if_added* procedure, as was done in Sect. 8-3 to supply the *uni* slot with a *default* value, is a good starting point for a solution to this problem!

The main reason for introducing the *generic frame* was to increase the robustness of our object base. It would be worthwhile to stop and consider what other "loopholes" remain, and how one might best close them. You should now have a sufficient grasp of the basics to do so!

9 The Representation and Use of Constraints

All the systems we have thus far presented have one thing in common –they all process the user request or some hypothesis systematically and, indeed, somewhat single-mindedly, and – with some luck –resolve them too! This is, however, not always the case. Configuration and planning systems, in particular, must search for a satisfactory solution among myriad possible ones. *Constraints* play a central role, not only in the evaluation of a suggested solution found by exhaustive search of the solution space, but also in the heuristic control of the selection process, to reduce the cost of finding a solution to a reasonable one. A system for selecting couplings and coupling components is presented to demonstrate the use of constraints. Moreover, we shall be using contraints to introduce an alternative user interface, based on menus.

9.1 Configuration and Selection Systems

In Sect. 2.8 we discussed a classification of different types of expert systems. This was based partly on the different areas of application, but, more importantly, on differences in the structure of the respective knowledge bases and the techniques applied.

Up to now we have dealt primarily with information or diagnostic systems. We were able to illustrate a number of common design and programming methods. Nonetheless, several "knowledge types" remain which we could not even touch upon on the basis of the examples, although they are certainly of interest to the developer of an expert system. Perhaps the most important one is the type of rule embodying what is referred to as *constraint*.

In our taxonomy of expert systems, we encountered this concept initially in the context of *configuration systems*. This makes sense, inasmuch as such systems attempt to construct systems from components to satisfy a variety of demands: customer requests, economic criteria, spatial limitations, physical laws, technical rules and numerous other *constraints*. Given that such aspects can play a role in the application of expert knowledge in other situations, i.e. beyond the area of equipment configuration or the planning of activities or processes, it is absolutely necessary to learn the fundamentals of representing and applying such knowledge in a knowledge base.

Thus, we wish to discuss these topics based on the simplest example of a configuration system: a *selection system* for a particular component. The only difference with respect to a large-scale configuration system is that there is only one free parameter; the other components of the total configuration are, in all relevant details, already given and the final component is to be selected from a catalogue of possible alternatives, such that all the given constraints are satisfied.

Typically, a larger configuration system would permit the variation of several or all components, indeed, often across many hierarchically embedded sub-component groups. This, however, leads to the previously discussed *combinatoric explosion* of the set of candidates, when a solution is sought via an exhaustive search, and makes it necessary to employ some *heuristics.* That is where constraints can be exploited.

Nevertheless, we shall restrict ourselves to the simpler selection system example. And, even there, it makes sense to limit the search by breaking off the investigation of a given candidate as soon as one of the associated constraints is clearly unfulfilled.

9.2   The "Coupling Expert"

We shall be examining a modified version of an existing expert system: a *coupling expert*[1]. The version described here is an object-oriented extension thereof. We have, for simplicity's sake, radically reduced the set of data and technical formulas involved. Extending the knowledge base to its technically complete level is merely a quantitative problem, yielding no further qualitative insights.

The task of the coupling expert is to help the mechanical engineer choose the proper *torsionally elastic coupling.* Such couplings are employed whenever, for reasons of design, the drive – e.g. a motor shaft – and the load to be coupled – e.g. a transmission –cannot be mounted rigidly.

Figure 9-1 illustrates the schematic structure of such an aggregate: the *Coupling* is housed in an *Assembly,* which connects a *Drive* on the one (drive) side with a *Load* on the other (load) side.

Correspondingly, in our problem, we are dealing with four different types of objects: the coupling to be selected, the assembly (or housing), the drive and the load. Each of these has associated with it some *characteristic data,* which must be compatible if the right coupling is to be found. A trivial *constraint,* immediately obvious even to the layperson, is that there must be enough room in the assembly housing for the coupling to fit in.

Other constraints relate to technical concepts and formulas, which are presumably as difficult for the reader to understand as they were for us. This is the lot of the *knowledge engineer:* she must often take the statements made by the *expert in the field* with whom she is working together and prepare the knowledge base, without necessarily really fully understanding its contents.

---

[1] The original system was developed jointly by the RWTH Aachen, West Germany (*Benner, Blatt* and *Spielvogel*) and InterFace Computer, Munich (*Leibrandt, Gschwind*).

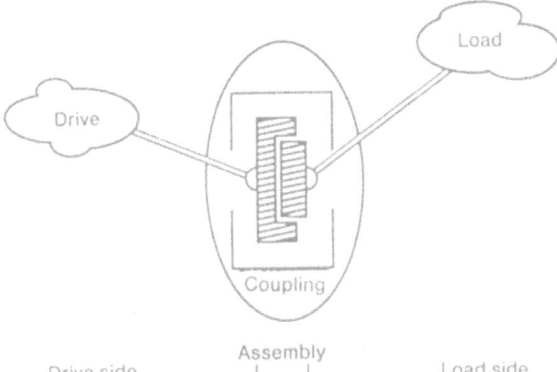

Fig. 9-1. The objects *Coupling,*
Drive, Assembly and *Load*

Thus, we must ask you to bear with us, and not attempt to comprehend all the technical details of couplings, etc., unless you happen to be a mechanical engineer yourself. We intentionally chose a problem area which would not be particulary familiar to most of the readers, just as it was unfamiliar to us. The transformation of relatively "foreign" knowledge from one formal representation (the technical data tables and formulas) into another (a knowledge base in Prolog) is a skill which must be "drilled" just as much as programming in Prolog itself.

9.3 Functions and the Structure of Knowledge

The expert system should make the following functions available to the user:

- the compilation (creation) of new objects in the knowledge base, i.e. the registration of characteristic data for couplings and assemblies, and drive and load sides,
- the display of objects and their attributes, and
- the selection of couplings for a given combination of assemby, drive and load.

Figure 9-2 illustrates the process of coupling selection. It is the consequence of numerous *constraints* which are contained in the knowledge base. The *result* is displayed to the user. We shall provide a number of alternative display methods.

It should be possible to demand a "*primitive selection*", where a thorough, and thus very slow check of all the couplings known to the system is made. Every constraint is tested for each coupling. As soon as a constraint is not satisfied for the *current coupling*, it gets rejected and the next coupling is examined.

If, however, a coupling fulfills all the constraints, then a message like

```
The coupling selected is 11
with the designation Stromag gr 10.
```

Case Data

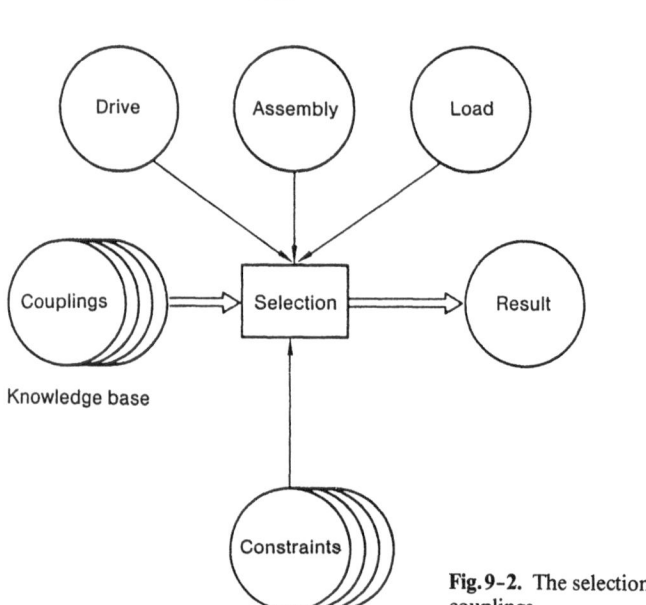

Knowledge base

Fig. 9-2. The selection of torsionally elastic couplings

is issued. A detailed justification or explanation of the selection is not necessary here, since the search process is designed such that the coupling found satisfies *all* technichal contraints.

This relatively slow, sequential search through all the objects can, of course, be accelerated by drawing on *meta- knowledge*, i.e. the appplication of suitable *heuristics.* This may be achieved via the analysis of protocols of previous selections, or perhaps via suitable multi-level selection techniques, e.g. first according to groups and then considering only those couplings in those groups which merit investigation.

If a suitable coupling cannot be found, then the system not only prints a message to that effect, but also, based on the constraints, makes a *suggestion* as to which characteristics an appropriate coupling should have.

```
A suitable coupling was not found.

Suggestion for an appropriate coupling:

        - type_of_mounting is axial
        - axial_clearance
          must be greater than 0.5
        - radial_clearance
          must be greater than 0.7
```

- angular_clearance
  must be greater than 1
- length must be less than 500
- diameter must be less than 400
- torque_rating must be greater than 41.8

The user can use the suggestion as a basis for building her own coupling or to call for tenders for a custom fabrication.

Lastly, the coupling expert should also be able to give *"why not"* explanations. This capability requires a *complete investigation* of the given coupling. A report should be made of all the constraints which the coupling does not satisfy with respect to the current assembly, drive and load side characteristics.

An object-oriented approach to structuring the knowledge base is again most appropriate. The characteristic data of the object classes and instances can be

```
frame(drive,general,
      rpm_independent_drive_frequency,
      value,[0]).

frame(drive,1,
      identifying_name,value,['AC_Motor I']).
frame(drive,1,
      ako,value,[general]).
frame(drive,1,
      torque_rating,value,[55]).
frame(drive,1,
      continuous_rpm,value,[710]).
frame(drive,1,
      angular_momentum,value,[0.0064]).

frame(drive,2,
      identifying_name,value,
      ['Rotary_Current_Motor 160 M4']).
frame(drive,2,
      ako,value,[general]).
frame(drive,2,
      torque_rating,value,[72.5]).
frame(drive,2,
      continuous_rpm,value,[1450]).
frame(drive,2,
      angular_momentum,value,[0.0735]).

%        . . . . .
```

Fig. 9-3. Examples of *drive* frames

represented as frames, along the lines of our previous system. The main difference is that we must distinguish four different *object types*: couplings, assemblies, drives and loads. Consequently, we must administer a separate *frame structure* and *frame hierarchy* for each *type of object*. This means that the entries for the various frames are facts of arity five instead of arity four:

> frame(*Type, Name, Characteristic, Facet, Value*),

for instance

> frame(drive,4,torque_rating,value,[162]).

In this knowledge base too, the *Value* argument is always a list, permitting us to assign multiple values to a characteristic, if so desired.

For each of the object hierarchies we provide a separate *general* frame, i.e. a descriptive *generic object*, as well as *default, prefer* and *require* facets to assist the user when compiling new objects.

```
frame(load,general,
      rpm_independent_drive_frequency,
      value,[0]).

frame(load,1,
      identifying_name,value,['Fan']).
frame(load,1,
      ako,value,[general]).
frame(load,1,
      torque_rating,value,[38]).
frame(load,1,
      angular_momentum,value,[5]).

frame(load,2,
      identifying_name,value,['Rotary_Pump']).
frame(load,2,
      ako,value,[general]).
frame(load,2,
      torque_rating,value,[69]).
frame(load,2,
      angular_momentum,value,[0.53]).

%        . . . . .
```

Fig. 9-4. Examples of *load* frames

9.4   Characteristic Object Data

Rather than going into great detail about frames for the individual objects –they are listed in Appendix D – we prefer to outline the fundamental structure.
     The description of two typical drives is shown in Fig. 9–3, together with their

```
frame(assembly,general,
      type_of_mounting,value,[axial]).

frame(assembly,1,
      identifying_name,value,['Assembly 1']).
frame(assembly,1,
      ako,value,[general]).
frame(assembly,1,
      temperature,value,[30]).
frame(assembly,1,
      axial_shaft_alignment,value,[0.5]).
frame(assembly,1,
      radial_shaft_alignment,value,[0.7]).
frame(assembly,1,
      angular_shaft_alignment,value,[1]).
frame(assembly,1,
      length_of_housing,value,[500]).
frame(assembly,1,
      diameter_of_housing,value,[400]).

frame(assembly,2,
      identifying_name,value,['Assembly 2']).
frame(assembly,2,
      ako,value,[general]).
frame(assembly,2,
      temperature,value,[50]).
frame(assembly,2,
      axial_shaft_alignment,value,[0.7]).
frame(assembly,2,
      radial_shaft_alignment,value,[0.9]).
frame(assembly,2,
      angular_shaft_alignment,value,[1.1]).
frame(assembly,2,
      length_of_housing,value,[200]).
frame(assembly,2,
      diameter_of_housing,value,[700]).

%        . . . . .
```

Fig. 9-5. Examples of *assembly* frames

common *general* frame, which sets the *rpm_independent_drive_frequency* (whatever that is!) to the normal value of 0.

Similar frames describe the load side and the assembly. Figures 9-4 and 9-5 illustrate some typical frames for each.

The more interesting object structure is the one for couplings. Here, too, we have a highest-level frame *general*, specifying the usual *type_of_mounting*, namely *axial*.

Like many other technical components, couplings are classified into "series" by their producers, according to specific common characteristics, such as "clearance" or "memory function"; the differences between the members of a series, on the other hand, relate to performance characteristics, such as *torque rating*, or physical dimensions or the *angular momentum*. As a consequence, a multilevel *object hierarchy*, as shown in Fig. 9-6, seems to be a practical way of representing the characteristic data of couplings.

Every coupling series has its own *class* frame which all *instances* of the different coupling models of that series refer to via their individual *ako* slots. Figure 9-7 shows sample descriptions of such series.

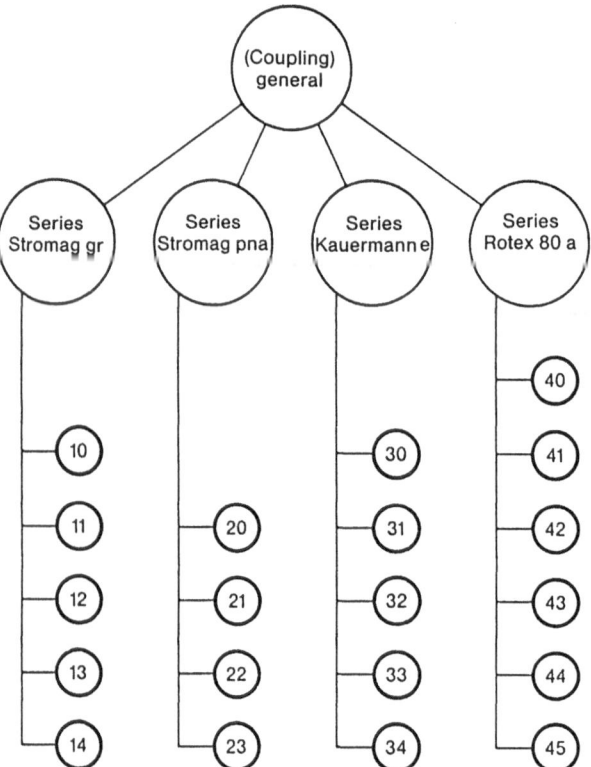

Fig. 9-6. The object hierarchy for couplings

Some frames describing specific instances of couplings can be seen in Fig. 9-8.

```
frame(coupling,general,
      type_of_mounting,value,[axial]).

frame(coupling,'Series Stromag gr',
      ako,value,[general]).
frame(coupling,'Series Stromag gr',
      memory_function,value,[0.5]).
frame(coupling,'Series Stromag gr',
      semi_static_friction,value,[0.8]).
frame(coupling,'Series Stromag gr',
      characteristic,value,[1.1]).
frame(coupling,'Series Stromag gr',
      nominal_twisting_angle,value,[3.5]).
frame(coupling,'Series Stromag gr',
      angular_clearance,value,[2]).
frame(coupling,'Series Stromag gr',
      radial_clearance,value,[1]).
frame(coupling,'Series Stromag gr',
      axial_clearance,value,[4]).

 %        . . . . .

frame(coupling,'Series Rotex 80a',
      ako,value,[general]).
frame(coupling,'Series Rotex 80a',
      memory_function,value,[0.43]).
frame(coupling,'Series Rotex 80a',
      semi_static_friction,value,[0.59]).
frame(coupling,'Series Rotex 80a',
      characteristic,value,[1.5]).
frame(coupling,'Series Rotex 80a',
      nominal_twisting_angle,value,[3.2]).
frame(coupling,'Series Rotex 80a',
      angular_clearance,value,[1.5]).
frame(coupling,'Series Rotex 80a',
      radial_clearance,value,[0.8]).
frame(coupling,'Series Rotex 80a',
      axial_clearance,value,[2]).
```

Fig. 9-7. Sample frames for coupling series

```
frame(coupling,10,
      identifying_name,value,['Stromag gr 2']).
frame(coupling,10,
      ako,value,['Series Stromag gr']).
frame(coupling,10,
      torque_rating,value,[25]).
frame(coupling,10,
      angular_momentum,value,[0.03]).
frame(coupling,10,
      diameter,value,[75]).
frame(coupling,10,
      length,value,[80]).

frame(coupling,11,
      .identifying_name,value,['Stromag gr 10']).
frame(coupling,11,
      ako,value,['Series Stromag gr']).
frame(coupling,11,
      torque_rating,value,[100]).
frame(coupling,11,
      angular_momentum,value,[0.22]).
frame(coupling,11,
      diameter,value,[112]).
frame(coupling,11,
      length,value,[125]).

%           . . . . .
```

Fig.9-8. Sample frames for specific instances of couplings

9.5   Entering and Displaying Objects

The incremental construction of the knowledge base is, again, achieved by enter-ing the individual objects under the guidance of the *generic frame*, whereby a separate *generic object* exists for each of the four object types mentioned earlier. Figure 9-9 illustrates this for *drive*.

```
frame(drive,gen_Frame,
      identifying_name,default,[new_drive]).
frame(drive,gen_Frame,
      identifying_name,prefer,[]).
frame(drive,gen_Frame,
      identifying_name,require,[]).
```

```
frame(drive,gen_Frame,
     ako,default,[general]).
frame(drive,gen_Frame,
     ako,prefer,[in_list([general])]).
frame(drive,gen_Frame,
     ako,require,[in_list([general])]).

frame(drive,gen_Frame,
     rpm_independent_drive_frequency,
     default,[0]).
frame(drive,gen_Frame,
     rpm_independent_drive_frequency,
     prefer,[less_than_or_equal_to(2000)]).
frame(drive,gen_Frame,
     rpm_independent_drive_frequency,
     require,[less_than_or_equal_to(5000)]).

frame(drive,gen_Frame,
     angular_momentum,default,[1]).
frame(drive,gen_Frame,
     angular_momentum,
     prefer,[between(0.5,500)]).
frame(drive,gen_Frame,
     angular_momentum,
     require,[less_than_or_equal_to(12000)]).

frame(drive,gen_Frame,
     continuous_rpm,default,[1500]).
frame(drive,gen_Frame,
     continuous_rpm,
     prefer,[between(500,4000)]).
frame(drive,gen_Frame,
     continuous_rpm,
     require,[less_than_or_equal_to(10000)]).

frame(drive,gen_Frame,
     torque_rating,default,[150]).
frame(drive,gen_Frame,
     torque_rating,
     prefer,[between(50,200)]).
frame(drive,gen_Frame,
     torque_rating,
     require,[less_than_or_equal_to(100000)]).
```

Fig. 9-9. The generic object for *drive*

The *default, prefer* and *require* facets are used to assist the user when entering information into the system, by validating the input and giving instructional help.

The following is a dialog excerpt illustrating the compilation of a *drive* object. In the next chapter we will be seeing how this and all other system functions are activated from a menu. That is the reason why the familiar Prolog prompt "**?-**" is missing here!

```
Number : 0
identifying_name: Drive 0
ako: general
rpm_independent_drive_frequency: help

Possible responses are :
assistance,help            ==> display this list.
?                          ==> display some typical values.
??                         ==> display limits on values.
*                          ==> display the default value.
                           ==> take the default value.
<return>                   ==> omit this slot.

rpm_independent_drive_frequency: ?
The value must be less than or equal to 2000.

rpm_independent_drive_frequency: ??
The value must be less than or equal to 5000.

rpm_independent_drive_frequency: *
Default-Value : 0

rpm_independent_drive_frequency: .

angular_momentum: ?
The value must lie between 0.5 and 500.

angular_momentum: ??
The value must be less than or equal to 12000.

angular_momentum: 30
continuous_rpm: 12345
The value must be less than or equal to 10000.

continuous_rpm: 3000
torque_rating: ?
The value must lie between 50 and 200.
```

```
torque_rating: 400

New frame : 0
torque_rating : 400
continuous_rpm : 3000
angular_momentum : 30
identifying_name : Drive 0
rpm_independent_drive_frequency : 0
ako : general
```

After the new frame has been registered in the knowledge base, it is displayed for verification.

The display of objects on demand has the same format. After selecting the display function from the menu, the system asks for the code number of the object to be displayed. Let us look at another dialog excerpt where the user asks to see the frame of a *coupling* instance.

```
Please enter the code number ==> 34

identifying_name : Kauermann 02 e
ako : Series Kauermann e
torque_rating : 1405
angular_momentum : 3.2
diameter : 272
length : 223
```

The predicate used here differs from the one shown in Fig. 7–11 for the *license* knowledge base only with respect to the arity of *display_frame(Type, Name)* and of *frame* itself. The same is true of the other output predicates *display_instances(Type, Name)* and *display_existing_objects(Type)*, as well as the procedure for defining new frames *new_frame(Type, Name)*. Thus, we refer you to Appendix D for further implementation details.

9.6 Primitive Access Predicates

As in Chap. 7, we provide a set of *primitive operations* like *search_for, ask, add, delete* and *execute*, for accessing objects. Because we now have a concrete data model and a specific application in mind, we can implement these to be somewhat less general and, thus, more efficient than in the previous chapters. There our objective was to write a general set of functions for object-oriented data management, and our license and memoranda administration system served merely as a means of illustrating their employment.

It is instructive to compare the primitive predicates. They show quite clearly how much simpler even basic functions can be when they are being developed for a specific, rather than generalized, application. Indeed, the license administrator by no means fully exploited the potential functionality of the primitive operations presented in Chaps. 7 and 8.

Nonetheless, the new primitive predicates present an extension to the earlier ones in one regard: because of the additional *Type* argument required, they have an arity, one greater than the old ones.

```
ask(Type,Frame,Slot,Data_Item) :-
    (    search_for(Type,Frame,Slot,value,
                                    Data_Item)
    ;    search_for(Type,gen_Frame,Slot,
                                    if_needed,Proc),
         execute(Proc,Type,Frame,Slot,Data_Item)
    ;    search_for(Type,Frame,ako,value,
                                    [Parent_Frame]),
         ask(Type,Parent_Frame,Slot,Data_Item)
    ),
    !.

search_for(Type,Frame,Slot,Facet,Data_Item) :-
    clause(frame(Type,Frame,Slot,Facet,Data_Item),_).

execute([Proc],Type,Frame,Slot,[Data_Item]) :-
    Attachment =.. [Proc,Type,Frame,Slot,Data_Item],
    Attachment.

ask_coupling(Slot,Data_Item) :-
    current(coupling,Name),
    ask(coupling,Name,Slot,[Data_Item]).

ask_drive(Slot,Data_Item) :-
    current(drive,Name),
    ask(drive,Name,Slot,[Data_Item]).

ask_load(Slot,Data_Item) :-
    current(load,Name),
    ask(load,Name,Slot,[Data_Item]).

ask_assembly(Slot,Data_Item) :-
    current(assembly,Name),
    ask(assembly,Name,Slot,[Data_Item]).

ask_requirement(Slot,Data_Item) :-
    ask(requirement,current,Slot,[Data_Item]).
```

Fig. 9-10. The *ask* predicates for the various object types

We do not intend to discuss these primitive predicates completely here - they can be found in their entirety in Appendix D. In Fig. 9-10 we merely show the predicate *ask*.

There is more than one predicate because we have, in addition to the generalized, quaternary *ask* predicate, some abbreviated ones, without the arguments *Type* and *Frame*. Among them is *ask_requirement*. The reason for introducing the object type *requirement* will be a topic of discussion later.

The particular object type being dealt with by the various abbreviated *ask* predicates is indicated by their functor names. And the frame that gets processed by each of them should be quite clear, based on their implementation as shown in Fig. 9-10, a *current Frame* of the corresponding type, whose *Name* is recorded in the knowledge base as a status fact of the form

```
current(ObjectType,Name).
```

These entries are made at the beginning of a coupling selection session according to the input given by the user and the coupling currently being investigated. As the selection process progresses they get updated or deleted.

9.7   Representation of the Computational Formulas

In sharp contrast to license administration, this area of application is heavily dependent on mathematical formulas for the derivation of numerous values. Whereas in the licensing problem we merely calculated the actual price from the gross price with a potential discount, here the mechanism of the *if_needed* attributes plays a far more important role - a typical characteristic of technical/scientific data processing.

The major problem in this context is deciding *which* object the calculated values should be assigned to. The values often do not simply relate to a single component, e.g. assembly, drive load or coupling, but rather to *sub-assemblies* consisting of some combination of these objects. For example, "total load mass moment of inertia" I_Ltot is derived from the "load mass moment of inertia" I_L and the "coupling mass moment of inertia" I_C according to the formula

```
I_Ltot = I_C/2 + I_L,
```

and the "normalized torque" T is derived from the "torque rating of the drive side" T_DN, the "torque rating of the load side" T_LN and the "torque rating of the coupling" T_CN where

```
T = T_N/T_CN
```

and

```
T_N = min(T_DN,T_CN).
```

The easiest way to solve this "assignment" problem is to introduce a new object "current requirements on the total aggregate", which we will simply call *current* and which will be of the type *requirement.*

In the generic frame for *requirement* one finds, in the *if_needed* facet of the corresponding slot, a reference to the formula needed to derive each of those *values* which is not stored directly as a component's attribute. If the formula is applied during the investigation of a coupling, then a corresponding *value* facet is entered in the *requirement* frame *current.* That is where the access predicate

```
frame(requirement,gen_Frame,
    dynamic_coupling_stiffness,if_needed,
    [calculate_dynamic_coupling_stiffness]).

frame(requirement,gen_Frame,
    elastic_coupling_stiffness,if_needed,
    [calculate_elastic_coupling_stiffness]).
```

%   . . . . .

```
calculate_dynamic_coupling_stiffness(
            Type,Frame,Slot,Data_Item) :-
    ask_coupling(nominal_twisting_angle,Phi),
    ask_coupling(torque_rating,T_CN),
    ask_coupling(semi_static_friction,Gdr),
    ask_coupling(memory_function,Mma),
    ask_requirement(
            elastic_coupling_stiffness,C_Tel),
    Data_Item is (Gdr + Mma) * T_CN / Phi + C_Tel,
    asserta(frame(Type,Frame,Slot,value,[Data_Item])).

calculate_elastic_coupling_stiffness(
            Type,Frame,Slot,Data_Item) :-
    ask_coupling(nominal_twisting_angle,Phi),
    ask_coupling(torque_rating,T_CN),
    ask_requirement(characteristic_curve_factor,M_1),
    ask_requirement(stretching,Epsilon),
    Data_Item is (Epsilon ^ 2 * (1 - M_1) * 3 + M_1)
                    * T_CN / Phi,
    asserta(frame(Type,Frame,Slot,value,[Data_Item])).
```

%   . . . . .

Fig.9-11. The calculation of characteristic data *requirement*

ask_requirement finds it, so that when values are needed repeatedly, they get calculated only once.

After completing the analysis of the current combination of components the *current* requirement is then deleted. This leaves *requirement* with only the if_needed facets of the generic frame. This causes the characteristic data for the next "current" coupling to be recalculated.

Figure 9-11 shows an excerpt from the *if_needed* facet of the generic frame of the *requirement* object, as well as a few of the associated formulas.

In the excerpt, one can already see that the formulas themselves sometimes draw on other *requirement* values. These are acquired by the *ask_requirement* primitive, which also initiates the calculation of a value should it not already exist. In this manner a *calling hierarchy*, similar to one in traditional programming, is established for the *if_needed* functions too; the difference here, of course, is that the functions are only called when the values needed are not present as *value* facts in the knowledge base.

9.8   Constraints on the Coupling Selection

The most important technique to be introduced in this chapter, however, is the use of *constraints* to sift information out of the knowledge base –in our specific case, to select the appropriate coupling for an aggregate consisting of a drive, a load and an assembly.

This coupling must satisfy the following constraints:

(1) The mounting of the coupling must be identical to that of the assembly.

(2) The axial clearance of the coupling must be greater than the axial shaft alignment of the assembly.

(3) The radial clearance of the coupling must be greater than the radial shaft alignment of the assembly.

(4) The angular clearance of the coupling must be greater than the angular shaft alignment of the assembly.

(5) The length of the coupling must be less than the length of the housing into which it will be placed.

(6) The diameter of the coupling must be less than the diameter of the housing.

(7) The torque rating of the coupling must be greater than the product of the temperature factor and the angular velocity.

(8) The rpm-independent drive frequency of the drive side should not be close to the intrinsic oscillation at the rated load (F), i.e. should not lie between $0.9 * F$ and $1.1 * F$.

(9) The rpm-dependent drive frequency of the load side should also not be too close to the intrinsic oscillation at the rated load.

(10) The nominal frequency should not be too close to the intrinsic oscillation at the rated load.

If the characteristic data mentioned in the constraints are not present in the object frames, they will be calculated as needed by the corresponding *if_needed* formula.

We must now define a scheme for a predicate according to which we can formulate the *constraints*. Since the status facts *current* already determine which objects are to be examined, a unary predicate *constraint(Criterion)* would, in principle, be adequate. The predicate returns successfully or unsuccessfully, depending on whether the criterion passed in as argument is satisfied or not.

If we merely test the suitability of a specific coupling, "aborting" as soon as the first unfulfilled constraint is encountered, then the *failure* of the *constraint* predicate can be considered to represent the unsuccessful check.

This is not very elegant, however, when we are doing a complete analysis of a coupling's suitability. In such cases, it is not desirable to stop the analysis when a single constraint is not satisfied, since we wish to gather all unfulfilled criteria into a list. Here we would prefer to have the *constraint* predicate always succeed. Thus, it would be more practical if it would return the results of its analysis via a second argument – an *empty* list, if the criterion is satisfied, and otherwise (i.e. in case of failure) a list with the name of the criterion (the first argument) as its sole element.

This is best illustrated with an example:

```
?- constraint(type_of_mounting,Result).
```

returns, when the *type_of_mounting* is suitable,

```
Result = []

yes
?-
```

and, when the constraint cannot be satisfied,

```
Result = [type_of_mounting]

yes
?-
```

For the complete analysis of the suitability of a coupling we need only call the binary predicate

```
constraint(Criterion, Result)
```

with the name of the particular *Criterion* to be checked and then concatenate all the *Result* lists for the given set of constraints.

The implementation of a binary *constraint* predicate which itself never fails, but which returns the current *Criterion* as a *Result* list when it *fails* to be satisfied, is simply achieved by placing the fact

```
constraint(Criterion,[Criterion]).
```

at the *end* of the set of *constraint* rules in the knowledge base. The rules themselves have the following general format

```
constraint(Criterion,[]) :-
    % . . . . . ,
    % the body consists of the "ask"
    % and test goals
    % . . . . . ,
    !.
```

i.e. when the constraint is tested and *fails*, the final, general fact is automatically activated (as last resort) and it announces an implicit failure by returning the original constraint *Criterion*.

Figure 9-12 illustrates some of the previously specified constraints formulated according to the scheme just described.

Our first application of the predicate is the procedure *examine(Coupling,Result)*. It is controlled by a *list of criteria* containing the names of the criteria to be checked. The list is stored in the fact

```
criteria(CriteriaList).
```

The implementation of *examine* is shown in Fig. 9-13.

Before beginning to actually investigate a coupling whose *Name* is passed in as the first argument, *examine* first declares it to be the *current* one and deletes the current requirement frame (should one exist). It then proceeds to analyze the coupling, but only in a "superficial" way, i.e. it stops any further investigation as soon as a criterion found in the list cannot be satisfied. Like *constraint*, it returns the name of the problematic criterion as a list via the second argument *Return*. Should the coupling satisfy all the criteria then *Result* is an empty list.

This predicate is adequate for selecting couplings which must satisfy all constraints, but inapplicable for extracting an explanation as to why a given coupling is unsuitable for use in a specific situation (complete analysis).

```
constraint(type_of_mounting,[]) :-                      /* 1 */
    ask_assembly(type_of_mounting,Assembly_Type),
    ask_coupling(type_of_mounting,Coupling_Type),
    Assembly_Type == Coupling_Type.

constraint(axial_shaft_alignment,[]) :-                 /* 2 */
    ask_assembly(axial_shaft_alignment,S_ax),
    ask_coupling(axial_clearance,C_ax),
    S_ax < C_ax.

constraint(radial_shaft_alignment,[]) :-                /* 3 */
    ask_assembly(radial_shaft_alignment,S_r),
    ask_coupling(radial_clearance,C_r),
    S_r < C_r.

% . . . . . .

constraint(coupling_torque_rating,[]) :-                /* 7 */
    ask_coupling(torque_rating,T_CN),
    ask_requirement(temperature_factor,S_theta),
    ask_requirement(torque,T_N),
    T_CN > TN * S_theta.

% . . . . . .

constraint(rated_frequency,[]) :-                       /* 10 */
    ask_requirement(rated_frequency,F_e),
    ask_requirement(rated_frequency,F),
    (          F_e < 0.9 * F
    ;          F_e > 1.1 * F
    ).

constraint(Criterion,[Criterion]).
```

Fig. 9-12. Examples of a few constraints

```
examine(Name,Result) :-
     note(coupling,Name,current),
     delete(requirement,current),
     criteria(List),
     member(Criterion,List),
     examine_constraint(Criterion,Result),
     Result = [],
     % Cut aborts the predicate when the first
     % unfulfillable criterion is encountered:
     !.
examine(_,[]) :-

examine_constraint(Criterion,Result) :-
     constraint(Criterion,Result),
     % the following Cut ensures that this constraint
     % is skipped when backtracking occurs and that
     % "member" returns the next criterion:
     !.

note(Type,Name,current) :-
     retract(current(Type,_)),
     asserta(current(Type,Name)).

current(coupling,0).      % Initialization
current(drive,0).
current(load,0).
current(assembly,0).

criteria([
        type_of_mounting,
        axial_shaft_alignment,
        radial_shaft_alignment,
        angular_shaft_alignment,
        length_of_housing,
        coupling_torque_rating,
        drive_frequency,
        load_frequency,
        rated_frequency
        ]).
```

Fig. 9-13. The predicate *examine* for conducting a complete analysis of a coupling

9.9   The Complete Analysis of a Coupling

In order to be able to produce a list of reasons *why* the coupling the operator would like to use is *not* suitable, we must have a procedure capable of conducting a complete investigation. It must test all the constraints and present a summary of the results to the user in a readable form. Figure 9-14 illustrates the predicate *examine_coupling* designed for this purpose.

In order to permit the complete analysis of a particular coupling at any stage of the dialog, the predicate always records the name of the coupling being pro-

```
examine_coupling(Coupling) :-
    retract(current(coupling,Current)),
    asserta(current(coupling,Coupling)),
    criteria(List),
    compare(Coupling,List,Result),
    write_protocol(complete,Result),
    explain(Coupling,Result),
    note(coupling,Current,current).

compare(_,[],[]).
compare(Coupling,[Criterion|Rest],Result) :-
    constraint(Criterion,Partial_Result),
    compare(Coupling,Rest,Final_Result),
    append(Partial_Result,Final_Result,Result).

explain(Coupling,[]) :-
    nl, write('The coupling '),
    write(Coupling),
    write(' is suitable!'),
    nl, nl.
explain(Coupling,Result) :-
    nl, write('The coupling '),
    write(Coupling),
    write(' is not suitable:'),
    nl,
    write_explanations(Result),
    nl, nl.

write_explanations([]).
write_explanations([Constraint|Rest]) :-
    write_this_explanation(Constraint),
    write_explanations(Rest).
```

Fig. 9-14. The complete analysis of a coupling

cessed at the time of invocation in a local variable *Current*. When it is finished with the investigation requested, the coupling whose name was stored is made *current* again. In addition, the predicate registers its *Result* in an internal protocol. This is done by *write_protocol*, which we shall be discussing in greater detail later.

Due to the complexity of the constraints, it is too much effort to derive the explanatory texts from their internal representation, as was done in the case of the simpler rule structures of the defect diagnosis for the auto heaters. It is not so difficult to extract and prepare the formulas from the Prolog rules – many expert systems do just that – but it is questionable that such explanations would help most users. What is needed is a short explanation summarizing the constraint problems in "plain English" (or whatever the language of the system may be). Figure 9-15 shows a few clauses implementing the predicate *write_this_explanation* employed in our system.

```
write_this_explanation(type_of_mounting) :-
        indent('- The mounting of the coupling and'),
        indent('  the assembly do not match').

write_this_explanation(axial_shaft_alignment) :-
        indent('- The axial clearance of the'),
        indent('  coupling is less than the axial'),
        indent('  shaft alignment of the assembly').

write_this_explanation(radial_shaft_alignment) :-
        indent('- The radial clearance of the'),
        indent('  coupling is less than the radial'),
        indent('  shaft alignment of the assembly').

%  .  .  .  .  .  .

write_this_explanation(rated_frequency) :-
        indent('- The nominal frequency is too close'),
        indent('  to the intrinsic oscillation').

indent(Text) :-
        nl, tab(10),
        write(Text).
```

Fig. 9-15. Presenting explanations

The best way to demonstrate how *examine_coupling* produces the "*why not*" explanations is to simply invoke it directly and see what happens:

```
?- examine_coupling(20).
```

```
The coupling 20 is not suitable:
```

```
            - The mounting of the coupling and
              the assembly do not match
            - The torque rating of the coupling
              is too low
```

As mentioned earlier, however, we shall, in general, not be employing the predicates for registering and displaying objects and analyzing couplings developed in this chapter directly from the Prolog interface. Instead, these will be embedded in a more comfortable user interface. That is the topic of the next chapter.

10   Embedding the System

Up to now we have not paid much attention to the overall environment in which the expert system operates. Essentially, we have relied upon the dialog-oriented features of Prolog itself. This is certainly adequate for a prototype system, where one's interest is more the demonstration and verification of the functionality of a given system concept. Indeed, we have often indicated that the Prolog interface should be "hidden" by a more robust and user-friendly interactive user interface. We shall be presenting one possible approach involving a menu-driven system environment. In addition, we will be examining techniques for exploiting "metaknowledge" to make the search process more intelligent and, thus, more efficient, for example, by having the system environment provide for a protocol of previous results ("experience"), which can be drawn upon as needed.

10.1   Dialog Flow

The employment of the "naked" *Prolog command interpreter interface* as the user interface to an expert system is a practical solution for prototyping purposes. It allows us, for example, to exploit the full functionality of the underlying Prolog system for testing purposes, without any further effort.

For the final product, however, this is neither useful nor advisable, because the standard Prolog interface is simply not robust enough and contains far too many syntactic and related peculiarities to be even halfway acceptable for a normal, "lay" user. For instance, one has to write all words with a lowercase initial letter and/or phrases as a single string connected by the underline symbol or to *quote* an input string with single quotes.

Consequently, a "commercial" expert system always provides a *user front-end* module for managing the dialog interaction; in our model of the general architecture of systems, in Fig. 4-1, we designated it as the *I/O control* component. There are a number of different approaches for constructing such a front-end.

A very common, but not all too popular approach is that of *interactive case data compilation* or *consultation in dialog*: the system poses the user a (frequently, very lengthy) series of questions, before delivering the desired information, advice or other service. The MTA expert and the system for finding defects in an automobile heating system typified this approach.

We have already discussed the idea of an *assistant system*, whose front-end consists of a normal text gathering or documentation system, which extracts the necessary data automatically from the text written.

A third alternative is the well known *menu-driven interface*, where the user selects system services from a series of display menus, either via the keyboard, a "mouse" or similar interactive input devices. Typically, one selects one's way through a hierarchy of menus until a level is reached where results are actually delivered. One advantage is that the mode of interaction can be varied, so that, as needed, i.e. once the "problem" has been sufficiently refined per menu, the user gets switched over into a more suitable mode, e.g. a compilation dialog. Such combination allows for a less tiresome interaction for the user.

10.2   The Menu Interface

We would like to embed the basic functions developed in the previous chapter for selection a coupling in a menu system with occasional dialog-oriented input. We have two possibilities: we employ a *menu shell*, i.e. a general menu system applications package, which is adapted to the specific task via driver tables, or we program the *menu control* functions needed especially for our specific task ourselves.

In Prolog, in sharp contrast to most other programming languages, the latter alternative is no more complicated and costly than the former. Therefore, we shall be programming our own menu control features[1]. To get an idea of just how the services of the coupling expert are embedded in the menu system, we will show you a few sample user interactions.

As soon as the user responds to the Prolog prompt with the command "start", she finds herself in the main menu, which offers her the following system services:

```
?- start.

**************************************************
                Main Menu
**************************************************

1               enter objects
2               select objects
3               show objects

end             end

**************************************************
Please enter your choice ==> 1
```

---

[1] Two versions of a generally applicable menu sub-system, programmed in Prolog, can be found in the literature [SCHN87], as already mentioned above.

By entering the number "1" the user selects the system service *enter objects.* Figure 10-1 outlines the hierarchical arrangement of the individual menus. The input moves the user to the next deeper level in the state tree defined.

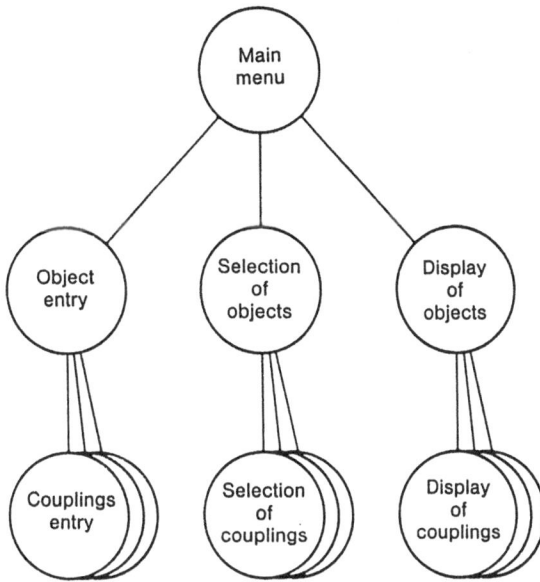

Fig. 10-1. The menu hierarchy

At that next deeper level the user can select a specific class of objects which she wishes to compile, select or display. Based on the following menu excerpt, if she enters the code number "2" in order to define a new *load*, then she finds herself in a direct dialog for compiling new objects, running unter the control of the generic object *load*. This should be familiar to us from the discussion in Sect. 9.5, where we also showed a detailed excerpt from just such a dialog, including error handling and help functions. We shall limit ourselves here to a simple dialog.

```
*************************************************
            Compiling Objects
*************************************************

1              Drive Side
2              Load Side
3              Assembly
4              Coupling

end            back to the Main Menu

*************************************************
Please enter your choice ==) 2
```

```
Number: 4
identifying_name: Marine_Propeller
ako: .
rpm_independent_drive_frequency:
angular_momentum: 18
torque_rating: 150

New frame: 4
torque_rating: 150
angular_momentum: 18
identifying_name: Marine_Propeller
rpm_independent_drive_frequency: 0

********************************************
              Compiling Objects
********************************************

1               Drive Side
2               Load Side
3               Assembly
4               Coupling

end             back to the Main Menu

********************************************
Please enter your choice ==>  end
```

Choosing *end* takes one back to the main menu of the menu tree shown in Fig. 10-1. By entering a "3" the user could then, for example, have the system display the various objects known to it.

Before we look at any of the other services offered at the main menu level, we would like to discuss the procedures involved in controlling the dialog.

As mentioned earlier, we are programming the entire menu driver entirely in Prolog itself. This is done according to a single, unified scheme, which is illustrated, with respect to the main menu, in Fig. 10-2.

menu_title(Text) is a trivial procedure for outputting *Text*, i.e. the title of the menu, with a line of asterisks as a visual separator. *end_of_menu* prints the closing line of separating asterisks followed by the standard prompt to make a selection. We do not show them here, because their implementation is quite simple and can be found in Appendix D for those interested in the details. Similarly, we are familiar with the predicate *read_in*, which we saw earlier in Fig. 8-3.

The *Function* returned by *transform* when the user enters end is *true*. This allows *deal_with* to end successfully and causes the procedure *start* to continue. If the user enters an unforeseen *Input*, then the last *transform* fact returns *invalid* as the *Function. invalid* then displays the corresponding message. Every "legal"

```
start :-
        repeat,
        main_menu(Input),
        % repeat until "end" has been entered:
        Input = end.

main_menu(Input) :-
        menu_title('Main Menu'),
        nl,write('1        enter objects'),
        nl,write('2        select objects'),
        nl,write('3        show objects'),
        nl,
        nl,write('end      end'),
        end_of_menu,
        read_in(Input),
        deal_with(main_menu,Input), !.

deal_with(main_menu,Input) :-
        transform(main_menu,Input,Function),
        Function, !.
%         . . . . .
% "deal_with" clauses for the remaining menus
%         . . . . .

transform(main_menu,1,enter).
transform(main_menu,2,select).
transform(main_menu,3,display_it).
transform(main_menu,end,true).
%         . . . . .
% "transform" facts for the remaining menus
%         . . . . .
transform(_,_,invalid).

invalid :-
        nl,write('Input is invalid !').
```

Fig. 10-2. Control procedures for the main menu

response is transformed into the associated, executable *Function.* If this happens to be a new, hierarchically lower-level *menu* -which is certainly the case for all responses possible at the highest level – then *Function* is the name of the procedure for processing the related menu, corresponding to the *start* clause of the main menu in both structure and function. Figure 10-3 illustrates this scheme based on the sub-menu *enter,* which is activated by the choice "1".

Here we can see how the utility functions for administering the objects are invoked via the various menus: in Fig. 10-3 it is the compilation procedure *new-*

frame, which is activated by the predicate _enter_object_ should the user _Input_ the correct code number.

The control of the other sub-menus is realized in the same manner.

```
enter :-
        repeat,
        enter(Input),
        Input = end.

enter(Input) :-
        menu_title('Compiling Objects'),
        nl,write('1        Drive Side'),
        nl,write('2        Load Side'),
        nl,write('3        Assembly'),
        nl,write('4        Coupling'),
      . nl,
        nl,write('end      back to the Main Menu'),
        end_of_menu,
        read_in(Input),
        deal_with(enter,Input), !.

%          . . . . .
deal_with(enter,Input) :-
        transform(menu,Input,Type),
        enter_object(Type), !.
%          . . . . .

%
% The following "transform" predicates are used to
% decode all object selection menus:
transform(menu,1,drive).
transform(menu,2,load).
transform(menu,3,assembly).
transform(menu,4,coupling).
transform(menu,end,back).
%          . . . . .

enter_object(back) :-
        !.
enter_object(invalid) :-
        invalid, !.
enter_object(Type) :-
        nl, nl, write('Number: '),
        read_in(Name),
        new_frame(Type,Name).
```

Fig. 10-3. The sub-menu _enter_

10.3 Displaying Objects

The second service offered is the *displaying of objects*. The following excerpt from the menu-driven dialog shows an example of this:

```
**************************************************
                  Main Menu
**************************************************


1             enter objects
2             select objects
3             show objects

end           end


**************************************************
Please enter your choice ==> 3


**************************************************
                Display Object
**************************************************


1             Drive Side
2             Load Side
3             Assembly
4             Coupling

end           back to the Main Menu


**************************************************
Please enter your choice ==> 4


**************************************************
              Display Couplings
**************************************************


all           show all instances
current       show current object
N             show object N

end           back to the Main Menu


**************************************************
Please enter your choice ==> 34
```

```
identifying_name: Kauermann 02 e
ako: Series Kauermann e
torque_rating: 1405
angular_momentum: 3.2
diameter: 272
length: 223


***************************************************
                Display Couplings
***************************************************


all             show all instances
current         show current object
N               show object N

end             back to the Main Menu

***************************************************
Please enter your choice ==> end
```

Figure 10-4 illustrates how the function *display_it*, activated by the choice
"2" in the main menu, controls the display of objects.

```
display_it :-
        repeat,
        display_it(Input),
        Input = end.

display_it(Input) :-
        menu_title('Display Objects'),
        nl,write('1       Drive Side'),
        nl,write('2       Load Side'),
        nl,write('3       Assembly'),
        nl,write('4       Coupling'),
        nl,
        nl,write('end     back to the Main Menu'),
        end_of_menu,
        read_in(Input),
        deal_with(display_it,Input), !.

%       . . . . .
deal_with(display_it,Input) :-
        transform(menu,Input,Type),
        display_objects(Type), !.
%       . . . . .
```

```
display_objects(back) :-
        !.
display_objects(invalid) :-
        invalid, !.
display_objects(Type) :-
        repeat,
        display_objects(Type,Input),
        Input = end.
```

Fig. 10-4. The sub-menu *display_it*

If the user selects a legitimate object *Type*, a second sub-menu is activated –
display_objects. In contrast to the menus discussed to date, this one is supplied
with the *Type* of object the user wishes to see via the input variable by the same
name. Figure 10-5 shows the procedure which displays the objects.

```
display_objects(Type,Input) :-
        menu_title('Display ',Type),
        nl,write('all      show all instances'),
        nl,write('current show current object'),
        nl,write('N        show object N'),
        nl,
        nl,write('end      back to the Main Menu'),
        end_of_menu,
        read_in(Input),
        deal_with(display_objects,Type,Input), !.

%        . . . . .
deal_with(display_objects,_,end).
deal_with(display_objects,Type,all) :-
        display_instances(Type,general,1).
deal_with(display_objects,Type,current) :-
        current(Type,Name),
        display_frame(Type,Name).
deal_with(display_objects,Type,Name) :-
        (        not is_instance(Type,Name),
                 nl, write('No such object exists.'),
                 nl
        ;        display_frame(Type,Name)
        ).
%        . . . . .
```

Fig. 10-5. Displaying objects

The binary version of *menu_title* used in this figure is a trivial extension of the unary one: it merely displays the two atoms passed in as arguments as a concatenated header.

We assume that the activation of the output primitives *display_instances* and *display_frame* in the respective *deal_with* clauses is self-explanatory.

10.4 The Selection of Objects

Having discussed the principle of menu management and the embedding of the utility functions in some detail, we can now focus our attention on the fundamental task of our coupling expert: the selection and analysis of couplings. Since the system can perform its duty only once a specific drive, load and assembly have been established as the *current objects* involved, the user must first choose the menu for selecting objects, as shown in Fig. 10-1, and, from there, branch to the appropriate sub-menus. There she can choose, respectively, from the drives, loads or assemblies listed as currently available in the object base. The following dialog illustrates how this is done:

```
?- start.

*********************************************
                Main Menu
*********************************************

1             enter objects
2             select objects
3             show objects

end           end

*********************************************
Please enter your choice ==> 2

*********************************************
               Object Selection
*********************************************

1             Drive Side
2             Load Side
3             Assembly
4             Coupling

end           back to the Main Menu

*********************************************
Please enter your choice ==> 1
```

```
**************************************************
                 Available Drive Sides
**************************************************

1               AC_Motor I
2               Rotary_Current_Motor 160 M4
3               AC_Motor II
4               Diesel_Motor 4 Cylinder
5               DC_Motor 160M


**************************************************
Please enter your choice ==> 3
```

By entering "3" the user selects "AC_Motor II" as the current drive. The system displays the Object Selection Menu once again, so that the load and the assembly can be selected too.

```
**************************************************
                 Object Selection
**************************************************

1               Drive Side
2               Load Side
3               Assembly
4               Coupling

end             back to the Main Menu

**************************************************
Please enter your choice ==> 3



**************************************************
                 Available Assembly
**************************************************

1               Assembly 1
2               Assembly 2
3               Assembly 3

**************************************************
Please enter your choice ==> 1
```

If the user should ask the system to select a suitable coupling before she has specified the assembly and load involved, then the system refuses to do so, issuing the explanatory message:

```
*************************************************
               Object Selection
*************************************************

1              Drive Side
2              Load Side
3              Assembly
4              Coupling

end            back to the Main Menu

*************************************************
Please enter your choice ==> 4

The load side remains to be selected


*************************************************
               Object Selection
*************************************************

1              Drive Side
2              Load Side
3              Assembly
4              Coupling

end            back to the Main Menu

*************************************************
Please enter your choice ==> 2


*************************************************
               Available Load Sides
*************************************************

1              Fan
2              Rotary_Pump
3              Rotary_Current_Generator I
4              Marine_Propeller

*************************************************
Please enter your choice ==> 1
```

After the user has selected the Fan as the current load, she can then request the system to select an appropriate coupling.

```
*************************************************
                Object Selection
*************************************************


1                Drive Side
2                Load Side
3                Assembly
4                Coupling

end              back to the Main Menu


*************************************************
Please enter your choice ==) 4
```

The system now offers three different methods of selection. The *primitive selection* searches through the available set of couplings until it finds one that satisfies all the constraints in the (internal) list of criteria. *Selection using metaknowledge*, as we shall see later, attempts to optimize this search by exploiting existing knowledge, i.e. previous experience. And, last but not least, the user can request a *complete investigation* of a particular coupling, whose number is entered in response to the menu prompt.

The following dialog excerpt shows a primitive selection and the complete investigation of a specific coupling.

```
AAAAAAAAAAAAAAAA*********************************
                Coupling Selection
*************************************************


p                primitive selection
m                selection using metaknowledge
N                analyze coupling N

end              end


*************************************************
Please enter your choice ==) p

The coupling selected is 11
with the designation Stromag gr 10
```

```
**************************************************
                Coupling Selection
**************************************************

p               primitive selection
m               selection using metaknowledge
N               analyze coupling N

end             end

**************************************************
Please enter your choice ==> 24

No such coupling exists !


**************************************************
                Coupling Selection
**************************************************

p               primitive selection
m               selection using metaknowledge
N               analyze coupling N

end             end

**************************************************
Please enter your choice ==> 33

The coupling 33 is not suitable:

                - The angular clearance of the
                  coupling is less than the angular
                  shaft alignment of the assembly


**************************************************
                Coupling Selection
**************************************************

p               primitive selection
m               selection using metaknowledge
N               analyze coupling N

end             end

**************************************************
Please enter your choice ==> end
```

Let us see just how this is implemented in terms of Prolog predicates. The menu control procedure *select* in Fig. 10-6 differs from *enter* of Fig. 10-3 - as we mentioned earlier - practically only with respect to the services invoked, represented here by the predicate *select_objects.*

```
select :-
        repeat,
        select(Input),
        Input = end.

select(Input) :-
        menu_title('Object Selection'),
        nl,write('1      Drive Side'),
        nl,write('2      Load Side'),
        nl,write('3      Assembly'),
        nl,write('4      Coupling'),
        nl,
        nl,write('end    back to the Main Menu'),
        end_of_menu,
        read_in(Input),
        deal_with(select,Input), !.

%        . . . . .
deal_with(select,Input) :-
        transform(menu,Input,Type),
        select_objects(Type), !.
%        . . . . .

select_objects(back) :-
        !.
select_objects(invalid) :-
        invalid, !.
%        . . . . .
% The predicates which actually perform the
% object selection appear here (see below)
%        . . . . .
```

Fig. 10-6. The sub-menu for selecting objects

As we have already seen, the selection of objects is handled differently, according to whether we are dealing with a coupling or some other type of object:

• In the case of a coupling, making the selection is the *job of the system.* Because it needs complete information about the environment involved, the decision can only be made when the current drive and load side, as well as assembly, are known.

- The latter three components, however, must be chosen *by the user*, who, on the other hand, must be presented a menu containing the list of currently available instances of the component types to be chosen from.

```
select_objects(coupling) :-
         (          current(assembly,0),
                    nl, nl,
                    write('The assembly')
         ;          current(drive,0),
                    nl, nl,
                    write('The drive side')
         ;          current(load,0),
                    nl, nl,
                    write('The load side')
         ),
         write(' remains to be selected'),
         nl, nl, !.
select_objects(coupling) :-
         repeat,
         select_objects(coupling,Input),
         Input = end.
select_objects(Type) :-
         menu_title('Available ',Type),
         display existing objects(Type),
         end_of_menu,
         read_in(Input),
         note(Type,Input,current),
         !.

select_objects(coupling,Input) :-
         menu_title('Coupling Selection'),
         nl,write('p        drive side'),
         nl,write('m        load side'),
         nl,write('N        assembly'),
         nl,
         nl,write('end      end'),
         end_of_menu,
         read_in(Input),
         deal_with(select_objects,coupling,Input),
         !.
```

Fig. 10-7. The predicate for selecting objects

```
deal_with(select_objects,coupling,end) :- !.
deal_with(select_objects,coupling,m) :-
        metaknowledge, !.
deal_with(select_objects,coupling,p) :- !,
        (       is_instance(coupling,Name),
                examine(Name,List),
                write_protocol(partial,List),
                List == [], !,
                write_result(Name)
        ;       nl,
                write('A suitable coupling could '),
                write('not be found !'),
                nl
        ).
deal_with(select_objects,coupling,Name) :-
        (       not is_instance(coupling,Name),
                nl,
                write('No such coupling exists.'),
                nl
        ;       examine_Coupling(Name)
        ).

search_for(Type,Frame,Slot,Facet,Data_Item) :-
        clause(frame(Type,Frame,Slot,Facet,
                                Data_Item),_).

is_instance(Type,Name) :-
        search_for(coupling,Name,
                                identifying_name, _,_).

write_result(Coupling) :-
        nl, nl, write('The coupling selected is '),
        write(Coupling), nl,
        write('with the designation '),
        search_for(coupling,Coupling,
                identifying_name,value,[Name]),
        write(Name), nl, nl.
```

Fig. 10-8. Selecting the coupling

10.5 Maintaining a Protocol

Testing all the couplings of a large set is extremely costly – particularly when, in the final system, even more constraints and formulas are involved than in our somewhat simplified prototype. Consequently, it pays to record the results attained in the form of an *internal protocol* in the knowledge base.

This ever-growing body of knowledge corresponds to the *experience* of a (human) coupling expert, which often enables her to pick out the correct coupling right away. This sort of experience, and its application as a simple and yet effective *heuristic* for finding solutions without resorting to the complex technical data and formulas, can be characterized as metaknowledge: knowledge *about* knowledge, in this case knowledge about the consequences of applying the "actual" technical knowledge in specific, relevant situations.

Such "prefabricated" (meta-)knowledge is all the more important when one is dealing with a complete *configuration system* or perhaps a *planning system*, where, in the course of numerous different steps, many sub-assemblies or sub-plans must be combined before the final product can be constructed. For example, the configuration of one or more disk units with controllers and housing assemblies is a typical sub-task of a computer configuration system. Since the same combination of peripheral equipment is required every so often, it would pay to keep track of the sub-assemblies involved for the particular case, so that one could call for it instantly and avoid having to "recalculate" it each time.

In our coupling system, we protocol the component combination for a specific aggregate with the help of the procedure *write_protocol* shown in Fig. 10-9.

```
write_protocol(Type,Result) :-
        current(drive,Drive),
        current(load,Load),
        current(assembly,Assembly),
        current(coupling,Coupling),
        !,
        store_protocol(Drive,Load,Assembly,
                       Coupling,Type,Result).

store_protocol(Drive,Ld,Assbly,Cltch,complete,Result) :-
        retract(protocol(Drive,Ld,Assbly,Cltch,_,_)),
        fail.
store_protocol(Drive,Ld,Assbly,Cltch,partial,Result) :-
        clause(protocol(Drive,Ld,Assbly,Cltch,_,_),_), !.
store_protocol(Drive,Ld,Assbly,Cltch,Type,Result) :-
        asserta(protocol(Drive,Ld,Assbly,Cltch,Type,Result)).
```

Fig. 10-9. The internal protocolling of results

We distinguish here between two different types of results, i.e. *complete* and *partial.* The actual procedure for maintaining the protocol, *write_protocol,* is formulated such that the result of a complete analysis will always replace that of a partial one.

Since the internal protocol is not intended for the user, the menus provide no opportunity to inspect its contents. For test purposes, however, we, as system developer, can access the information via the normal Prolog interpreter interface. Just how this can be done is demonstrated in the following example:

```
?- protocol(_,_,_,Coupling,Type,Result),
   write(Coupling),nl,write(Type),nl,
   write(Result),nl,nl,fail.
33
complete
[angular_shaft_alignment]

20
complete
[type_of_mounting, coupling_torque_rating]

11
partial
[]

10
partial
[coupling_torque_rating]

0
_1816
[]
```

We let the system display the couplings investigated to date, together with the associated results. Since we have specified the drive, load and assembly to be anonymous variables in our request, and do not display their values (which we could easily have done), we merely learn that the couplings 33 and 20 are the only ones which have been completely analyzed. In the current combination of components - which, although fixed, remains unknown to us here - we learn that coupling 33 did not satisfy the criterion for the *angular_shaft_alignment* and 22 failed with respect to the *type_of_mounting,* as well as the *coupling_torque_rating.* The couplings 11 and 10 were only partially analyzed, whereby 11 was found suitable and 10 failed due to its *coupling_torque_rating.* The last information displayed in the list output relates to the information with which a protocol is initialized, which is of the form

```
protocol(0,0,0,0,_,[]).
```

The exploitation of the "experience" recorded in this form is one of the ways one can optimize the selection process and improve the user's informational resources through metaknowledge.

10.6 Applying Metaknowledge

By *metaknowledge*, we mean *knowledge about knowledge*, i.e. knowledge about the structure and meaningful manipulation thereof, as well as implicit relationships between the facts and rules stored in the knowledge base (which we consider to be the *primary knowledge* about the special area of knowledge being dealt with). In more general terms, metaknowledge embodies characteristics of the primary knowledge which are neither directly evident nor derivable from it.

Let us look at some examples of such metaknowledge and its exploitation by procedures and rules, in the context of our coupling expert. Like the menu interface, the metaknowledge can also be considered a part of the system environment (embedding) of the primary knowledge. A good user interface may make the primary knowledge more convenient to use, but good metaknowledge should make it more efficient.

```
metaknowledge :-
        check_if_already_dealt_with.
metaknowledge :-
        examine_groupwise.
metaknowledge :-
        make_suggestion.

check_if_already_dealt_with :-
        current(drive,Drive),
        current(load,Load),
        current(assembly,Assembly),
        protocol(Drive,Load,Assembly,Coupling,_,[]),
        write_result(Coupling).

examine_groupwise :-
        search_for(coupling,Group,ako,_,[general]),
        examine_multilevel(1,Group,Preliminary_Result),
        Preliminary_Result == [],
        search_for(coupling,Coupling,ako,_,[Group]),
        examine_multilevel(2,Coupling,Final_Result),
        Final_Result == [],
        write_result(Coupling).
```

Fig. 10-10. Clauses for exploiting metaknowledge

Our predicate *metaknowledge*, which is activated by the coupling selection in Fig. 10-8 whenever the user chooses "m" rather than "p" for "primitive search", pursues the following strategy:

- If the aggregate being sought has already been investigated, then the result is merely extracted from the internal protocol.
- If no usable result can be found in the protocol, then it takes advantage of the fact that the different coupling series are classified into groups with common features. Thus, it pays to first check those constraints which depend on the common characteristics of a coupling group. If such criteria are not fulfilled, then one can eliminate the entire group from further investigation.
- The existing metaknowledge is also used to increase the usefulness of the system: if a suitable coupling cannot be found, then a summary of the necessary characteristics of a potential candidate are presented in the form of a *suggestion*, which can then be used for its custom fabrication or purchase.

```
examine_multilevel(Step,Name,Result) :-
        note(coupling,Name,current),
        delete(requirement,current),
        criteria(Step,List),
        member(Criterion,List),
        examine_constraint(Criterion,Result),
        Result \= [],
        !.
examine_multilevel(_,_,[]).

criteria(1,
        [
        type_of_mounting,
        axial_shaft_alignment,
        radial_shaft_alignment,
        angular_shaft_alignment
        ]).

criteria(2,
        [
        length_of_housing,
        diameter_of_housing,
        coupling_torque_rating,
        drive_frequency,
        load_frequency,
        rated_frequency
        ]).
```

Fig. 10-11. Breaking up the constraints list for multilevel investigation of couplings

The three clauses shown in Fig. 10-10 provide for this sequence of system actions.

The procedure implementing the first *metaknowledge* clause, which is to look for a result in the protocol based on the investigation of the same aggregate, is shown in the same figure. If a protocol entry with an empty list is found for the corresponding aggregate, implying that the coupling selected fulfills the current combination of *Drive*, *Load* and *Assembly*, then the *Coupling* recorded therein is returned as the result of the search.

The second search procedure, *examine_groupwise*, is somewhat more complicated. In the first stage, the procedure *examine_multilevel* is applied to each *Group*, to determine if the group-specific characteristics satisfy all the relevant constraints. The result is a *Preliminary_Result* list, which, if empty, indicates that no conflict exists at the group level, and it can now proceed to the second stage of groupwise examination, where the individual couplings in the group are searched for a suitable one.

As can be seen in Fig. 10-11, this multilevel search is achieved by simply breaking the list of constraints up into two lists. The first one contains the group-specific criteria and the second one the coupling-specific criteria, i.e. those relevant within a given series.

Finally, we still want to use the accumulated metaknowledge to prepare a suggestion for the construction of a suitable coupling, even if the two search procedures fail to find one among those in the object base.

10.7   Preparing a Suggestion for Coupling Construction

Just what a suggestion might look like is illustrated in our final sample dialog:

```
***************************************************
                 Coupling Selection
***************************************************


p               primitive selection
m               selection using metaknowledge
N               analyze coupling N

end             end


***************************************************
Please enter your choice ==) m

A suitable coupling was not found.
```

Suggestion for an appropriate coupling:

    - type_of_mounting is axial

    - axial_clearance must be greater than 0.5

    - radial_clearance must be greater than 0.7

    - angular_clearance must be greater than 1

    - length must be less than 500

    - diameter must be less than 400

    - torque_rating must be greater than 41.8

The procedure *make_suggestion*, which displays this suggestion for constructing a suitable coupling, is shown in Fig. 10-12.

```
make_suggestion :-
     nl,
     write('A suitable coupling was not found.'),
     nl, nl,
     write('Suggestion for an appropriate coupling:'),
     suggestion_list(List),
     member(Requirements, List),
     write_suggestion(Requirements),
     fail.
make_suggestion.

suggestion_list([
     type_of_mounting,
     axial_clearance,
     radial_clearance,
     angular_clearance,
     length,
     diameter,
     torque_rating
     ]).
```

Fig. 10-12. The compilation of a suggestion for the construction of a coupling

The output of the proposal is driven by a *suggestion_list*, according to which the procedure *write_suggestion* prepares the individual requirements, one at a time, for display. A few exemplary clauses are to be seen in Fig. 10-13.

```
write_suggestion(type_of_mounting) :-
     ask_assembly(type_of_mounting,Mount_Type),
     write_requirement(type_of_mounting,is,
                              Mount_Type).
write_suggestion(axial_clearance) :-
     ask_assembly(axial_shaft_alignment,S_ax),
     write_requirement(axial_clearance,
                              greater_than,S_ax).

%       . . . . .


write_suggestion(torque_rating) :-
     ask_requirement(temperature_factor,S_theta),
     ask_requirement(torque,T_N),
     T_max is T_N * S_theta,
     write_requirement(axial_clearance,
                              greater_than,T_max).

write_requirement(Criterion,Relationship,Data_Item) :-
     nl,nl, tab(2), write('- '),
     write(Criterion),
     write_relation(Relationship),
     write(Data_Item).

write_relation(is) :-
     write(' is ').
write_relation(greater_than) :-
     write(' must be greater than ').
write_relation(less_than) :-
     write(' must be less than ').
```

Fig. 10-13. Producing suggestions for a suitable coupling

The standardized, auxiliary predicates *write_requirement* and *write_relation* make the preparation of the information a matter of simply transforming the respective constraint into a text component.

10.8   Shortcomings and Possible Improvements

The sample coupling expert system presented in the last two chapters is, obviously, still very much a prototype. This is not only due to the small size of the knowledge base and the limited services offered, compared to the commercial system from which it has been distilled. The "real" system, for example, contained an integrated package of Fortran functions for calculating and graphically displaying characteristic curves and dynamic characteristics.

The prototype, however, could be improved in other ways as well:

- The user interface is, despite the menu orientation, "cruder" then one would like to see. In the dialog excerpt in Sect. 10-2, for example, one is confronted with compound technical terms, such as

```
rpm_independent_drive_frequency
```

in their internally defined form, i.e. as Prolog atoms, with their usual underline symbol connectors.

- The awkward style of expressing such compound terms, i.e. phrases derives from the fact that these text components are derived from the constant values in Prolog clauses. A simple solution, requiring more "brawn than brains" is to edit all the source code such that the respective identifiers (phrases) are "expressed" normally, i.e. with intervening blanks and the like, and the entire phrase is then made into an atom by enclosing it in *single quotes*. Since the Prolog interpreter accepts, for example,

```
'rpm independent drive frequency'
```

or

```
'angular velocity'
```

as atoms, the semantics of the Prolog programs are in no way changed. On the other hand, it makes the code a bit more difficult to read, in many cases, and, thus, we recommend that one make such modifications only after the knowledge base has been validated.

- The checking for improper user input is more limited in scope than we would expect in a commercial system. A good example of this can be found in Fig. 10-7, where, in the clause *select_objects(Type)*, we neglect to check if the user actually entered the name of one of the object instances which were listed. With blind faith in the user's infallibility and good will, we set the identifier of the current object to the unchecked *Input* entered.

You have probably found other, similar shortcomings. Indeed, many of the criticisms made in Chaps. 7 and 8 with respect to the robustness and comfort afforded by our frame-based implementation are in some way applicable here; in some cases, in fact, even more so. For example, we simplified the more generalized form of the primitive predicates, streamlining them to fit the specific application. While this increased the overall efficiency, it also decreased the stability and integrity of the system.

Thus, if the reader has not yet done so, we are certain that it would pay to scrutinize the prototype with an eye for these and other weaknesses. This is especially advisable, if the coupling expert is to be used as the basis for the development of practical, commercial expert system applications.

11 Software Development Methodology

Knowledge-based programming also requires some form of project management. One should not assume, however, that one can simply apply the methodology of "classical" software development. The distinction between algorithms and data upon which many traditional approaches and techniques are based is no longer applicable. Since "knowledge" is more dynamic than "data", activities such as *specification* and *design* involve goals quite different from their traditional counterparts and must be redefined accordingly. Thus, the "evolutionary prototyping" technique permeates all "phases" of the project. Consequently, this final chapter of our book attempts to introduce a "knowledge-based" software engineering methodology, based on the traditional *phase model* of software development. It explains why the "phases" are no longer phases. And it discusses concepts which were not conceivable in the traditional approach, but which now play an important role in the theory and practice of system design, the major one being that of "metaknowledge" and its application. Above all, however, we offer practical advice on how to best manage the development of an expert system.

11.1 "Knowledge-Based" Software Technology

Software engineering is more than just programming and also more than just design. We have known this since about 1970, when the notion of *software engineering* was born, and because it proceeded, in the decade that followed, to acquire widespread acceptance not only in the field of computer science, but also among experienced data processing practitioners –indicating that there was a real need for a systematic methodology for fabricating software as an industrial product.

It would be quite amazing if this were suddenly no longer the case with respect to the development of knowledge-based software. Since we focused our attention, in the previous ten chapters, exclusively on design and programming techniques, it is only proper that we now devote ourselves to the methodological issues. The fact that we need a methodology for developing expert systems does not necessarily imply that the techniques should be the same ones with which we are familiar from traditional software development. For one thing, the products which we are producing are fundamentally distinct from those implemented in the traditional programming languages.

For example, the amalgamation and administration of facts and rules, i.e. data-like and procedural elements, in the same knowledge base is the quintessential characteristic of knowledge-based software. This immediately renders one of the fundamental prerequisites of classical design and programming methodology inoperative, namely the strict separation of the *database* from the *algorithms*. This inevitably has consequences for the *modularization* of Prolog programs. Modularization, naturally, remains a vital aspect of the engineering methodology, but it serves different purposes and obeys rules different from those postulated by classical software technology.

We commented on this issue earlier. For a more detailed discussion we suggest you read a suitable textbook on the subject (e.g. [SCHN87]). We mention these design and programming issues here only to make a case for the fact that we must be prepared for deviations from the familiar with respect to the methods with which a project is carried out.

The "familiar", in the case of classical software engineering, is the *project model* for the structuring and stepwise construction of a software product, and the *phase model* for the individual steps in the development process derived from it[1]. The basic assumption is that the phases are distinct units, delineated by so-called *milestones*, defined concretely as the completion of specific intermediate "products".

As we have already seen, a kind of "evolutionary prototyping" technique is frequently employed in the development of expert systems. This implies the emergence of the final product through a continuous, stepwise refinement and extension of an originally minimal model of the system with a correspondingly limited knowledge base. And since the knowledge embodying most areas of knowledge and applications is constantly growing and being modified, one cannot be sure that the "final product" is not a chimera.

But what becomes of the well-defined, intermediate products and the milestones derived from them? They no longer exist!

11.2   Project Flow

Does this mean that there is no phase model for the planning and verification of the *flow of a project* to develop a knowledge-based system?

Yes and no.

With the disappearance of "cleanly" defined milestones, we are going to have to get used to the fact that we no longer have such "phases" in which, for example, an activity - such as *specifying, designing, coding* or *testing* - is done exclusively, exhaustively and definitively. Instead, at any given time, *all* these

---

[1] It is noteworthy that the concept of project phases is itself a controversial issue among practitioners of classical software engineering (e.g. see [FLOY81]).

activities will be overlapping and – at best – be conducted with shifting emphasis[2].

Nonetheless, we can also draw up a project plan which "resembles a phase
model". A sample plan, upon which we shall be basing further discussion, can be
seen in Fig. 11-1. We have essentially followed an outline developed by *P. Jackson* [JACK86].

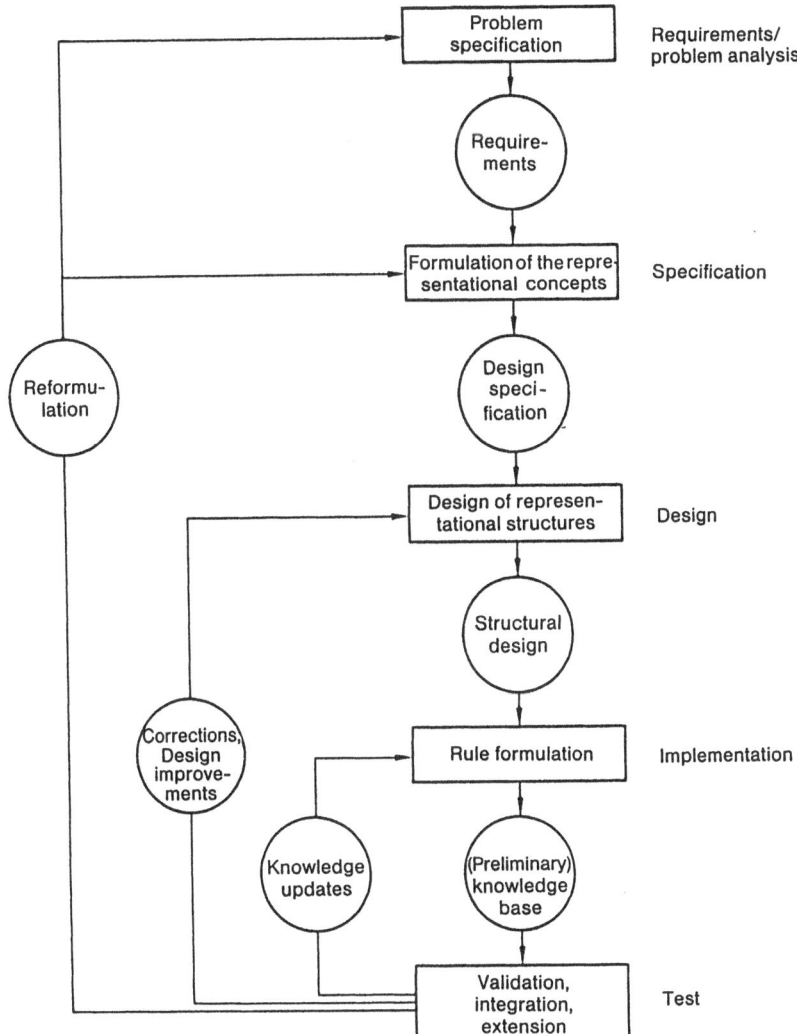

Fig. 11-1. The "phase model" of knowledge-based system development

---

[2] Cynics will now say "just like it has always been in reality". But at least now we need not have a
guilty conscience!

To simplify the comparison with a traditional project model, we have included the roughly corresponding concepts from conventional plans, in addition to the description of the associated activities. It is, however, important to recall that the actual meaning, i.e. the particular action to be carried out, is not the same as in the classical phase model.

The **specification of the problem**

pursues essentially the same goals as *problem* or *requirements analysis* in the traditional project model: determining which problems are to be solved, ascertaining if it makes sense to employ computerized data processing (and, in this case, knowledge-based techniques), what costs are involved and an estimate of the time frame and resource requirements for the project. We shall see, however, that, in the case of knowledge-based software development, we must already begin to consider problems in this phase which in the classical model are assigned to later phases. We believe that the "milestone" bounding this phase is not only a document describing the *requirements*, but in fact a *minimal prototype* as well, which illustrates the essential structural characteristics and, at least in principle, the user interface.

The **formulation of the representation concepts**

corresponds to the classical *specification phase*. The goal here is the establishment of the *knowledge organization*: What knowledge must be formalized and stored? In what form and from which *area experts* will the knowledge be acquired? Does one need a *knowledge compiling component*, with which the experts can enter and maintain their knowledge, or will this task be dispatched directly by the *knowledge engineers*, in Prolog or the knowledge representation language of the shell employed? Can part or all of the knowledge be acquired via traditional data processing, or is the expert system intended to be the control system or supplier of data for some conventionally written software? Must an existing *databank* or other software, as a consequence, be integrated into the knowledge-based system? Which modification and maintenance activities are to be expected with respect to the knowledge involved. How is the knowledge base to be modularized? And how can one meaningfully break the knowledge down into facts, rules and metaknowledge?

The **design of the representation structures,**

while corresponding most closely to the *design phase*, must essentially be conducted concurrently with the formulation of the representation concepts. Here is where the *knowledge representation* is planned. It is decided which structures shall be employed for representing the facts, the rules and the meta- knowledge, how the *inference engine* and the *dialog interface* function and interact, how the internal data structures and the *state information* should be stored and if and how a *protocol* should be realized. If the knowledge is not to be stored directly as production rules, but rather in

frames or some other structure, then their representation and manipulation must be specified – much in the way we did in Chaps. 7 and 8 – and
implemented as a prototype. Likewise, the necessary mechanisms and primitive procedures should be developed and implemented for those services
not directly provided by either Prolog or the shell employed, e.g. *explanatory components* or the representation and processing of *vague knowledge.*
The most important *design goal* when defining the *representational struc-
ures* is to achieve as uniform and symmetric a coding as possible of the
various facts, rules, frame slots and/or whatever other structural elements
are involved. The decisions made in this regard will later determine the
ease, elegance and efficiency with which the implementation and refinement of procedures can be achieved. In Prolog it is always inadvisable to
define predicates constituting a "class" of actions with different arities,
because arity is a basic attribute of a functor and accessing predicates of
unknown arity is complicated and *inefficient.* If the problem requires the
facility to process a variable number of arguments in the same manner, the
experienced Prolog programmer will resort to a list representation[3].

The **formulation of rules**

then begins, corresponding to the structures decided upon for representing
the knowledge, with the *specification of knowledge*, i.e. the actual formulation of the expert knowledge in terms of facts and rules. In the process, the
first knowledge base is created for a preliminary system, so that we could
equate this activity with the *coding* or *implementation* phase of the traditional project model. Admittedly, this activity overlaps, once again, with
the specification and design of the representation structures, since the
primitive auxiliary system procedures written in those "phases" must be
developed and tested on the basis of "genuine" expert knowledge.

The **validation, full integration** and **extension**

of the knowledge base correspond to the conventional *test, integration* and
maintenance phases of the system. Once again, however, there exist some
fundamental differences with respect to traditional programming practice.
Whereas "maintenance" classically implies, above all, the correction of
"bugs", and the addition of new features is thought of more in the context
of customization, i.e. a marketing instrument for follow-up business, in the
case of knowledge-based software the need to continuously make *knowledge updates* is the norm: a knowledge base is, virtually by definition,
"never complete", because not only the desires of the user evolve with

---

[3] We present this example intentionally for the "moral" involved: the belief that one can design
software independently of the programming language in which it is to be implemented has been
the cause of many a "classical software" development disaster. We should, therefore, take advantage of the opportunity given by the introduction of a "new" software technology to lay this fable
to rest.

time, but the knowledge itself is constantly subject to change and development. The need for a fundamentally unproblematic modification and extension of the procedural, i.e. rule based knowledge, not to mention the pure, factual information, was perhaps the most important motive for the development of the new, knowledge-based methods and languages.

Naturally, we must qualify this statement. The updating of knowledge is only unproblematic if the organization and representation of that knowledge is such that a rapidly growing body of facts and rules does not lead to structural difficulties, inefficiencies and, simply, bottle-necks. In addition to the aforementioned issue of predicates with varying numbers of arguments (what happens if we need some new arguments in order to record new kinds of knowledge?), this is a key consideration in the modularization of a system. We shall be dealing with the latter topic a little further on.

Of course, as in (honest) conventional phased plans, there are "backward" references, or elements of feedback between the final phase and the previous ones[4], as is indicated in the illustration in Fig. 11-1:

- The knowledge updates during the integration of the knowledge base in the "final" system require a continuous formulation of new rules and facts.

- If in this process of "fleshing out", i.e. filling the knowledge base, weaknesses are discovered in the internal knowledge representation, then these must be corrected by design modifications, i.e. introducing extended or improved representational structures.

- It may, however, turn out that these modifications are not sufficient to solve the problems, so that the specification of the representational concepts or even the requirements analysis itself must be modified.

Since the continuous adjustment of the knowledge content of the knowledge base is, so to speak, a basic assumption of the methodology, the first sort of feedback is essentially non-critical. The last two forms of feedback, however, require fundamental changes to a "finished" product, and are as costly and disagreeable in the "new" methodology as in the classical ones. It is worthwhile, then, taking the necessary measures to avoid their occurrence.

The best place to start is apparently at the level of the problem specification: if we define the problem correctly, then we will not have to later reformulate it. To do so, however, we must know if it is at all possible to implement the system as defined – to which end we must at least consider, in principle, the representational concept and structural organisation. All of which, in a Prolog environment, is best done directly on the computer, as a *formal specification* of those structures. The advantage is that we can immediately "run" the specification (or *validate* it, to use a more esoteric term), and at least minimize the chances that we were mistaken about the implementability of our specification.

---

[4] Since, as we already mentioned, the intermediate phases of our project model involve overlapping activities, we have dispensed with these implicit lines of feedback in our diagram.

The idea here, essentially, is to use *rapid prototyping* during the problem specification phase to establish a firm base for the following phases, in the hopes of avoiding any disagreeable surprises much later on.

To the extent that you are still caught up in the concepts of traditional software development methodology, the idea of performing those activities which are "normally" done in "later" phases in the course of the initial "problem analysis" probably strikes you as being somewhat unorthodox and sinister. If it is reasonable – why was it not done so all along?

The reason is that, until recently, one *could not* do so. The development of Prolog provided us with the linguistic means to write formal specifications so compactly and yet, at the same time, so readably, that we can treat them as a part of the requirements analysis. And once Prolog appeared embedded in modern system environments, like Unix, we could expand these specifications with minimal effort into prototypes, test them and present them to the customer, together with the documentation of the requirements analysis as proof of their implementability.

Thus, the following tips for developing expert systems are primarily with respect to the first activity overall, i.e. that which is designated in Fig. 11-1 as problem specification. As already mentioned, we can consider this phase analogous to the classical problem analysis, whereby the goals and tasks involved are considerably further reaching. Nevertheless, thanks to modern techniques and the many possibilities given by Prolog as a specification and prototyping tool, we can safely assume that the amount of time required for this is approximately of the same order of magnitude as we are accustomed to from traditional project models. Thus, if one devotes between two to four man-months to the problem analysis, one can expect a prototype approximately as comprehensive as that which is found in this book and its appendices. We hope that our sample systems might prove to be helpful starting points.

11.3   Problem Specification

Problem specification, as already mentioned, involves more than that which we are accustomed to in classical methodologies. Implied are the issues of knowledge specification and representation, as well as suitable prototype solutions for them and for the intended user dialog interactions.

Let us first, however, concentrate on those questions which, in like form, also play a role in the first phase of a classical project model:

(1) What problem is actually to be solved?

(2) Is it possible to solve the problem with an expert system and does it make sense to do so?

As you can see, the second question goes a bit further than in traditional problem analysis. Classically, the issue is only whether a computerized data processing solution pays. Here, however, one must consider whether a traditional programming solution would not be more suitable for the problem at hand, or at least some part of it.

In Chap. 2, we discussed when and where expert systems are sensible and promising solutions. Let us limit ourselves here to a review of a few critical issues.

- Do any experts exist who are already able to solve the given problem according to some partially formalized or presumably formalizable methods?
  Problems which are not currently solvable, or which cannot be formally solved, for example, conflicts between individuals or the invention of cooking recipes, cannot be solved by expert systems either.
- Is a suitable expert available who can actively participate in the development project to the extent her knowledge expertise is necessary?
  One must assume that the transfer of knowledge and related advisory work will involve several weeks, if not months, of concrete involvement on the part of the area expert(s). Needless to say, one cannot assume that good experts can be placed at the developer's disposal or engaged as consultants for such lengths of time.
- Are the tasks and methods of the experts too diverse?
  One should be able to identify and describe one, or at most a few, classes of standard methods with which the experts dispatch a substantial portion of their given tasks. If each problem requires, essentially, a new approach and must be treated individually – as is the case with upper management or with the creative professions, such as artists, advertising consultants, writers, etc. – then an expert system can, at best, only provide some assistance with respect to routine peripheral tasks, such as gathering decision-making information or providing some sort of "intelligent" documentation and text processing services.
- Is the expert's problem solving method (currently) difficult to describe algorithmically?
  The more algorithmic the description, the more likely a solution programmed in a conventional language will prove more efficient (whereby the use of Prolog for the specification and rapid prototyping can still be useful).
- Is the problem too simple?
  If an expert requires less than a few minutes to come up with a solution, then an expert system probably does not pay. Naturally, there are exceptions to this rule: tiresome, routine activities, such as the monitoring of industrial processes, or relieving experts of distracting interruptions, such as inquiries, or supervisory tasks, such as correcting exercises, tests, etc.
- Is the problem too complex?
  If an expert needs more than a few hours to solve a problem, then this activity is probably too costly to formalize and implement. Naturally, here too, there are exceptions. For example, it is quite possible that in optimization problems the necessary calculations and testing of diverse alternatives is very time-con-

The idea here, essentially, is to use *rapid prototyping* during the problem spec-
ation phase to establish a firm base for the following phases, in the hopes of
iding any disagreeable surprises much later on.

To the extent that you are still caught up in the concepts of traditional soft-
re development methodology, the idea of performing those activities which
"normally" done in "later" phases in the course of the initial "problem analy-
' probably strikes you as being somewhat unorthodox and sinister. If it is rea-
iable – why was it not done so all along?

The reason is that, until recently, one *could not* do so. The development of
ilog provided us with the linguistic means to write formal specifications so
npactly and yet, at the same time, so readably, that we can treat them as a part
the requirements analysis. And once Prolog appeared embedded in modern
item environments, like Unix, we could expand these specifications with mini-
il effort into prototypes, test them and present them to the customer, together
th the documentation of the requirements analysis as proof of their implemen-
iility.

Thus, the following tips for developing expert systems are primarily with
ispect to the first activity overall, i.e. that which is designated in Fig. 11–1 as
oblem specification. As already mentioned, we can consider this phase analo-
ius to the classical problem analysis, whereby the goals and tasks involved are
insiderably further reaching. Nevertheless, thanks to modern techniques and
e many possibilities given by Prolog as a specification and prototyping tool, we
in safely assume that the amount of time required for this is approximately of
ie same order of magnitude as we are accustomed to from traditional project
iodels. Thus, if one devotes between two to four man-months to the problem
ialysis, one can expect a prototype approximately as comprehensive as that
'hich is found in this book and its appendices. We hope that our sample systems
iight prove to be helpful starting points.

.1.3   Problem Specification

'roblem specification, as already mentioned, involves more than that which we
ire accustomed to in classical methodologies. Implied are the issues of knowl-
:dge specification and representation, as well as suitable prototype solutions for
hem and for the intended user dialog interactions.

Let us first, however, concentrate on those questions which, in like form, also
ilay a role in the first phase of a classical project model:

(1) What problem is actually to be solved?

(2) Is it possible to solve the problem with an expert system and does it make
sense to do so?

As you can see, the second question goes a bit further than in traditional
problem analysis. Classically, the issue is only whether a computerized data pro-

(3) The user (dialog) interface should be implemented and tested to the degree that one can give the customer or eventual end-user an approximate idea of the behavior, functionality and performance of the system.

This is, undoubtedly, a far more comprehensive set of objectives than is typical in conventional prototyping, where usually only the user interface or a few, as yet untested, technical solutions are to be checked out. This is because the development of an expert system necessarily involves three other (groups of) participants, in addition to the software engineer herself, and the prototype has, in essence, the function of demonstrating and testing, and as such, co-ordinating the interplay of their respective contributions to the system:

(1) the extraction of the knowledge from the *area expert,*

(2) the preparation of the knowledge by the *knowledge engineer* and

(3) the presentation of the knowledge via the *user interface.*

These three aspects are very tightly coupled, both conceptionally, as well as in their technical implementation, and must therefore be planned and developed in parallel.

This is probably the reason why the classical method of making a detailed specification of the system before beginning to implement anything is (still) somewhat more problematic in knowledge-based software development than in traditional programming. Even the most experienced software engineer would have trouble producing a useful, consistent specification of the system to be developed, from all three points of view simultaneously, without having the chance to test each idea continuously in the form of a prototype.

A Prolog prototype eliminates this problem entirely   the three aspects converge in the *one* knowledge base and every weakness or error in the one or the other becomes self-evident through the fact that it becomes impossible to either formulate the knowledge correctly, manipulate it or make inquiries about it.

Typically, the development of the prototype begins by having the area expert and the knowledge engineer jointly attempt to delineate the knowledge which the system is to master. This implies the attempt to meaningfully define a (useful) portion of the expert's total expertise. It has been estimated that an experienced professional or specialist has approximately between fifty and one hundred thousand so-called *chunks*[5] of knowledge readily available in her brain ([HARM85], p. 32). The few hundred to a few thousand clauses of a knowledge base – disregarding those which merely serve to support the structural aspects of the system architecture and the realization of the user interface, etc. – can thus only represent a small percentage of the expert's total knowledge. As such, it makes sense to start by trying to clearly and unambiguously define the modest subset with which one will be working.

---

[5] A "chunk" is defined, somewhat vaguely, as the "quantity" of knowledge which a person grasps and (somehow) stores as a unit of coherent (circumstantial) information. This might reasonably be considered approximately equivalent to a clause in a knowledge base.

The expert and the knowledge engineer spend perhaps a week attempting to extract the basic set of knowledge pertaining to the relevant field. The knowledge engineer seeks, of course, to formalize this knowledge sufficiently, that it might flow directly into the prototype; in the event that it will be programmed in Prolog, this implies a formulation in terms of facts and rules.

This direct translation of the specialist's expertise into "useful" knowledge is perhaps the most efficient method to compile the necessary knowledge in a reasonable amount of time, with a sufficient amount of structure. It is not of much practical use to ask the expert to:

"Please tell me everything you know about XYZ"

A more productive approach would be to start the dialog by saying:

"This machine is intended to be an expert system for the field of XYZ. Please tell me what it should know about in order to function as such. And please be sure to let me know when it does something incorrectly and what its proper behavior should be."

This is especially true if the knowledge engineer, either between or during the sessions with the actual expert, is constantly transforming the information received directly into rules and is in a position to correct such errors immediately, allowing for continuous feedback with the expert in the initial phase of building the knowledge base.

This proto-knowledge base, along with the necessary administrative procedures and, possibly, explanatory text components (which themselves represent more expert knowledge and thus flow automatically into the documentary specification), can then be coded and tested. This occurs along the lines described in the sample system for couplings, i.e. at first direct via the Prolog interpreter -without a comfortable, dialog-oriented user interface. This should be adequate for testing the system together with the expert and, based on the trial results, correcting and extending the knowledge accumulated and the manipulative procedures provided.

This preliminary knowledge base should exhibit a satisfactory level of stability before one then proceeds to work on the prototype user interface in which the knowledge base is to be embedded. Presenting the end user with a model of the system prematurely is, in any case, very dangerous. If the functionality of the proto-knowledge base is not yet adequate or robust enough, then it runs the risk of acquiring the reputation of being "trivial" and/or "unreliable", which becomes increasingly difficult to shake.

If the intention is to ultimately leave the maintenance and extension of the knowledge base to the expert(s), or some correspondingly trained personnel, and not the knowledge engineer, then a suitable component for assisting the user when *compiling new knowledge* should also be planned and prototyped. The sooner it is provided, the easier it becomes for the expert(s) to construct a nontrivial, complex knowledge base and the sooner one will be able to demonstrate a system which gives a realistic impression of the performance of the final product.

To help the reader *estimate the development time* of an expert system prototype, we have made a list of the number of man-weeks invested in the preparation of the sample systems presented in this book:

Prototype-System	man-weeks
MTA expert	3
auto heater diagnosis	8
license administration	5
memoranda management	3
coupling expert	8

These figures include the planning by the knowledge engineer, the time invested by the area expert(s), where needed, and, naturally, the actual programming involved.

11.5   The Organization of Knowledge

One of the first tasks to be dispatched when *organizing knowledge* is the *classification of knowledge*. We mean this in a very pragmatic sense, i.e. with respect to the storage, consultation, processing and updating of the knowledge involved.

We distinguish, essentially, between *well* and *poorly-structured knowledge or problems*. This is primarily a function of the degree to which a *deterministic, algorithmic processing* of the knowledge is feasible: A problem and the knowledge needed to solve it are *well structured*, if

- they are represented by numerical variables or "equivalent" data (such as formatted fields of text),
- the starting and terminating (goal) states, as well as the state transitions are, described by precisely defined, objective functions, and
- a not-all-too-complex and *completely correct algorithm*[6] for solving the problem exists.

If these prerequisites are not fulfilled, then we consider the problem to be *poorly structured*. This is exactly the sort of problem for which the knowledge-based techniques are primarily intended and for which we would like to employ expert systems, using heuristic, non-deterministic methods.

---

[6] By *completely* correct, we mean that the algorithm always terminates and delivers the solution defined by its specification; if it cannot be guaranteed that the algorithm always terminates, then we designate it as being only *partially* correct.

In most practical applications which are not terribly small-scale, it usually turns out that one part of the problem and the data to be processed is well structured while the other is not. For instance, in our coupling expert from Chaps. 9 and 10, the technical, mathematical formulas were quite well structured, whereas the basis for the actual selection process itself was considerably poorer. In the full-blown version of the coupling expert system, where the technical algorithms are significantly more comprehensive, particularly for preparing the results for graphical display, the two software components are kept separate: the "actual" expert system, written in Prolog, calls a set of programs written in Fortran to make the necessary, well-structured calculations.

Thus, it is advisable to attempt to classify the problem and knowledge involved according to their *degree of structure*, as described above. If they prove to be highly structured, then it would be wise to consider the feasibility of using classical methods. If, however, this is only true of larger portions of the problem, then one should examine the possibility of separating off those tasks for a conventional implementation, in the context of a mixed or hybrid system. This requires, of course, that the knowledge-oriented programming language or environment being used easily permit this. This is not true of all Prolog implementations and especially of many shells and dedicated AI-machines, as already mentioned.

A further classification of the rules in the knowledge base is of a dynamic nature: In which order should the different applicable rules be evaluated? Each such set of possible rules is called the *conflict set*. The order in which the rules of a given set are to be selected for consideration is essentially a function of the *strategy of the inference engine* employed in dealing with the problem. The two most common alternatives are *backward* and *forward chaining*. These are already built into some languages and most tools (*shells*) and are, thus, "automatically" activated. Prolog, as we have already said, supparts backward chaining. One could call it a *goal-oriented strategy*, since it starts with the user query and recursively reduces it, corresponding to the particular rule involved, to a set of subgoals, and applying the unification algorithm, searches, at each new level, for the subsequent rule(s) for achieving the new sub-goal(s).

Another example of a strategy built into a language is OPS 5. It implements a *data-driven strategy*, based on a forward chaining mechanism. Here, the rules in the knowledge base determine the flow of the process, under the influence of certain priorities associated with the rules. These priorities can be partially modified by the programmer.

Usually, however, it remains the job of the knowledge engineer or the system developer to determine, when specifying the knowledge representation, what sort of inference stategy is optimal for the knowledge to be processed. Only in the simplest cases - as, for example, our MTA expert -will it be possible to merely apply the strategy built into the programming language or shell used.

11.6   Inference Strategies

Just how the desired strategy is to be implemented depends, among other things, on the possibilities given by the language employed. "Genuine" programming languages, such as Lisp and Prolog, give the programmer a great deal of freedom in this respect. Shells, on the other hand, frequently permit one or a few strategies, but make it extremely difficult to implement new, custom alternatives.

Two methods frequently employed to implement custom strategies involve the use of metarules or content-driven inference.

The use of *metarules* involves the inclusion of special control rules in the knowledge base, which determine which rules apply under which conditions, i.e. assign particular rules to the current *focus* of processing activity. A general format for such metarules for controlling the inference strategy might be:

```
applicable_Rule(Focus, Rule_List).
```

A concrete example for the case of an automobile diagnosis system would be

```
applicable_Rule(heater, [10, 11, 12, 13, 24, 37, 38]).
```

The *Rule_List* lists those rules which the inference engine should activate if the focus of the investigation relates to the heating system.

In the *content-driven strategy* the knowledge engineer defines the *applicability of a rule* directly in the body of each rule. The inference engine then compares this information with the current focus to decide if the corresponding rule should be applied. The general format for rules when taking this approach could be as follows:

```
rule(Number,
        Applicability_Information,
        Constraints_Section_of_Rule,
        Actions_Section_of_Rule).
```

A concrete example, based again on our automobile diagnosis system, would be

```
rule(10,
        [heater, v-belt, heater_blower],
        ['V_belt is defective'],
        ['heater blower is defective']).
```

The interpretation of this rule 10 is that it is applicable when the focus is either the *heater*, the *v-belt* or the *heater blower*, and, in these cases, a defective V-belt is a possible cause for a malfunctioning heater blower.

11.7 Modularization of the Knowledge Base

A third, very important "dimension" of the classification of the knowledge to be processed is the issue of *modularization of the knowledge base*, with respect to the (pure) facts (i.e. "data" in traditional terms), rules, metaknowledge and other information (e.g. descriptive or informal text).

This is a problem often neglected by novices in knowledge-based programming. It should, however, be resolved *definitively* in the planning stage of the knowledge representation, i.e., as far as foreseeable, for the total assumed "life" of the system, and should include all the mechanisms necessary to support the chosen modularization strategy. This is a critical issue, in both traditional and knowledge-based programming, insofar as mistakes or omissions made in modularization are almost impossible to correct at some later date.

The risk of making a planning error is, indeed, even greater when employing the evolutionary-oriented development methodology of prototyping than with classical methods, where the product is planned more completely from the very beginning. The reason is, quite simply, that many program and data structures are merely "outlined" in a prototype and "provisionally" solved using dummy procedures or a minimal set of facts. This can often distort the proportions of the prototype with respect to the actual dimensions of the final system. One can easily overlook the modularization necessitated by memory, compilation or structural constraints, which only later become self-evident.

Even experienced knowledge engineers find it sometimes "absurd" to code a few facts and rules in an independent module and to "consult" them, as such, separately, only because they could possibly grow to contain a few hundred at some later time. But one need ignore this advice but once and have to pay the consequences, before one tends to "over-modularize" to avoid the catastrophe at all costs[7].

When establishing a modularization concept and the associated mechanisms, you should, above all, consider two reasons which might make the partitioning and storage of portions of the knowledge base in separate modules seem desirable:

(1) The presumed volume of portions of the expert knowledge or even specific, auxiliary procedures (metaknowledge) can grow to be so large, that you would like to load it into the workspace only as needed. This is, of course, easily done with *consult*. But should you then wish to remove the "specific" knowledge, e.g. to make room for another "portion", then you must take this into consideration at the planning stage and provide the necessary mechanisms for doing so. This may involve a software implemented "virtualization" of oversized fact bases or a *garbage-collection* mechanism implemented

---

[7] Unix programmers are likely to accept this recommendation more readily than others. And just as experienced Unix programmers usually begin developing a new program by creating a *directory* structure, it is a good idea to begin planning a large Prolog system by defining a *consulting* structure.

with *abolish* or *retract*-based procedures (which should be defined as uniformly, i.e. generally as possible, so that one can manage the process with a just a few "delete" clauses). Both possibilities can be realized quite simply in Prolog – one must only have given it some thought early enough in the development process.

(2) Long *texts*, intended purely for display, such as explanations or operating instructions, are probably the most space-consuming, as well as the most complex and maintenance-intensive parts of the knowledge base. It is, thus, often preferable to store these, either in their final form or as text assemblies, in the normal file system of the underlying operating system. One can then fetch them, as needed, directly onto the screen or filter them through some formatting procedure. In addition, it is usually more comfortable to compile and modify (maintain) these texts using a normal, powerful text editor, than to "construct" them using the built-in Prolog predicates *write*, *put* and *tab*. This is reason enough to plan and provide for the procedures necessary to permit such a simplified approach during the knowledge representation phase. If the volume of such texts should prove to be greater than that which one would like to store in a "one-dimensional" file system, one should consider how one might best modularize the texts in the form of a file hierarchy in the early planning stages; to access the files one must define the Prolog access predicates such that they can deal with the relevant file system data structures and naming policies.

Needless to say, these are not the only parts of a Prolog program which one should give early consideration with respect to modularization. In our experience, however, they are those which are most often overlooked or ignored when prototyping, and yet cause the most problems when the attempt is later made to move them into an independent module.

11.8   Knowledge Representation

Despite the rather fluid boundary between "data" and "algorithms" in knowledge-based programming, it is useful to distinguish between *declarative knowledge* and *procedural knowledge*. A declarative representation of knowledge describes "what" attributes a specific result should have, whereas a procedural one explains "how", i.e. the process involved in acquiring a particular result.

Here we have a sample of a declarative representation of a sort algorithm for lists (see [SCHN87], p. 185ff.)

```
sort(Unsorted,Sorted) :-
        permutation(Unsorted,Sorted),
        is_sorted(Sorted).
```

This representation assumes the existence of suitable *permutation* and *is_sorted* predicates, presumably formulated declaratively too. *permutation* takes the list passed in via *Unsorted* and passes out a permuted version via *Sorted*. The permuted list is then tested to see if it, coincidentally, *is_sorted*.

A procedural representation of the sorting algorithm would involve a description of the process chosen to perform the sort, e.g. a *bubble* or a *heap* or a *quicksort*:

```
sort(Unsorted,Sorted) :-
        quicksort(Unsorted,Sorted,[]).

quicksort([],AuxiliaryList,AuxiliaryList).
quicksort([Element|Rest],Sorted,AuxiliaryList) :-
        split(Element,Rest,ListA,ListB),
        quicksort(ListB,ListC,AuxiliaryList),
        quicksort(ListA,Sorted,[Element|ListC]).
```

Here we have *split*, a *procedure* for dividing the list *Rest* into two new lists to be sorted, *ListA* and *ListB*. *ListA* contains only those entries from *Rest* which are less than *Element*, and *ListB* is assigned all the other entries.

The comparison of the two representational approaches should make clear that, as a rule, the declarative form is more general, more compact and easier to understand than the procedural one. It describes straightforwardly the characteristics of a *Sorted* list. On the other hand, it is hardly self-evident that the procedure *quicksort* really always delivers a sorted list: one must first try it out (seeing is believing) or – better still – prove it! This can be done, for example, by treating the declarative representation as the *formal specification* of the task and then demonstrating that the *Sorted* list returned by *quicksort* always satisfies the two predicates

```
permutation(Unsorted,Sorted)
```

and

```
is_sorted(Sorted).
```

In light of the greater universality and ease of comprehension, the declarative representation of knowledge would seem to be generally preferable to the procedural one. And, in fact, perhaps one of the most important goals of knowledge-based programming is the substitution of procedural knowledge representations with declarative ones. This is, however, not always completely possible.

A trivial example is the process of conducting a dialog with the user. This is clearly a "procedure", characterized, essentially, by the time sequence of events. It is quite obvious that it is *not* irrelevant as to when a particular (information) display is made to the user and when an input is accepted from her.

A less trivial issue is that of efficiency, as we can imagine with respect to our sample *sort* predicate above. The declarative procedure will, more often than not, run far slower than the procedural version, even if we were to compare it with a much slower algorithm, like the bubble-sort.

Of course, a declarative solution need not always be less efficient than a procedural one. Prolog, after all, always interprets the "declarative" predicates procedurally, according to its built-in evaluation strategy. If this is efficient for a given case, then there is no conflict. And, if you recall our calculation of the *Fibonacci numbers* in Sect. 4.4, you can see that even a very time-consuming solution process – such as the doubly recursive calculation algorithm therein – can be dramatically accelerated by taking an (essentially declarative) table-look-up approach.

Thus, the choice between the two approaches is by no means simple. On the contrary, it is often crucial for both the efficiency of the the knowledge representation and compilation, as well as its processing. The ability to choose the right approach from the many alternatives, with all their disadvantages and risks, is one of the most important qualifications of the experienced knowledge engineer and developer of knowledge-based software. It is, frequently, virtually impossible to determine the optimal form of representation, e.g., in our example above the best sort algorithm, right from the start. If one wishes to make it dependent on the actual state of the system, case data or some other parameter at runtime, then one must introduce another class of knowledge, *control knowledge*. This "knowledge about knowledge" is commonly referred to as *metaknowledge*; we shall be talking about this in more detail in the following section.

Before we do so, however, let us briefly summarize a few characteristics which serve as points of orientation when deciding if a problem is best solved "declaratively" or "procedurally".

A *procedural description* is particularly advantageous – aside from those obvious cases, such as the aforementioned programming of the user dialog or other inherently sequential processes – when dealing with

• complete knowledge
• vague knowledge or
• the integration of the knowledge of several experts.

The latter is especially the case if the sources of the total knowledge are not to be treated as being equal. For instance, if the value or reliability of the knowledge is dependent on the alleged "quality" of its source or, perhaps, depending on the current case involved, is to be evaluated with differing priority, then it is usually easier to formulate the circumstances procedurally than declaratively.

A *declarative description*, on the other hand, is usually advantageous when

• the knowledge is well structured
• initial values or *default* values, based on experience, are to be taken into consideration,
• inheritance mechanisms are to be formulated and applied,
• very complex relationships prevail among the data.

Naturally, one will seldom find a clear predominance of one or the other characteristic in typical, complex problems. Thus, one should accustom oneself to continuously changing between the two perspectives during the implementation of an expert system and its associated knowledge base, so as to achieve an optimal system in the end.

Languages and representation methods for knowledge-based systems tend to emphasize one of the two representational aspects. For example, *production rules, actor languages, Plasma, Lisp* and *OPS 5* are predominantly procedural in focus. A more declarative emphasis can be found in *frames* along with the (sub-)languages designed for their description, such as *Loops, Unit, semantic networks or scripts.*

One of Prolog's great advantages is that the programmer can view and employ it both declaratively and procedurally. The examples in this book should serve as adequate proof of the ease with which one can express both approaches in this language and, indeed, even mix them arbitrarily in one and the same program.

11.9   Representing Metaknowledge

We have already presented examples of the distinction between *knowledge and metaknowledge*. Metaknowledge is particularly important for the structuring and efficient implementation of comprehensive, knowledge-based systems.

By "knowledge", we mean an expert's informational "know-how", which is stored directly in the form of facts and rules. This might be knowledge of flight connections or – to return to our last example – about the characteristics of couplings and the formulas for technical calculations in mechanical engineering.

"Metaknowledge", on the other hand, is "knowledge about knowledge", i.e. about its structure, its meaningful employment (e.g. in heuristics) and the derivation of new knowledge from existing information. Indeed, it is conceivable that many *levels of metaknowledge* exist: "lower order" metaknowledge, dealing with the mathematical characteristics of formulas, for example, may be the focus of "higher order" metaknowledge, which employs new formulas derived by applying certain formal operations, such as differentiation and integration.

There are obviously many different kinds of metaknowledge and certainly as many different ways of applying it. Thus it makes little sense to even try and outline them. Instead we prefer to present a few examples as orientation:

• For an airline reservation system, facts about flight connections such as

```
connection(munich,frankfurt,Depart_MUC,Arrive_FRA)
```

or

```
connection(frankfurt,new_york,Depart_FRA,Arrive_JFK)
```

constitute "knowledge". Metaknowledge, here, would be knowledge about the *transitivity* of the relation *connection*, i.e. a rule of the type

```
connection(Start,Destined,Depart,Arrive) :-
      connection(Start,X,Depart,Time),
      connection(X,Destined,T1,Arrive),
      T1 › Time + 30.
```

That these rules are typically placed at the end of the associated table of facts, in Prolog, should not blind the programmer to the fact that she is dealing with two fundamentally different "kinds" of knowledge.

- If there are a number of potentially applicable rules, then the (heuristic) meta-knowledge determines the order in which they should be employed. A variety of different criteria may play a role here. One might be metaknowledge about the *quality of the knowledge* involved: the knowledge of a medical specialist could have "priority" over the remedies of an experienced pharmacist. Or metaknowledge regarding the *previous success* of specific rules under given circumstances: we saw examples of this in the auto heater diagnosis and coupling selection systems.
- Similarly, one can not only make the "triggering" of particular rules dependent on such metaknowledge – in Prolog, by sorting the rules in the knowledge base accordingly – one can also make the rules themselves more efficient by reorganizing the constraints within the respective rule body, such that those which cause the highest rejection rates occur closer to the beginning.
- Another kind of metaknowledge revolves around the problem of deciding which of the "intermediate results" produced one should, perhaps, store as independent facts or rules in the knowledge base, to eliminate the need to repeatedly "recalculate" them. You recall the example with the Fibonacci numbers in Sect. 4.4. There we exploited our metaknowledge, regarding the fact that our formula was double-recursive and, thus, very computationally intensive, by having our procedure build a table of Fibonacci numbers and use table-look-up to minimize the number of recursions necessary to produce "new" values.
- The automatic ticket printing system used by the German National Railway Service is a very complex system, due to the large number of train stations and whistle stops, not to mention all the discounts available to various different customer groups (junior and senior citizens, students and families) and the forever changing "specials" involving many and varied restrictions. It is, without a doubt, a kind of expert system. And only by exploiting metaknowledge is it capable of working with reasonable response times: it is based on the very plausible assumption that most of the tickets requested at any given point-of-sale have to do with routes between the major cities. The majority of the remainder involve similar, standard routes, but of a local or regional nature. Thus, a trip between Bremerhaven, on the North Sea, and a suburb called

Varel, some 35km away, is almost never purchased at a train station in Bavaria, the most southeasterly province of Germany. As a consequence, almost 90% of the fares actually needed can be stored, pre-compiled, making the calculation of some fare according to the many and complex rules an exceptional case.

We hope that the reader has been able to get a better idea of which knowledge can be treated as metaknowledge in a particular field, and how it might best be applied. The "particular field" is, by the way, an essential aspect of the "meta" attribute of knowledge. What is "knowledge" to the developer of a specific expert system –e.g. the *rules for differentiation* for the author of a system for symbolic formula processing – may be "metaknowledge" to someone else – e.g. the mechanical engineer, for whom the formulas themselves represent the "knowledge".

11.10   Metasystems

Since metaknowledge embraces the knowledge above and beyond the primary knowledge specific to a given field, it makes sense to collect it into a "package", which we shall call a *metasystem,* that can serve as the superstructure for diverse knowledge bases. The concept is probably a familiar one: it is nothing more than the idea of a pre-fabricated *shell* for constructing simple expert systems.

Whereas a shell is the pragmatic approach to *metasystems* –indeed, many such shells were created by "culling" the field specific knowledge from an existing expert system –the formulation of metaknowledge and its implementation as a metasystem is a more theoretically-based process, which, nonetheless, has the same goal.

One advantage of taking a theoretical view of an idea that has been previously pursued quite pragmatically is that one is more likely to detect the subtle weaknesses and limitations thereof.

As we saw in our earlier discussion, large portions of so-called metaknowledge are still very tightly bound to the structural characteristics, manipulative possibilities and goals typical for a special field, in much the same way as the basic facts and rules constituting the actual expert knowledge. Thus, it is quite foolish to assume that meta- knowledge –and its implementation as a metasystem or shell – is readily transferable from one area of knowledge to another.

If one is considering using a shell, then one of the crucial issues in the *problem analysis* is whether the problem to be dealt with and the associated knowledge base "match" the functionality of the particular shell. Naturally, one of the best ways of determining this is by doing some rapid prototyping – the "proof of the metaknowledge is in the usage", so to speak.

Inasmuch as the particular shell is available for such purposes, this is a simple and rather risk-free test. Even if it should prove to be unsuited, not all is for nought –one will have learned a good deal about the nature of the knowledge involved, while trying to formulate it in the input language of that shell, which should prove useful when it comes to the organization and representation thereof in a more appropriate programming language (or another shell).

If, however, the shell is not available and must first be purchased, then the problem becomes more acute. Such tools are usually not cheap – many cost tens of thousands of dollars. Not all projects can bear the financial burden of investing in such tools (not to mention the time expense for training the developers who are expected to use it) "just to see if the shoe happens to fit".

In such a case, one must insist that the product be installed on a *trial basis*. Since at least one or two months preparation and about three months for the implementation and analysis of the prototype must be realistically reckoned with, and given the usual additional inevitable delays and mishaps, less than 6 months for the trial installation is foolhardy.

Indeed, one should strive for at least a year-long trial period, especially since one should really investigate several other aspects of the shell beyond its usefulness for the specific prototyping task. Many characteristics which are vital to the evolutionary, further development and integration of the final expert system may prove difficult or impossible to determine in the sole context of the prototype.

The following is a checklist of some of the more important aspects to be considered:

• What facilities for modularization does the shell provide? Will these be adequate for the expected volume of the knowledge base in the next five to ten years?
• (How) can the shell connect up with existing data banks, conventional software packages and communications software?
• Can the programmer(s) and enduser(s) continue to use existing tools, such as text editors or menu-driven front-ends, or must they change over to those built into the shell (if at all available)?
• How does one get (input) information from existing data processing into the shell and, vice versa, get data out of the knowledge base (e.g. case data or statistics) into conventional data bases? Or must certain information be manually re-entered, which is not only a major source of errors, but, in our experience, typically so costly that it is then dropped altogether?
• Can explanatory and (error) message texts be created, modified and possibly translated into other languages?
• Is the tool at all portable, so that there is a chance that it and the applications produced with it will run on the next generation of hardware, or on equipment of the same generation but different manufacture?

Undoubtedly there are shells for which all these questions can be answered positively. In particular, those which have been implemented "with feeling" for the underlying programming language - be it Lisp or Prolog, or even some conventional programming language like C -and deliver not only their special services, but also provide the programmer access to all the power of the language of implementation. Such shells reduce the risk considerably; the worst that may happen on smaller systems, such as PCs, is that the tool itself requires so much memory and computational power, that the actual application "does not fit". This should be easy enough to estimate, however, based on the experience gained with the prototype.

These hints should, however, not be misconstrued as a warning against the employment of shells in general. We merely wish to correct the widespread impression that such a tool will necessarily reduce the costs and risks of developing an expert system, under the assumption that it simplifies the design and implementation. The latter may indeed be true in specific cases, but it is important to realize that this advantage may be outweighed by the considerable additional effort and risk involved in the problem analysis and prototyping, if the selection of the specific shell is not to be treated as a gamble.

11.11   Project Execution

As we have mentioned several times before, one cannot begin prototyping the desired system early enough. The classic model of project execution, where detailed studies, specifications and designs are produced before the computer is used for anything other than text processing, is, at the very least unproductive, if not counterproductive, in the realm of knowledge-based programming. If for no other reason, this is certainly so because the dialog and the knowledge compilation together with the expert(s) can only be successful if it is continuously being entered and formalized in a prototype.

This "preliminary" knowledge base is, naturally, typically incomplete and inconsistent. Since it is being used in a practical, concrete situation, under the continuous supervision of the special experts, the weaknesses and "bugs" surface quickly and are far more easily corrected than if one were to try to detect them in the most comprehensive and detailed written specification of the knowledge to be dealt with.

Once the system dispatches the routine cases to the satisfaction of the experts, one can then begin to integrate the exceptional cases, stepwise, into the knowledge base. As a rule, one would still use the "naked" Prolog interpreter for this purpose. Any system functions which are already to be built into the prototype should only be "attacked" once the knowledge base has achieved a reasonable level of stability.

The steps involved in the *development of a prototype* are approximately as follows, whereby this scheme can certainly be varied according to the specific circumstances, should it appear to be expedient (e.g. because certain components already exist).

(1) Determination of the organization and representation of the expert knowledge; implementation of the important primitives for manipulating the knowledge base.

(2) Compilation of the preliminary (first prototype of a) knowledge base in close co-operation with the expert(s) in the field.

(3) Building up of the rule base for processing the knowledge base and organization and representation of the metaknowledge.

(4) Construction of the inference engine by connecting the knowledge base and the rule base.

(5) Design, implementation and testing of a simple dialog component.

(6) Development and integration of the explanatory components, if possible, in close co-operation with the expert(s) who assisted in defining the original (preliminary) knowledge base.

(7) Development of the definitive user model and the apparently most favorable user interface, possibly in different versions (e.g. one for lay users and another for expert users).

(8) Testing the system model with end users.

(9) Extension of the system by help functions and integration of changes suggested by users during the trials. Addition of new utilities and simultaneous documentation of the prototype.

The documentation should mostly be "written" in the form of user assistance and explanatory "messages" integrated into the knowledge base (self-documentation). This principle is also promoted in "conventional structured programming", where one of the goals is to limit the technical documentation of a program as much as possible to the program code and in-line comments. Knowledge-based software technology is an advocate of this methodology. The typically greater compactness and transparence of a Prolog program, compared with "well-structured" solutions in other high level languages, is of great practical help in achieving this goal. Indeed it should, in many cases, be possible to reduce the *documentation external to the expert system* to a few pages describing its purpose, the significant services and the system interaction with the user.

A thus documented prototype then serves as the basis for the further development and maintenance of the final system, which should be conducted according to the principles of *evolutionary prototyping*, i.e. by employing as many and as much of the components from the preliminary (pilot) model as possible. This is the reason why we repeatedly emphasized the importance of a detailed and well-considered modularization concept at the very earliest stages.

On this basis, the *implementation* of the final system consists of the following overlapping activities:

(1) A concept for the final system is worked out, whereby every effort should be made to foresee (potential) later extensions, such as possible, alternative uses for the knowledge base, either for other purposes or other user communities,

perhaps even its integration in a general purpose data processing environment.

(2) Time, cost and activity plans are made for the essential participants involved (the experts, knowledge engineers, software engineers).

(3) Since the tasks now involved build upon a sufficiently well-defined base, they can – and should – be specified and documented according to the rules of classical development methodology.

(4) The user interface gets tended to, extended and finalized. The help functions are supplemented, the interactions are made more robust with respect to incorrect usage and the correctness and comprehensibility of system messages are checked and improved.

(5) The knowledge base is built up further and continuously checked for inconsistencies. This is particularly necessary if the knowledge in the knowledge base is the collective expertise of many experts.

(6) The system should collect statistics about the frequency with which individual rules are applied and provide an analysis thereof. This information is useful for detecting superfluous rules or rules which require modification, as well as revealing errors in the system's control structures and metaknowledge.

(7) The prototype system presumably had no component for acquiring knowledge. Such a component will be needed, however, if one plans, at some point, to become independent of the knowledge engineer and let the qualified (expert) users take on the task of collecting additional knowledge and maintaining the knowledge base. This component must be designed and implemented.

Since knowledge and its applications are constantly developing in their own right, only an unsuccessful expert system can really ever be "finished". We hope that, with our book, we have made a substantial contribution to having *your* systems avoid this fate.

Appendix

A The "MTA Expert"

A.1 Start-up Procedure

```
# This exec procedure starts the "MTA Expert" in a Unix
# system by consulting the first module.
# The module "mta" displays an explanatory text and then
# proceeds to- consult the remaining components

ifprolog -c mta
```

A.2 Module "mta"

```
:-
        write('I am a small Prolog program, '),
        write('my name is MTA.'),
        nl,
        write('MTA stands for Munich Transport Authority.'),
        nl,nl,
        write('My job is to help you select '),
        write('the proper ticket '),
        nl,
        write('for travel in the central city zone.'),
        nl,nl,
        write('You must cancel 2 fields of a ticket '),
        write('for a single trip.'),
        nl,
        write('The following tickets are available:'),
        nl,
        write('- Single trip tickets, with 2 fields '),
        write('for 2.30 DM,'),
        nl,
        write('- Type A multiple trip tickets, with '),
        write('7 fields for 6.50 DM and'),
        nl,
        write('- Type B multiple trip tickets, '),
```

```
write('with 13 fields for 12.00 DM.'),
nl,nl,
write('In addition, for persons under '),
write('15 or pets, we have'),
nl,
write(' - Kiddie tickets, with 8 fields for 5.00 DM.'),
nl,nl,
write('Passengers travelling less than '),
write('5 kilometers can'),
nl,
write('use a kiddie ticket regardless of age.'),
nl,nl,
write('If you would like my help '),
write('in selecting a ticket, '),
write('enter "mta."'),
nl,
write('With "restart." you can start a '),
write('fresh session, i.e. '),
nl,
write('any recorded facts will be forgotten.'),
nl.

:-

[
controlling,
dialog,
explanation,
aux_programs,
rule_base
].
```

A.3 Module "controlling"

```
mta :-
        enter_current_rule(100),
        is_a_Kiddie_Ticket_possible,
        recommend_childrens_ticket.
mta :-
        enter_current_rule(101),
        is_a_Multi_Trip_Ticket_B_possible,
        recommend_multi_trip_ticket_B.
```

```
mta :-
        enter_current_rule(102),
        is_a_Multi_Trip_Ticket_A_possible,
        recommend_multi_trip_ticket_A.
mta :-
        enter_current_rule(103),
        is_a_Single_Trip_Ticket_possible,
        recommend_single_trip_ticket.
mta :-
        enter_current_rule(104),
        must_one_ride_without_paying,
        recommend_non_payment_of_fare.
mta :-
        enter_current_rule(105),
        must_one_walk,
        recommend_walking.

recommend_multi_trip_ticket_A :-
        write('You should buy a Type A Multi '),
        write('Trip Ticket for 6.50 DM.'),
        two_fields.

recommend_multi_trip_ticket_B :-
        write('You should buy a Type B Multi '),
        write('Trip Ticket for 12 DM.'),
        two_fields.

recommend_childrens_ticket :-
        write('You should buy a Kiddie Ticket '),
        write('for 5 DM.'),
        two_fields.

recommend_single_trip_ticket :-
        write('You should buy a Single Trip Ticket '),
        write('for 2,30 DM.').

recommend_non_payment_of_fare :-
        write('You should ride without buying a ticket!!!.').

recommend_walking :-
        write('You should go on foot.').

two_fields :-
        nl,
        write('And remember to cancel two fields!').
```

A.4   Module "dialog"

```
recognize(Input,yes) :-
        member(Input,[yes,certainly,'of course',yeah]),
        !.
recognize(Input,no) :-
        member(Input,[n,no]),
        !.
recognize(Input,why) :-
        member(Input,[why,'how come']),
        !.
recognize(Input,'not sure') :-
        member(Input,
        ['who knows','not sure','no idea',perhaps]),
        !.
recognize(Input,Input) :-
        !.

non_interpretable :-
        nl,
        write('I cannot interpret your response.'),
        nl,
        write('Please re-enter your answer.'),
        nl.

ask(cash,F1) :-
        write('How much money do you have ?    '),
        read(Input),
        recognize(Input,Money),
        test_f1(Money,F1).

test_f1(Money,Money) :-
        numeric(Money),
        !.
test_f1(none,0) :-
        !.
test_f1(enough,13) :-
        !.
test_f1(why,F1) :-
        !,
        write_explanation,
        enter_current_level,
        ask(cash,F1).
test_f1(_,F1) :-
        non_interpretable,
        ask(cash,F1).
```

```
ask(distance,F2) :-
      write('How great is the distance ?    '),
      read(Input),
      recognize(Input,Distance),
      test_f2(Distance,F2).


test_f2(Distance,near) :-
      numeric(Distance),
      Distance =< 5,
      !.
test_f2(Distance,far) :-
      numeric(Distance),
      !.
test_f2('not sure',far) :-
      !.
test_f2(why,F2) :-
      !,
      write_explanation,
      enter_current_level,
      ask(distance,F2).
test_f2(_,F2) :-
      non_interpretable,
      ask(distance,F2).


ask(age,F3) :-
      write('How old are you ?    ')
      read(Input),
      recognize(Input,Age),
      test_f3(Age,F3).


test_f3(Age,child) :-
      numeric(Age),
      Age =< 14,
      !.
test_f3(Age,adult) :-
      numeric(Age),
      !.
test_f3('not sure',adult) :-
      !.
test_f3(why,F3) :-
      !,
      write_explanation,
      enter_current_level,
      ask(age,F3).
```

```
test_f3(_,F3) :-
        non_interpretable,
        ask(age,F3).

ask(boldness,F4) :-
        write('Are you daring ?   '),
        read(Input),
        recognize(Input,Courage),
        test_f4(Courage,F4).

test_f4(yes,daring) :-
        !.
test_f4(no,timid) :-
        !.
test_f4('not sure',timid) :-
        !.
test_f4(why,F4) :-
        !,
        write_explanation,
        enter_current_level,
        ask(boldness,F4).
test_f4(_,F4) :-
        non_interpretable,
        ask(boldness,F4).
```

A 5   Modulo "explanation"

```
write_explanation :-
        level(Level),
        step(Step),
        tree(Step,Rule),
        nl, nl,
        explanation(Level,Rule),
        !.

and_so :-
        nl, nl,
        write('Now: ').

explanation(1,_) :-
write('I want to find the least expensive '),
write('ticket for your trip.'),
and_so.
```

```
explanation(2,No) :-
        member(No,[1,2,4]),
        write('Because a Kiddie Ticket is the cheapest.'),
        and_so.
explanation(2,_) :-
        write('Since you do not have enough money.'),
        write('for a ticket,'),
        nl,
        write('I must look for another solution.'),
        and_so.

explanation(3,1) :-
        write('To buy a Kiddie Ticket you must: '),
        nl,
        write('  - have at least 5 DM and'),
        nl,
        write('  - be under 15 years of age.'),
        nl, nl,
        write('So I would like to know '),
        write('if you have at least 5 DM.'),
        and_so.
explanation(3,2) :-
        write('I know that you have more than 5 DM.'),
        nl,
        write('Consequently, if you are under '),
        write('15 years of age,'),
        nl,
        write('you can buy a Kiddie Ticket.'),
        nl,
        write('So I would like to know '),
        write('if you are under 15.'),
        and_so.
explanation(3,4) :-
        write('I know that you have more than 5 DM.'),
        nl,
        write('Consequently, if you are making a short trip'),
        nl,
        write('you can buy a Short Trip Ticket '),
        write('(Kiddie_Ticket).'),
        nl,
        write('A short trip is less than 5 kilometers.'),
        nl,
        write('So, I would like to know how long '),
        write('the route is.'),
        and_so.
```

```
explanation(3,6) :-
        write('You must have at least 12.00 DM to '),
        write('buy a Type B Multi Trip Ticket.'),
        nl, nl,
        write('That is why I want to know '),
        write('if you have at least 12 DM?'),
        and_so.
explanation(3,8) :-
        write('You must have at least 6.50 DM to '),
        write('buy a Type A Multi Trip Ticket.'),
        nl, nl,
        write('That is why I want to know '),
        write('if you have at least 6.50 DM?'),
        and_so.
explanation(3,10) :-
        write('You must have at least 2.30 DM to '),
        write('buy a Single Trip Ticket.'),
        nl, nl,
        write('That is why I want to know '),
        write('if you have at least 2.30 DM?'),
        and_so.
explanation(3,12) :-
        write('You should only ride without paying '),
        write('if you'),
        nl,
        write('   - have less than 2.30 and'),
        nl,
        write('   - are willing to risk a fine if caught.'),
        nl, nl,
        write('Therefore, I first want to know '),
        write('if you have more than 2.30 DM.'),
        and_so.
explanation(3,15) :-
        write('You must go on foot, if you'),
        nl,
        write('   - have less than 2.30 DM and'),
        nl,
        write('   - are unwilling to risk being caught.'),
        nl, nl,
        write('Therefore, I first want to know '),
        write('if you have more than 2.30 DM.'),
        and_so.
explanation(3,_) :-
        write('I want to know if you are willing to take'),
        nl,
```

```
        write('a risk to get to your destination quickly?'),
        and_so.

explanation(_,_) :-
        write('How about fewer questions and more answers!'),
        and_so.
```

A.6 Module "aux_programs"

```
assistance :-
        nl, nl,
        write('Possible questions are: '),
        nl,
        write('- mta.'),
        nl,
        write('- is_a_Kiddie_Ticket_possible.'),
        nl,
        write('- is_a_Multi_Trip_Ticket_A_possible.'),
        nl,
        write('- is_a_Multi_Trip_Ticket_B_possible.'),
        nl,
        write('- is_a_Single_Trip_Ticket_possible.'),
        nl,
        write('- must_one_ride_without_paying.'),
        nl,
        write('- must_one_walk.'),
        nl,
        write('- restart.           -> deletion of old data.'),
        nl,
        write('- tree(Step,Rule).  -> show tree.'),
        nl, nl.

restart :-
        abolish(status,2),
        assertz(status(_,unknown)),
        abolish(tree,2),
        assertz(tree(0,0)),
        set(step,0),
        set(level,0),
        set(increment,2).

status(_,unknown).
```

```
step(0).
tree(0,0).
level(0).
increment(2).

query(Status,Number) :-
        enter_current_rule(Number),
        set(level,3),
        ask(Status,Answer),
        !,
        asserta(status(Status,Answer),!).

enter_current_rule(Rule_Number) :-
        retract(step(State)),
        New is State + 1,
        assertz(step(New)),
        assertz(tree(New,Rule_Number)),
        (       Rule_Number > 99,
                    set(increment,1)
        ;       true
        ),
        !.

enter_current_level :-
        retract(level(Old)),
        increment(Increment),
        New is Old   Increment,
        assertz(level(New)).

set(Functor,Argument) :-
        abolish(Functor,1),
        G =.. [Functor,Argument],
        asserta(G).
```

A.7   Module "rule_base"

```
is_a_Kiddie_Ticket_possible :-
        status(cash,Money),
        Money == unknown,
        query(cash,1),
        fail.
is_a_Kiddie_Ticket_possible :-
        status(cash,Money),
        Money >= 5,
```

```
        status(age,Age),
        Age == unknown,
        query(age,2),
        fail.
is_a_Kiddie_Ticket_possible :-
        status(cash,Money),
        Money >= 5,
        status(age,child),
        enter_current_rule(3).
is_a_Kiddie_Ticket_possible :-
        status(cash,Money),
        Money >= 5,
        status(distance,Distance),
        Distance == unknown,
        query(distance,4),
        fail.
is_a_Kiddie_Ticket_possible :-
        status(cash,Money),
        Money >= 5,
        status(distance,near),
        enter_current_rule(5).

is_a_Multi_Trip_Ticket_B_possible :-
        status(cash,Money),
        Money == unknown,
        query(cash,6),
        fail.
is_a_Multi_Trip_Ticket_B_possible :-
        status(cash,Money),
        Money >= 12,
        enter_current_rule(7).

is_a_Multi_Trip_Ticket_A_possible :-
        status(cash,Money),
        Money == unknown,
        query(cash,8),
        fail.
is_a_Multi_Trip_Ticket_A_possible :-
        status(cash,Money),
        Money >= 6.50,
        enter_current_rule(9).

is_a_Single_Trip_Ticket_possible :-
        status(cash,Money),
        Money == unknown,
```

```prolog
        query(cash,10),
        fail.
is_a_Single_Trip_Ticket_possible :-
        status(cash,Money),
        Money >= 2.30,
        enter_current_rule(11).

must_one_ride_without_paying :-
        status(cash,Money),
        Money == unknown,
        query(cash,12),
        fail.

must_one_ride_without_paying :-
        status(cash,Money),
        Money < 2.30,
        status(boldness,Courage),
        Courage == unknown,
        query(boldness,13),
        fail.

must_one_ride_without_paying :-
        status(cash,Money),
        Money < 2.30,
        status(boldness,daring),
        enter_current_rule(14).

must_one_walk :-
        status(cash,Money),
        Money == unknown,
        query(cash,15),
        fail.
must_one_walk :-
        status(cash,Money),
        Money < 2.30,
        status(boldness,Courage),
        Courage == unknown,
        query(boldness,16),
        fail.
must_one_walk :-
        status(cash,Money),
        Money < 2.30,
        status(boldness,timid),
        enter_current_rule(17).
```

B   The System for Finding Defects in Automobile Heaters

B.1   Start-up Procedure

```
# This command file starts up the "Auto Heater Expert"
# in a Unix environment by consulting all the components

ifprolog -c knowledge_base -c test_aids -c learn
         -c explanation -c init -c aux_predicates
         -c dialog  -c main_prog -c hypotheses
```

B.2   Module "main_prog"

```
start :-
      note_phase(1),
      hypotheses(Hypotheses_List),
      examine(Hypotheses_List).

start :-
      note_phase(2),
      new_priorities,
      hypotheses(New_Hypotheses_List),
      examine(New_Hypotheses_List).

examine([]) :-
      phase(2),
      nl,
      write('I cannot find any defects.').

examine([Alternative|Others]) :-
      (       check(Alternative)
      ;       examine(Others)
      ).
```

```
check(R_No) :-
        delete_previous_steps,
        defect(R_No,A,B,C),
        increment(R_No),
        store_this_step(R_No),
        print_result(R_No,A,B,C).


cause(Cause_No,A,B,C) :-
        clause(defect(_,A,B,C),_),
        !,
        defect(R_No,A,B,C),
        nl,
        store_this_step(R_No).

cause(Cause_No,A,B,C) :-
        fact(A,B,C,true),
        !.

cause(Cause_No,A,B,C) :-
        fact(A,B,C,false),
        !,
        fail.

cause(Cause_No,A,B,C) :-
        fact(A,B,C,uncertain),
        !,
        fail.

cause(Cause_No,A,B,C) :-
        fact(A,B,C,unknown),
        phase(1),
        !,
        fail.

cause(Cause_No,A,B,C) :-
        note_do_not_know_entered(no),
        ask(Cause_No,A,B,C).

print_result(No,A,B,C) :-
        write_this_sentence_uppercase(A,B,C),
        write_the_rules_applied,
        nl.
```

```
/*
        Switch to "endless" search for defects by
        replacing predicate "print_result" :
*/

endless :-
        [-endless].
```

B.3   Module "knowledge_base"

```
defect(1,'the heater',is,defective) :-
        cause(1,'the heater blower',is,defective).
defect(2,'the heater',is,defective) :-
        cause(2,'the heating regulator',is,defective).
defect(3,'the heater',is,defective) :-
        cause(3,'the water pump',is,defective).
defect(4,'the heater',is,defective) :-
        cause(4,'the heat exchanger',is,defective).
defect(11,'the heater blower',is,defective) :-
        cause(11,'the fuse',is,defective).
defect(12,'the heater blower',is,defective) :-
        cause(12,'the switch',is,defective),
        cause(12,'the cable',is,defective).
defect(13,'the heater blower',is,defective) :-
        cause(13,'the blower',is,stuck),
        cause(13,'the jumper cable',is,defective),
        cause(13,'the blower motor',is,defective).
defect(14,'the heater blower',is,defective) :-
        cause(14,'the blower motor',is,defective),
        cause(14,'the battery',is,empty).
defect(21,'the heating regulator',is,defective) :-
        cause(21,'the Bowden cable',is,broken).
defect(22,'the heating regulator',is,defective) :-
        cause(22,'the Bowden cable',is,stuck),
        cause(22,'the heater valve',is,stuck).
defect(23,'the heating regulator',is,defective) :-
        cause(23,'the Bowden cable',is,stuck),
        cause(23,'the heater valve',
        is,clogged).
defect(31,'the water pump',is,defective) :-
        cause(31,'the V-belt',is,torn),
        cause(31,'the water pump',is,stuck).
```

```
defect(32,'the water pump',is,defective) :-
        cause(32,'the V-belt',is,loose),
        cause(32,'the water pump',is,clogged).
defect(33,'the water pump',is,defective) :-
        cause(33,'the V-belt',is,loose),
        cause(33,'the water pump',is,leaky).
defect(41,'the heat exchanger',is,defective) :-
        cause(41,'the heat exchanger',
        is,'dirty on the outside'),
        cause(41,'the heat exchanger',is,clogged).
defect(42,'the heat exchanger',is,defective) :-
        cause(42,'the heat exchanger',
        is,'dirty on the outside'),
        cause(42,'the heat exchanger',is,leaky).
defect(43,'the heat exchanger',is,defective) :-
        cause(43,'the heat exchanger',
        is,'dirty on the outside'),
        cause(43,'the coolant',is,frozen).
defect(44,'the heat exchanger',is,defective) :-
        cause(44,'the system',is,'low on coolant'),
        cause(44,'air','there is','in the coolant').
```

B.4   Module "test_aids"

```
test('the heater blower',is,defective) :-
        try(
        [],
        [
        'no air comes out the vents when',
        'the blower  is switched on.'
        ]).
test('the fuse',is,defective) :-
        try(
        [],
        [
        'voltage cannot be detected',
        'behind the blower fuse.'
        ]).

test('the switch',is,defective) :-
        try(
        [],
```

```
        [
        'the switch cannot be reset.'
        ]).

test('the cable',is,defective) :-
        try(
        [],
        [
        'the fan does not run when the',
        'cable has been bridged.'
        ]).

test('the blower',is,stuck) :-
        try(
        [],
        [
        'the blower does not run smoothly.'
        ]).

test('the jumper cable',is,defective) :-
        try(
        [],
        [
        '12 Volts of power cannot be measured',
        'on the jumper cable of the air cooling circuit.'
        ]).

test('the blower motor',is,defective) :-
        try(
        [],
        [
        'the blower motor does not run when',
        'directly supplied with operating voltage.'
        ]).

test('the battery',is,empty) :-
        try(
        [],
        [
        'the battery voltage less than 10 volts',
        'when the headlights are switched on.'
        ]).
```

```
test('the heating regulator',is,defective) :-
        try(
        [
        'budge the heating regulator'
        ],
        [
        'the heating regulator lever does not move'
        ]).
test('the Bowden cable',is,broken) :-
        try(
        [],
        [
        'the Bowden cable can be pulled out',
        'toward the motor'
        ]).
test('the Bowden cable',is,stuck) :-
        try(
        [
        'detach both ends of the Bowden cable.'
        ],
        [
        'the Bowden cable is not smooth.'
        ]).
test('the heater valve',is,stuck) :-
        try(
        [
        'detach the Bowden cable from the valve.'
        ],
        [
        'the valve cannot be easily actuated.'.
        ]).
test('the heater valve',is,clogged) :-
        try(
        [],
        [
        'a blockage is visible once the',
        'valve has been removed.'
        ]).


test('the V-belt',is,torn) :-
        try(
        [],
```

```
        [
        'the belt drive-wheel of the water',
        'pump does not rotate.'
        ]).

test('the V-belt',is,loose) :-
        try(
        [],
        [
        'the V-belt can be pressed more than 1 cm'
        ]).

test('the water pump',is,defective) :-
        try(
        [],
        [
        'the temperature gauge is in the red zone',
        'after the motor is running for 5 minutes.'
        ]).

test('the water pump',is,stuck) :-
        try(
        [],
        [
        'the water pump cannot be turned',
        'easily when the V-belt has been loosened.'
        ]).

test('the water pump',is,clogged) :-
        try(
        [
        'unmount the water pump.'
        ],
        [
        'some blockage is visible.'
        ]).

test('the water pump',is,leaky) :-
        try(
        [],
        [
        'some coolant is dripping',
        'out of the water pump.'
        ]).
```

```
test('the heat exchanger',is,defective) :-
        try(
        [],
        [
        'there is no temperatur gradient',
        'between incoming and outgoing',
        'heating pipe'
        ]).

test('the heat exchanger',is,'dirty on the outside') :-
        try(
        [
        'remove the heat exchanger casing.'
        ],
        [
    .   'any foreign bodies are visible.'
        ]).

test('the heat exchanger',is,clogged) :-
        try(
        [
        'unmount the heat exchanger.'
        ],
        [
        'compressed air cannot be blown',
        'through the heat exchanger.'
        ])

test('the heat exchanger',is,leaky) :-
        try(
        [],
        [
        'there are traces of water to be seen',
        'when the cooling system is under pressure.'
        ]).

test('the coolant',is,frozen) :-
        try(
        [],
        [
        'there is not enough anti-freeze',
        'in the radiator coolant.'
        ]).

test('the system',is,'low on coolant') :-
        try(
```

```
[],
[
'there is no more coolant in the reservoir.'
]).

test('air','there is','in the coolant') :-
       try(
       [
       'loosen the bleeder screw on the heat',
       'exchanger while the heater is switched on',
       'and the motor is running.'
       ],
       [
       'the heater runs now.'
       ]).
```

B.5   Module "dialog"

```
ask(No,A,B,C) :-
       (
       B == 'there is',
       write_this_sentence_uppercase('is there',A,C);
       write_this_sentence_uppercase(B,A,C)
       ),
       write(' ? '),
       read_in(Answer),
       !,
       recognize(Answer,No,A,B,C).

recognize(Answer,_,A,B,C) :-
       meaning(Answer,yes),
       !,
       asserta(fact(A,B,C,true)).

recognize(Answer,_,A,B,C) :-
       meaning(Answer,no),
       !,
       asserta(fact(A,B,C,false)),
       fail.

recognize(Answer,No,A,B,C) :-
       meaning(Answer,do_not_know),
       !,
       deal_with_vague_answers(No,A,B,C).
```

```
recognize(Answer,No,A,B,C) :-
        meaning(Answer,why),
        !,
        why(No),
        ask(No,A,B,C).

recognize(Answer,No,A,B,C) :-
        meaning(Answer,test),
        !,
        display_test(A,B,C),
        ask(No,A,B,C).

recognize(_,No,A,B,C) :-
        nl,
        write('I do not understand your response.'),
        nl,
        write('Please re-enter your answer.'),
        ask(No,A,B,C).


meaning([y|_],yes).
meaning([yes|_],yes).
meaning([yeah|_],yes).

meaning([n|_],no).
meaning([no|_],no).
meaning([nope|_],no).

meaning([test|_],test).
meaning(['Test'|_],test).
meaning([try|_],test).
meaning(['Try'|_],test).

meaning([do,not,know|_],do_not_know).
meaning(['I',do,not,know|_],do_not_know).
meaning([perhaps|_],do_not_know).
meaning([maybe|_],do_not_know).
meaning([],do_not_know).
meaning([char(C)|_],do_not_know) :-
        "?" = [C].

meaning([why|_],why).
meaning([how_come|_],why).
```

```
deal_with_vague_answers(No,A,B,C) :-
        do_not_know_entered(no),
        display_test(A,B,C),
        !,
        ask(No,A,B,C).

deal_with_vague_answers(No,A,B,C) :-
        asserta(fact(A,B,C,uncertain)),
        fail.

display_test(A,B,C) :-
        note_do_not_know_entered(yes),
        clause(test(A,B,C),try(Part_1,Part_2)),
        !,
        write_experiment(Part_1),
        write_text_module1,
        write_this_sentence_lowercase(A,B,C),
        write(','),
        write_text_module2,
        write_experiment(Part_2),
        write_text_module3.

display_test(A,B,C) :-
        write_text_module4,
        write_this_sentence_lowercase(A,B,C),
        write('.'),
        nl.

write_experiment([]).

write_experiment([A|B]) :-
        nl,
        write(A),
        write_experiment(B).

write_text_module1 :-
        nl, nl,
        write('To see if'),
        nl.

write_text_module2 :-
        nl,
        write('you can check if').

write_text_module3 :-
        nl, nl,
        write('Please do the above and'),
```

```
        nl,
        write('respond to the following question.'),
        nl.

write_text_module4 :-
        nl,
        write('I know of no simple method '),
        write('for testing'),
        nl,
        write('if ').

write_this_sentence_lowercase(A,'there is',C) :-
        !,
        write_this_sentence_lowercase('there is',A,C).
write_this_sentence_lowercase(A,B,C) :-
      · write(A),
        write(' '),
        write(B),
        write(' '),
        write(C).

write_this_sentence_uppercase(A,'there is',not) :-
        !,
        write_this_sentence_uppercase('there is',no,A).
write_this_sentence_uppercase(A,'there is',C) :-
        !,
        write_this_sentence_uppercase('there is',A,C)
write_this_sentence_uppercase(A,B,C) :-
        nl,
        write_this_term_uppercase(A),
        write(' '),
        write(B),
        write(' '),
        write(C).

write_this_term_uppercase(Term) :-
        name(Term,Word),
        write_uppercase(Word,Uppercase_Word),
        name(New_Term,Uppercase_Word),
        write(New_Term).

write_uppercase([LC_Letter|Rest],[UC_Letter|Rest]) :-
        [LC_a,LC_z] = "az",
        LC_a =< LC_Letter,
        LC_Letter =< LC_z,
        !, UC_Letter is LC_Letter - 32.
```

```prolog
write_uppercase(Term,Term).

write_the_rules_applied :-
        findall(Rule,applied_rule(S,Rule),L),
        write_rules(L).

write_rules([A|B]) :-
        write(' (Rule '),
        write(A),
        write_additional_rule(B).

write_additional_rule([]) :-
        write(').').

write_additional_rule([A|B]) :-
        write(','),
        write(' Rule '),
        write(A),
        write_additional_rule(B).

read_in(Line) :-
        get0(C),
        read_word(C,Word,C1),
        word_in_list(Word,C1,Line).

word_in_list(char(end),_,[]) :-
        !.

word_in_list(char(white),C,WordList) :-
        read_word(C,Word,C1),
        !,
        word_in_list(Word,C1,WordList).

word_in_list(Word,C,[Word|WordList]) :-
        read_word(C,Word1,C1),
        word_in_list(Word1,C1,WordList).

read_word(4,char(end),_) :-
        !.

read_word(10,char(end),_) :-
        !.

read_word(9,char(white),C) :-
        get0(C),
        !.
```

```
read_word(32,char(white),C) :-
        get0(C),
        !.

read_word(C,Word,C2) :-
        in_word(C),
        !,
        get0(C1),
        rest_of_word(C1,String,C2),
        name(Word,[C|String]).

read_word(C,char(C),C1) :-
        get0(C1).

rest_of_word(C,[C|String],C2) :-
        in_word(C),
        !,
        get0(C1),
        rest_of_word(C1,String,C2).

rest_of_word(C,[],C).

in_word(C) :-
        C > 64,
        C < 91.

in_word(C) :-
        C > 90,
        C < 123.

in_word(C) :-
        C > 47,
        C < 58.
```

B.6   Module "aux_predicates"

```
restart :-
        [-init].

rule(N) :-
        display_rule(N).

note_phase(P) :-
        retract(phase(_)),
        asserta(phase(P)).
```

```
note_do_not_know_entered(X) :-
        retract(do_not_know_entered(_)),
        asserta(do_not_know_entered(X)).

increment(No) :-
        retract(statistic(No,State)),
        !,
        Newer_State is State + 1,
        asserta(statistic(No,Newer_State)).

increment(_).

store_this_step(R_No) :-
        retract(step(S_No)),
        New_S_No is S_No + 1,
        asserta(step(New_S_No)),
        asserta(applied_rule(New_S_No,R_No)),
        clause(defect(R_No,A,B,C),_),
        fact(A,B,C,Degree),
        (       Degree == unknown,
                !
        ;       asserta(fact(A,B,C,true))
        ).

facts :-
        fact(A,B,C,B_Degree),
        (       B_Degree == true,
                write_this_sentence_uppercase(A,B,C)
        ;       B_Degree == false,
                write_this_sentence_uppercase(A,B,not),
                write(' '), write(C)
        ;       B_Degree == uncertain,
                nl, write('It is uncertain, if '),
                write_this_sentence_lowercase(A,B,C)
        ;       B_Degree == unknown,
                !
        ),
        fail.

assistance :-
        nl,
        write('Possible inputs :'),
        nl, nl,
        write('start.                         ==> '),
        write('Begin the diagnosis.'),
        nl, fail.
```

```
assistance :-
        write('rule_of_thumb.              ==> '),
        write('Defect search with preparatory tests.'),
        nl,
        write('reason.                      ==> '),
        write('Display the line of reasoning.'),
        nl,
        write('why_not(N).                  ==> '),
        write('Why does rule "N" not apply?'),
        nl, fail.

assistance :-
        write('rule(N).                     ==> '),
        write('Display rule "N".'),
        nl,
        write('facts.                       ==> '),
        write('Display all currently known facts.'),
        nl,
        write('restart.                     ==> '),
        write('Delete accumulated facts.'),
        nl, fail.

assistance :-
        write('statistic(N,How_often).  ==> '),
        write('How often has the cause "N"'),
        nl,
        write('                            '),
        write('already been diagnosed?'),
        nl,
        write('assistance.                  ==> '),
        write('Display this list.').

delete_previous_steps :-
        abolish(step,1),
        abolish(applied_rule,2),
        asserta(step(0)).
```

B.7   Module "init"

```
fact(X,Y,Z,unknown).

do_not_know_entered(no).

phase(2).
```

B.8   Module "explanation"

```
reason :-
     step(0),
     nl,
     write('It is the logical conclusion'),
     nl,
     write(' the facts given me').

reason :-
     retract(step(S_No)),
     applied_rule(S_No,R_No),
     clause(defect(R_No,A,B,C),Causes),
     nl,
     write_this_sentence_uppercase(A,B,C),
     nl,
     write('because '),
     write_causes(Causes),
     write('.'),
     New_S_No is S_No - 1,
     asserta(step(New_S_No)).

write_causes(cause(No,A,B,C)) :-
     write_this_sentence_lowercase(A,B,C).
write_causes((cause(No,A,B,C),Remainder)) :-
     write_this_sentence_lowercase(A,B,C),
     write(','),
     nl,
     write('and '),
     write_causes(Remainder).

display_rule(No) :-
     clause(defect(No,A,B,C),Causes),
     nl,
     write('If '),
     write_causes(Causes),
     write(','),
     nl,
     write('then '),
     write_this_sentence_lowercase(A,B,C),
     write('.').

why(No) :-
     display_rule(Nr).
```

```
why_not(No) :-
        clause(defect(No,_,_,_),Causes),
        !,
        separate(Causes,T,F,Uncertain,Unkn),
        something_is_false(F),
        something_is_uncertain(Uncertain),
        something_is_unknown(Unkn),
        (   check_if_still_applicable(F,Uncertain,Unkn)
        ;   true
        ),
        nl.

why_not(_) :-
        nl,
        write('No such rule exists !').

separate(cause(N,A,B,C),[(A,B,C)],[],[],[]) :-
        fact(A,B,C,true),
        !.
separate(cause(N,A,B,C),[],[(A,B,C)],[],[]) :-
        fact(A,B,C,false),
        !.
separate(cause(N,A,B,C),[],[],[(A,B,C)],[]) :-
        fact(A,B,C,uncertain),
        !.
separate(cause(N,A,B,C),[],[],[],[(A,B,C)]).
separate((cause(N,A,B,C),Causes),
        [(A,B,C)|True],False,Uncertain,Unknown) :-
        fact(A,B,C,true),
        !,
        separate(Causes,True,False,Uncertain,Unknown).
separate((cause(N,A,B,C),Causes),
        True,[(A,B,C)|False],Uncertain,Unknown) :-
        fact(A,B,C,false),
        !,
        separate(Causes,True,False,Uncertain,Unknown).
separate((cause(N,A,B,C),Causes),
        True,False,[(A,B,C)|Uncertain],Unknown) :-
        fact(A,B,C,uncertain),
        !,
        separate(Causes,True,False,Uncertain,Unknown).
separate((cause(N,A,B,C),Causes),
        True,False,Uncertain,[(A,B,C)|Unknown]) :-
        separate(Causes,True,False,Uncertain,Unknown).
```

```
something_is_false(False) :-
        write_the_false_facts(False).
something_is_false(_).


something_is_uncertain(Uncertain) :-
        write_the_uncertain_facts(Uncertain),
        write('.').
something_is_uncertain(_).


something_is_unknown(Unknown) :-
        write_the_unknown_facts(Unknown),
        write('.').
something_is_unknown(_).


write_the_false_facts([(A,B,C)]) :-
        nl,
        write_this_sentence_uppercase(A,B,not),
        write(' '),
        write(C),
        write('.').
write_the_false_facts([(A,B,C)|Facts]) :-
        write_the_false_facts([(A,B,C)]),
        write_the_false_facts(Facts).


write_the_uncertain_facts([]) :-
        !,
        fail.
write_the_uncertain_facts(Facts) :-
        nl,
        write('It is uncertain, if'),
        nl,
        write_an_uncertain_fact(Facts).


write_an_uncertain_fact([(A,B,C)]) :-
        write_this_sentence_lowercase(A,B,C).
write_an_uncertain_fact([Fact|Facts]) :-
        write_an_uncertain_fact([Fact]),
        write(' and if'),
        nl,
        write_an_uncertain_fact(Facts).


write_the_unknown_facts([]) :-
        !,
        fail.
```

```
write_the_unknown_facts(Facts) :-
        nl,
        write('It has not yet been clarified if'),
        nl,
        write_an_unknown_fact(Facts).

write_an_unknown_fact([(A,B,C)]) :-
        write_this_sentence_lowercase(A,B,C).
write_an_unknown_fact([Fact|Facts]) :-
        write_an_unknown_fact([Fact]),
        write(' and if'),
        nl,
        write_an_unknown_fact(Facts).

check_if_still_applicable([],[],[]) :-
      · nl,
        write('This rule could still be applied.'),
        nl.
```

B.9   Module "hypotheses"

```
rule_of_thumb :-
        make_hypothesis(List),
        test_hypotheses(List).

make_hypothesis(HypothesesList) :-
        nl,
        write('Do the headlights work ? '),
        read_in(Answer_1),
        test_questions1(Answer_1),
        nl,
        write('Does the motor start ? '),
        read_in(Answer_2),
        test_questions2(Answer_2),
        point(1,A,_),
        point(2,B,_),
        point(3,C,_),
        point(4,D,_),
        sort([A,B,C,D],_,
        [1,2,3,4],HypothesesList),
        retract(hypotheses(_)),
        asserta(hypotheses(HypothesesList)).
```

```
test_hypotheses([]) :-
      nl,
      write('I cannot find any defects.').
test_hypotheses([Next_Alternative|Remainder]) :-
      (       point(Next_Alternative,_,possible),
              check(Next_Alternative)

      ;
              test_hypotheses(Remainder)
      ).


test_questions1(Answer) :-
      meaning(Answer,yes),
      increase_probability(3,3),
      reduced_probability(2,6).
test_questions1(Answer) :-
      meaning(Answer,no),
      increase_probability(1,5),
      increase_probability(4,2).
test_questions1(_).


test_questions2(Answer) :-
      meaning(Answer,yes),
      reduced_probability(1,4),
      increase_probability(3,2).
test_questions2(Answer) :-
      meaning(Answer,no),
      impossible(4),
      increase_probability(2,2).
test_questions2(_).


increase_probability(Hypo,Points) :-
      retract(point(Hypo,Old_State,possible)),
      Newer_State is Old_State + Points,
      asserta(point(Hypo,Newer_State,possible)).
increase_probability(_,_).


reduced_probability(Hypo,Points) :-
      retract(point(Hypo,Old_State,possible)),
      Newer_State is Old_State - Points,
      asserta(point(Hypo,Newer_State,possible)).
reduced_probability(_,_).


impossible(Alternative) :-
      point(Alternative,0,impossible),
      !.
```

```
impossible(Alternative) :-
        retract(point(Alternative,_,_)),
        asserta(point(Alternative,0,impossible)).

display_hypothesis :-
        hypotheses(List),
        write_hypothesis(List).

write_hypothesis([]).
write_hypothesis([Alternative|Remainder]) :-
        (       point(Alternative,_,possible),
                clause(defect(Alternative,_,_,_),
                cause(_,A,B,C)),
                write_this_sentence_uppercase(A,B,C),
                fail
        ;
                write_hypothesis(Remainder)
        ).

point(1,0,possible).
point(2,0,possible).
point(3,0,possible).
point(4,0,possible).

hypotheses([1,2,3,4]).
```

B.10   Module "learn"

```
statistic(1,0).
statistic(2,0).
statistic(3,0).
statistic(4,0).

new_priorities :-
        statistic(1,A),
        statistic(2,B),
        statistic(3,C),
        statistic(4,D),
        sort([A,B,C,D],_,[1,2,3,4],New_List),
        retract(hypotheses(_)),
        asserta(hypotheses(New_List)).

sort([],[],[],[]).
sort([P|Points],New_Points,[H|Hypos],New_Hypos) :-
        split(P,Points,UP1,UP2,H,Hypos,UH1,UH2),
```

```
        sort(UP1,VP1,UH1,VH1),
        sort(UP2,VP2,UH2,VH2),
        append(VP1,[P|VP2],New_Points),
        append(VH1,[H|VH2],New_Hypos).

split(_,[],[],[],_,[],[],[]).
split(H,[H1|T1],[H1|U1],U2,
        HA,[HA1|TA1],[HA1|UA1],UA2) :-
        H1 > H,
        split(H,T1,U1,U2,HA,TA1,UA1,UA2).
split(H,[H1|T1],U1,[H1|U2],
        HA,[HA1|TA1],UA1,[HA1|UA2]) :-
        H1 =< H,
        split(H,T1,U1,U2,HA,TA1,UA1,UA2).
```

B.11   Module "endless"

```
print_result(Nr,A,B,C) :-
        write_this_sentence_uppercase(A,B,C),
        write_the_rules_applied,
        nl, nl,
        note_phase(2),
        write('Should more defects be searched for ? '),
        read_in(Continue),
        (       meaning(Continue,yes),
                !, delete_previous_steps,
                fail
        :       true
        ).
```

C The License and Memo Manager

C.1 Initialization Procedure

```
# This exec procedure initializes the license manager
# in a Unix system by consulting all components

rm MEMOS/*
ifprolog -c primitives -c frames -c attachments \
         -c help -c memos -c input_output
```

C.2 Start-up Procedure

```
# This exec procedure starts the license administrator
# in a Unix system, by consulting the file containing
# the system state last stored by a user

ifprolog -c license
```

C.3 Module "primitives"

```
/* Search for Frame : */

search_for(Frame,Slot,Data_Item) :-
      % Default facet is "value" :
      search_for(Frame,Slot,value,Data_Item).

search_for(Frame,Slot,Facet,Data_Item) :-
      (        var(Data_Item)
      ;        is_list(Data_Item)
      ),
      clause(frame(Frame,Slot,Facet,Data_Item),_).

search_for(Frame,Slot,Facet,Values_from_List) :-
      nonvar(Values_from_List),
      Values_from_List = evaluate([Data_Item|Rest]),
      search_for_x(Frame,Slot,Facet,[Data_Item|Rest]).
```

```
search_for(Frame,Slot,Facet,Data_Item) :-
        nonvar(Data_Item),
        Data_Item = evaluate([_|_]),
        not is_list(Data_Item),
        search_for_x(Frame,Slot,Facet,[Data_Item]).


search_for_x(Frame,Slot,Facet,[Data_Item|Rest]) :-
        nonvar(Data_Item),
        clause(frame(Frame,Slot,Facet,DataList),_),
        (       member(Data_Item,DataList)
        ;       search_for_x(Frame,Slot,Facet,Rest)
        ).

search_for_x(Frame,Slot,Facet,[Data_Item|Rest]) :-
        var(Data_Item),
        search_for_x(Frame,Slot,Facet,Rest).

/* Modify an entry : */

modify(Frame,Slot,Data) :-
        % Default facet is "value" :
        modify(Frame,Slot,value,Data).

modify(Frame,Slot,Facet,Data) :-
        nonvar(Frame), nonvar(Slot),
        nonvar(Facet), nonvar(Data),
        delete(Frame,Slot,Facet),
        new_data(Frame,Slot,Facet,Data).

new_data(_,_,_,[]) :- !.

new_data(Frame,Slot,Facet,[Data_Item|Rest]) :-
        % "add" does not accept
        % variable arguments :
        !, add(Frame,Slot,Facet,Data_Item),
        new_data(Frame,Slot,Facet,Rest).

new_data(Frame,Slot,Facet,Data_Item) :-
        add(Frame,Slot,Facet,Data_Item).

/* Determine the data for a slot : */

ask(Object,Slot,Data) :-
        nonvar(Object), nonvar(Slot),
```

```
(       var(Data)
;       is_list(Data)
),
(       search_for(Object,Slot,value,Data), !
;       procedure_call(if_needed,Object,Slot,Data),
        !
;       % A list is permitted for "ako"
        % Many fathers are processed in order;
        % the first one with something to
        % "bequeath" will be "adopted" :
        search_for(Object,ako,value,Fathers),
        member(Father,Fathers), !,
        ask(Father,Slot,Data)
).
```

```
/* Add a data value for a facet of a slot : */

add(Frame,Slot,Data_Item) :-
      % Default facet is "value" :
      add(Frame,Slot,value,Data_Item).

add(Frame,Slot,Facet,Data_Item) :-
      nonvar(Frame), nonvar(Slot),
      nonvar(Facet), nonvar(Data_Item),
      (     retract(frame(Frame,Slot,value,Previously)),
            (    member(Data_Item,Previously),
                 % each Data_Item should only
                 % appear once in the list :
                 !, Afterwards = Previously
            ;    append([Data_Item],Previously,Afterwards)
            )
      ;     Afterwards = [Data_Item]
      ),
      assertz(frame(Frame,Slot,value,Afterwards)),
      % activate "if_added" procedure if "value"
      % and "Afterwards" are not equal to "Previously"
      % (i.e. a new value was really added):
      (     Facet == value,
            Afterwards == Previously,
            procedure_call(if_added,Frame,Slot,Data_Item),
            !
      ;     true
      ).
```

```
/* Delete primitive for entry, always ends with fail (!) */

delete_x(Frame,Slot,Facet) :-
        retract(frame(Frame,Slot,Facet,Data)),
        % "if_removed" Proc., if "value" :
        Facet = value,
        procedure_call(if_removed,Frame,Slot,Data),
        fail.

/* Delete Facet of a Slot : */

delete(Frame,Slot,Facet) :-
        nonvar(Frame), nonvar(Slot),
        nonvar(Facet),
        (       delete_x(Frame,Slot,Facet)
        ;       true
        ).

/* Delete Slot : */

delete(Frame,Slot) :-
        nonvar(Frame), nonvar(Slot),
        (       search_for(Frame,Slot,Facet,_),
                delete_x(Frame,Slot,Facet)
        ;       true
        ).


/* Delete Frame : */

delete(Frame) :-
        nonvar(Frame),
        findall(Dependent,
                search_for(Dependent,ako,value,Frame),
                List),
        List = [],
        nl, write('The frame "'),
        write(Frame),
        write('" cannot be deleted.'), nl,
        write('The following frames are dependent on it:'),
        nl, write_list(List), nl,
        !, fail.

delete(Frame) :-
        % no dependent frames via "ako" :
        nonvar(Frame),
```

```
(           search_for(Frame,Slot,Facet,_),
            delete_x(Frame,Slot,Facet)
;           !
).
```

```
/* Show frame on the current output stream : */

display_frames :-
        display_frame(_).

display_frame(Frame) :-
        var(Frame),
        (       Frame = general
        ;       search_for(Frame,ako,value,_)
        ),
        nl,nl,
        write(Frame),
        nl,
        display_frame(Frame),
        fail.

display_frame(Frame) :-
        nonvar(Frame),
        search_for(Frame,Slot,value,Data),
        write_slot(Slot,Data),
        fail.

display_frame(_) :-
        nl, !.

/* Display object on the current output stream */

display_object(Object) :-
        nonvar(Object),
        display_values(Object,[],SlotsShown),
        findall(Slot,
                search_for(_,Slot,if_needed,_),
                IfNeededSlots),
        display_if_needed_slots(IfNeededSlots,Object,
                SlotsShown,AllSlots),
        display_father_slot(Object,AllSlots,_).

display_values(Object,Shown,Afterwards) :-
        search_for(Object,Slot,value,Data),
        not member(Slot,Shown),
```

```
        write_slot(Slot,Data),
        display_values(Object,[Slot|Shown],Afterwards).

display_values(_,Shown,Shown).

display_if_needed_slots([Slot|Slots],Object,
                        Shown,Afterwards) :-
        member(Slot,Shown),
        display_if_needed_slots(Slots,Object,
                                Shown,Afterwards).

display_if_needed_slots([Slot|Slots],Object,
                        Shown,Afterwards) :-
        not member(Slot,Shown),
        (       procedure_call(if_needed,Object,
                                Slot,Data),
                !,
                nonvar(Data),
                write_slot(Slot,Data)
        ;       true
        ),
        display_if_needed_slots(Slots,Object,
                        [Slot|Shown],Afterwards).

display_if_needed_slots([],_,Shown,Shown).

display_father_slot(Object,Shown,Afterwards) :-
        search_for(Object,ako,value,Fathers),
        display_fathers_slot(Fathers,Shown,Afterwards).

display_father_slot(_,Shown,Shown).

display_fathers_slot([Father|Fathers],Shown,Afterwards) :-
        display_values(Father,Shown,Now_Shown),
        display_father_slot(Father,Now_Shown,
                        To_Be_Shown),
        display_fathers_slot(Fathers,To_Be_Shown,
                        Afterwards).
display_fathers_slot([],Shown,Shown).

/* Display instances of a frame on the current output stream */

display_instances :-
        display_instances(all,0).
```

```prolog
display_instances(Frame) :-
        display_instances(Frame,0).

display_instances(all,I) :-
        !,
        display_instances(general,I).

display_instances(Frame,I) :-
        search_for_instance(Frame,I),
        indent(I),
        write(Frame),
        J is I + 1,
        search_for(Instance,ako,value,Frame),
        display_instances(Instance,J),
        fail.

display_instances(_,_).

search_for_instance(Frame,I) :-
        (       search_for(Frame,_,_,_),
                !
        ;       indent(I),
                write(Frame),
                write(' does not exist'),
                fail
        ).
write_slot(Slot,Data) :-
        nl,
        write(Slot),
        write(' :'),
        write_list(Data).

/* Store state of system in a file : */

store :-
        system_ident(SystemName),
        telling(Whom),
        tell(SystemName),
        listing,
        told,
        tell(Whom).

/* End session after saving system state : */

stop :- store, bye.
```

```
/* Create a new frame : */

new(ObjectName) :-
        search_for(ObjectName,_,_,_),
        nl,
        write('There already is an object "'),
        write(ObjectName),
        write('". Should it be modified? '),
        read_in(Input),
        (       meaning(Input,yes),
                delete(ObjectName),
                !,
                new(ObjectName)
        ;       !,
                fail
        ).

new(ObjectName) :-
        system_ident(Gen_Frame),
        new(Gen_Frame,ObjectName).

new(Gen_Frame,ObjectName) :-
        nonvar(Gen_Frame),
        search_for(Gen_Frame,Slot,default,_),
        read_value_entered(Gen_Frame,Slot,ObjectName),
        fail.

new(Gen_Frame,ObjectName) :-
        nonvar(Gen_Frame),
        nl,
        write('New Object: '),
        write(ObjectName),
        display_frame(ObjectName).

read_value_entered(Gen_Frame,Slot,Frame) :-
        nl, write(Slot),
        write(': '),
        read_in(Input),
        recognize(Input,Gen_Frame,Slot,Frame),
        !.

recognize(Input,Gen_Frame,Slot,Frame) :-
        meaning(Input,assistance),
        explain_input,
        read_value_entered(Gen_Frame,Slot,Frame).
```

```
recognize('.',Gen_Frame,Slot,Frame) :-
        % default only entered if the slot for
        % this frame does not yet have a value,
        % (e.g. a procedural attachment!)
        not search_for(Frame,Slot,value,_),
        search_for(Gen_Frame,Slot,default,Data),
        new_Slot(Frame,Slot,value,Data),
        !.

recognize('.',_,_,_) :-
        !.

recognize('?',Gen_Frame,Slot,Frame) :-
        % show possible inputs
        !,
        search_for(Gen_Frame,Slot,prefer,Data),
        nl,
        write_constraint(Data,prefer),
        read_value_entered(Gen_Frame,Slot,Frame),
        !.

recognize('??',Gen_Frame,Slot,Frame) :-
        % show all possible inputs
        !,
        search_for(Gen_Frame,Slot,require,Data),
        nl,
        (       Data = [],
                write('Arbitrary values are permitted.'),
                nl,nl
        ;       write_constraint(Data)
        ),
        read_value_entered(Gen_Frame,Slot,Frame),
        !.

recognize('',Gen_Frame,Slot,Frame) :-
        % no input ( only permitted if no "require"
        % list present in generic frame!
        (       search_for(Gen_Frame,Slot,
                        require,[in_list(_)]),
                nl,
                write('Obligatory entry, '),
                write('"." for default.'),
                % continue as if all possibilities requested
                recognize('??',Gen_Frame,Slot,Frame)
```

```
            ;          % no "require" entry
                       true
            ),
            !.

recognize(Input,Gen_Frame,Slot,Frame) :-
            (          search_for(Gen_Frame,Slot,require,Constr),
                       !
            ;          Constr = []
            ),
            (          check_these_constraints(Input,Constr),
                       !,
                       new_Slot(Frame,Slot,value,Input)
            ;          nl,
                       write_constraint(Constr),
                       read_value_entered(Gen_Frame,Slot,Frame)
            ).

new_Slot(Frame,Slot,Facet,Value) :-
            add(Frame,Slot,Facet,Value).

explain_input :-
            nl,
            write('Possible responses are :'),
            nl,
            write('assistance,help,info  ==> '),
            write('display this list.'),
            nl,
            write('?                      ==> '),
            write('display some possible values.'),
            nl,
            write('??                     ==> '),
            write('display limits on values'),
            nl,
            write('.                      ==> '),
            write('take the default value.'),
            nl,
            write('‹return›               ==> '),
            write('omit this slot.'),
            nl.

write_constraint(L) :-
            write_constraint(L,require).

write_constraint([],_).
```

```
write_constraint([Constr|Rest],Which) :-
        write_this_constraint(Constr,Which),
        write_constraint(Rest,Which).

write_this_constraint(in_list(L),Which) :-
        (       Which = require,
                !,
                write('The possible')
        ;       write('Some possible')
        ),
        write(' response are : '),
        nl,
        write_list(L),
        nl.
write_this_constraint(between(A,B),_) :-
        write('The value must lie between '),
        write(A),
        write(' and '),
        write(B),
        nl.

write_this_constraint(larger(A),_) :-
        write('The value must be greater than '),
        write(A),
        write('.'),
        nl.

write_this_constraint(less_than(A),_) :-
        write('The value must be less than '),
        write(A),
        write('.'),
        nl.

check_these_constraints(_,[]).

check_these_constraints(Input,[Constr|Rest]) :-
        not is_list(Input),
        check_this_constraint(Input,Constr),
        check_these_constraints(Input,Rest).

check_these_constraints(Input,[Constr|Rest]) :-
        is_list(Input),
        nl,
        write('List ('),
        write(Input),
```

```
                write(') for "check constraints" '),
                write('not provided'),
                nl.

check_this_constraint(Input,in_list(L)) :-
                member(Input,L).

check_this_constraint(Input,between(A,B)) :-
                integer(Input),
                Input >= A,
                Input =< B.

check_this_constraint(Input,larger(A)) :-
                integer(Input),
            _   Input > A.

check_this_constraint(Input,less_than(A)) :-
                integer(Input),
                Input < A.

/* invoke procedural attachment (if present) */

procedure_call(Facet,Frame,Slot,Data) :-
                system_ident(SystemName),
                search_for(SystemName,Slot,Facet,Proc),
                execute(Proc,Frame,Slot,Data).

/*      execute a set of procedures            */
/*      for a set of data                      */

execute([],_,_,_) :-
                !.

execute(Proc,Frame,Slot,Data) :-
                Data == [],
                !.

execute(Proc,Frame,Slot,Data_Item) :-
                not is_list(Data_Item),
                execute(Proc,Frame,Slot,[Data_Item]).

execute([Proc|Rest],Frame,Slot,Data) :-
                !,
                execute(Proc,Frame,Slot,Data),
                execute(Rest,Frame,Slot,Data).
```

```
execute(Proc,Frame,Slot,[Data_Item|Rest]) :-
        nonvar(Proc),
        !,
        Procedure =.. [Proc,Frame,Slot,Data_Item],
        clause(Procedure,_),
        !,
        activate(Procedure),
        execute(Proc,Frame,Slot,Rest).

execute(_,_,_,_).

activate(Procedure) :-
        Procedure,
        !.

activate(_).

is_list(X) :- var(X), !, fail.
is_list([_|_]) :- !.
is_list([]) :- !.
```

C.4 Module "frames"

```
/* System-Identification : */

system_ident(license).

/* Object classes : */


frame(general,quantity,value,[1]).
frame(general,language,value,[german]).
frame(general,uni,value,[no]).
frame(general,discount,value,[0]).
frame(general,currency,value,[dm]).

frame(normal,ako,value,[general]).
frame(normal,time_limit,value,[unlimited]).

frame(special,ako,value,[general]).

frame(oem,ako,value,[general]).

frame(on_loan,ako,value,[general]).
```

```
frame(ibm_pc,ako,value,[normal]).
frame(ibm_pc,gross_price,value,[1500]).
frame(ibm_pc,operating_system,value,[msdos]).
frame(ibm_pc,computer,value,[ibm_xt,ibm_at]).
frame(ibm_pc,medium,value,[diskette]).
frame(ibm_pc,storage,value,[256]).

frame(others,ako,value,[normal]).
frame(others,storage,value,[5000]).

frame(artificial_intuition,ako,value,[ibm_pc]).
frame(artificial_intuition,computer,value,[siemens_pcd]).
frame(artificial_intuition,storage,value,[512]).
frame(artificial_intuition,uni,value,[yes]).
frame(artificial_intuition,discount,value,[30]).

/* Generic frame for the license management : */

frame(license,ako,default,[ibm_pc]).
frame(license,ako,prefer,[in_list([ibm_pc,others])]).
frame(license,ako,require,
       [in_list([ibm_pc,others,oem,special,on_loan])]).

frame(license,computer,default,[ibm_pc]).
frame(license,computer,prefer,
        [in_list([ibm_pc,van,oadmus])]).
frame(license,computer,require,[]).

frame(license,operating_system,default,[unix]).
frame(license,operating_system,prefer,
       [in_list([unix,msdos,vms])]).
frame(license,operating_system,require,[]).

frame(license,storage,default,[5000]).
frame(license,storage,prefer,[in_list([256,5000])]).
frame(license,storage,require,[larger(0)]).

frame(license,gross_price,default,[1500]).
frame(license,gross_price,prefer,[between(1500,8100)]).
frame(license,gross_price,require,[between(1050,22600)]).

frame(license,currency,default,[dm]).
frame(license,currency,prefer,[in_list([dm,dollar])]).
frame(license,currency,require,[]).
```

```
frame(license,language,default,[german]).
frame(license,language,prefer,
        [in_list([german,english])]).
frame(license,language,require,[]).

frame(license,uni,default,[no]).
frame(license,uni,prefer,[in_list([yes,no])]).
frame(license,uni,require,
        [in_list([yes,no,unknown])]).

frame(license,discount,default,[0]).
frame(license,discount,prefer,[in_list([0,30,40,70])]).
frame(license,discount,require,[less_than(100)]).

frame(license,time_limit,default,[unlimited]).
frame(license,time_limit,prefer,[in_list([unlimited,3])]).
frame(license,time_limit,require,[]).

frame(license,keywords,default,[]).
frame(license,keywords,prefer,
        [in_List(['List',of,words,consisting,
                  of, letters,',',numbers,'-',
                  and,'_'])]).
frame(license,keywords,require,[]).

/* Procedural attachment */

frame(license,uni,if_added,[store_discount]).
frame(license,price,if_needed,[calculate_price]).
```

C.5   Module "attachments"

```
calculate_price(Frame,Slot,[Price]) :-
        ask(Frame,discount,[Discount]),
        ask(Frame,gross_price,[Gross]),
        Price is (100 - Discount) * Gross / 100.

store_discount(Frame,uni,yes) :-
        add(Frame,discount,value,30).

increase_instance_count(Frame,ako,Parent) :-
        retract(frame(Parent,number_of_instances,value,[Old])),
        New is Old + 1,
        add(Parent,number_of_instances,value,New).
```

C.6   Module "help"

```
assistance :-
        nl,
        write('Possible responses are :'),
        possibility([
          'new(Name)',
          'Records the license for the new customer named.'
          ]),
        possibility([
          'ask(Object,Slot,DataItem)',
          'Asks for the value of the slot in object.'
          ]),
        possibility([
        · 'add(Frame,Slot,DataItem)',
          'Enters the data item as value for slot in frame.'
          ]),
        possibility([
          'modify(Frame,Slot,Data)',
          'Enters the data values as value for slot in frame.'
          ]),
        possibility([
          'delete(Object,Slot,value)',
          'Deletes the value in slot in object.'
          ]),
        possibility([
          'delete(Object,Slot)',
          'Deletes the slot in object.'
          ]),
        possibility([
          'delete(Object)',
          'Deletes the object.'
          ]),
        continuation,
        possibility([
          'display_instances(Frame)',
          'Displays the instances of frame.'
          ]),
        possibility([
          'display_instances',
          'Displays all instances in existence.'
          ]),
        possibility([
          'display_frame(Frame)',
          'Displays the contents of a frame.'
```

```
     ]),
  possibility([
    'display_object(Object)',
    'Displays the complete object.'
    ]),
  possibility([
    'memo(Frame)',
    'Opens an editing window for a memo.'
    ]),
  possibility([
    'write_memos(Object)',
    'Outputs memos associated with object.'
    ]),
  possibility([
    'write_memos(Object,Keyword(list))',
    'Outputs memos containing keyword(s) for object.'
    ]),
  continuation,
  possibility([
    'store',
    'Stores the current state of the system.'
    ]),
  possibility([
    'stop',
    'Ends the session after storing state of the system.'
    ]),
  possibility([
    'assistance',
    'Displays this help information.'
    ]),
  nl.

possibility([Input|Explanations]) :-
     nl, nl,
     write(Input),
     nl,
     write('      ==> '),
     write_List(Explanations).

continuation :-
     nl, nl,
     write('------------ <return> to continue'),
     skip(10).
```

C.7   Module "memos"

```
/*
        Memo Management
        **************

        must be consulted after the
        generic frame module
*/

memo_prefix("MEMOS/").
editorname("tiptop ").

/* Enter a memo for a frame : */

memo(Frame) :-
        (       clause(frame(Frame,_,_,_),_), !,
                next_memo_name(Memo),
                compose_memo(Memo),
                add(Frame,memos,value,Memo)
        ;       nl, write('Unknown object'), nl
        ).

compose_memo(Memo) :-
        name(Memo,Filename),
        editorname(EditorCall),
        append(EditorCall,Filename,CommString),
        name(Command,CommString),
        sh(Command).

next_memo_name(MemoName) :-
        memo_prefix(NP),
        system_ident(System),
        name(System,SS),
        append(NP,SS,NPS),
        next_memo_number(N),
        number(N,NA),
        append(NPS,NA,Name),
        name(MemoName,Name).

next_memo_number(N) :-
        (       retract(memo_number(N))
        ;       N = 1
        ),
        N1 is N + 1,
        asserta(memo_number(N1)).
```

```prolog
/* Procedural attachment for "trigger" : */

:- ( system_ident(System),
     (          clause(frame(System,memos,if_added,_),_)
      ;         asserta(frame(System,memos,
                         if_added,memo_trigger))
     )
   ).

memo_trigger(Frame,_,MemoName) :-
        /* read memo into list a word-at-a-time : */
        words_from_file(MemoName,List_of_all_Words),
        unique_word(List_of_all_Words,WordList),
        word_trigger(Frame,MemoName,WordList).

word_trigger(_,_,[]).
word_trigger(Frame,MemoName,[Word|Words]) :-
        trigger(Frame,Frame,MemoName,Word),
        word_trigger(Frame,MemoName,Words).

trigger(InFrame,FromFrame,MemoName,Word) :-
        exec_trigger(InFrame,FromFrame,
                        MemoName,Word),
        search_for(InFrame,ako,value,Fathers), !,
        % several fathers are permitted
        member(Father,Fathers),
        trigger(Father,FromFrame,MemoName,Word).
trigger(_,_,_,_).

exec_trigger(InFrame,FromFrame,MemoName,Word) :-
        % A list of all actions to be
        % triggered may be inserted here :
        keyword_reference(InFrame,FromFrame,
                        MemoName,Word),
        !.
exec_trigger(_,_,_,_).

/* Add a reference to frame according to keyword : */

keyword_reference(InFrame,FromFrame,MemoName,Word) :-
        search_for(InFrame,keywords,value,Word), !,
        add(InFrame,references,value,
                        memo(FromFrame,MemoName,Word)).
keyword_reference(_,_,_,_).

/* Memo output*/
```

```
/* All memos of an object (with inheritance) : */

write_memos(Object) :-
        findall(Ancestor,
                ancestor(Object,Ancestor),
                FrameList),
        search_for_memo_list(FrameList,MemoList).
        show_memos(MemoList).

/* all memos associated with one or more keywords: */

write_memos(Object,KeywordList) :-
        is_list(KeywordList),
        memo_list(Object,KeywordList,Memos),
        unique(Memos,MemoList),
        show_memos(MemoList).
write_memos(Object,Keyword) :-
        not is_list(Keyword),
        write_memos(Object,[Keyword]).

memo_list(_,[],[]).
memo_list(Object,[Keyword|Rest],MemoList) :-
        findall([Memo,Frame],
                fetch_memo(Object,Keyword,
                           Memo,Frame),
                List),
        memo_list(Object,Rest,RestList),
        append(List,RestList,MemoList).

fetch_memo(Object,Keyword,Memo,Frame) :-
        search_for(Object,references,value,
              memo(Frame,Memo,Keyword)).
fetch_memo(Object,Keyword,Memo,Frame) :-
        search_for(Object,ako,value,Fathers),
        member(Father,Fathers),
        fetch_memo(Father,Keyword,Memo,Frame).

show_memos([]).
show_memos([MemoEntry|Rest]) :-
        conditional_output_memo(MemoEntry),
        show_memos(Rest).

conditional_output_memo([Memo,Frame]) :-
        not telling(user), !,
        show_memo_name(Memo,Frame),
        output_memo(Memo).
```

```prolog
conditional_output_memo([Memo,Frame]) :-
        show_memo_name(Memo,Frame),
        write('------- display (y/n) ? '),
        get0(C), skip(10),    % Skip to end of line
        (       [C] = "y",
                output_memo(Memo)
        ;       true
        ).

output_memo(Memo) :-
        write_line,
        output_file(Memo),
        write_line.

show_memo_name(MemoName,Frame) :-
        write('Frame: '), write(Frame),
        write('  Memo: '),write(MemoName), nl.

search_for_memo_list([],[]).
search_for_memo_list([Frame|Rest],MemoList) :-
        search_for_memo_list(Rest,RestMemos),
        (       search_for(Frame,memos,value,NewMemos), !,
                memos_insert(Frame,NewMemos,
                                RestMemos,MemoList)
        ;       MemoList = RestMemos
        ).

memos_insert(_,[],List,List).
memos_insert(Frame,[NewMemo|RestNew],[],
                [[NewMemo,Frame]|RestList]) :-
        memos_insert(Frame,RestNew,[],RestList).
memos_insert(Frame,[NewMemo|RestNew],
                [[OldMemo,OldFrame]|OldRestList],
                [[NewMemo,Frame]|RestList]) :-
        compare(>,NewMemo,OldMemo), !,
        memos_insert(Frame,RestNew,
                [[OldMemo,OldFrame]|OldRestList],
                RestList).

memos_insert(Frame,NewMemos,
                [X|OldRestList],[X|RestList]) :-
        memos_insert(Frame,NewMemos,
                OldRestList,RestList).


/* Auxiliary predicates */
```

```
unique([],[]).
unique([Word|Rest],UniqueRest) :-
        member(Word,Rest), !,
        unique(Rest,UniqueRest).
unique([Word|Rest],[Word|UniqueRest]) :-
        unique(Rest,UniqueRest).

unique_word([],[]).
unique_word([Word|Rest],UniqueRest) :-
        (       /* eliminate special chars : */
                Word = char(_)
        ;       member(Word,Rest)
        ), !,
        unique_word(Rest,UniqueRest).
unique_word([Word|Rest],[Word|UniqueRest]) :-
        unique_word(Rest,UniqueRest).

ancestor(Object,Object).
ancestor(Object,Ancestor) :-
        search_for(Object,ako,value,Fathers),
        member(Father,Fathers),
        ancestor(Father,Ancestor).
```

C.8   Module "input_output"

```
/*
        End-of-File Symbol
*/

is_EOF(4).
is_EOF(26).

/*
        Reading One Word at a Time
        **************************
*/

words_from_file(File,WordList) :-
        seeing(Was), see(File),
        (       read_file(WordList), !
        ;       true            % guarantees closing !
        ),
        seen, see(Was).
```

```
words_in_line(WordList) :-
        read_words(WordList,till_nl).

read_file(WordList) :-
        read_words(WordList,bis_EOF).

read_words(WordList,End) :-
        get0(C), read_a_word(C,Word,C1,End),
        word_in_list(Word,C1,WordList,End).

word_in_list(char(end),_,[],_) :- !.
word_in_list(char(white),C,WordList,End) :-
        read_a_word(C,Word,C1,End), !,
        word_in_list(Word,C1,WordList,End).
word_in_list(Word,C,[Word|WordList],End) :-
        read_a_word(C,Word1,C1,End),
        word_in_list(Word1,C1,WordList,End).

/* EOF can be 4 or 26 : */
read_a_word(4,char(end),_,_) :- !.
read_a_word(26,char(end),_,_) :- !.
read_a_word(10,char(end),_,till_nl) :- !.
read_a_word(9,char(white),C,_) :- get0(C), !.
read_a_word(10,char(white),C,bis_EOF) :- get0(C), !.
read_a_word(32,char(white),C,_) :- get0(C), !.
read_a_word(C,Word,C2,_) :-
        in_word(C), !, get0(C1),
        rest_of_word(C1,String,C2),
        name(Word,[C|String]).
read_a_word(C,char(C),C1,_) :- get0(C1).

rest_of_word(C,[C|String],C2) :-
        in_word(C), !, get0(C1),
        rest_of_word(C1,String,C2).
rest_of_word(C,[],C).

in_word(C) :-
        /* uppercase letters */
        C > 64, C < 91.
in_word(C) :-
        /* lowercase letters */
        C > 96, C < 123.
in_word(C) :-
        /* numbers */
        C > 47, C < 58.
```

```prolog
in_word(C) :-
        (       [C] == "-"
        ;       [C] == "_"
        ).

/*
        Print file directly to the standard output
        stream (typically user's terminal)
*/

file_output(Filename) :-
        seeing(Was), see(Filename),
        repeat,
        get0(C),
        (       is_EOF(C)
        ;       put(C),
                fail
        ),
        seen, see(Was).

/* Synonym list */

meaning(Input,yes) :-
        member(Input,[y,yup,yeah,yes]),
        !.

meaning(Input,no) :-
        member(Input,[n,no,nope]),
        !.

meaning(Input,assistance) :-
        member(Input,
                [h,help,assistance,explain,advise,info]),
        !.


/* Auxiliary procedures : */


read_in(Input) :-
        read_till_return(List),
        (       is_a_number(List),
                number(Input,List)
        ;       name(Input,List)
        ).
```

```
read_till_return([A|B]) :-
        get0(A),
        A = 10,
        !,
        read_till_return(B).

read_till_return([]).

is_a_number([Element]) :-
        Element >= 48,
        Element =< 57.

is_a_number([Element|Rest]) :-
        Element >= 48,
        Element =< 57,
        is_a_number([Element]),
        is_a_number(Rest).



write_list([]).

write_list([Element|Rest]) :-
        tab(1),
        write(Element),
        write_list(Rest).


indent(I) :-
        nl,
        T is I * 3,
        tab(T).


write_line :-
        [Output_Separator] = "-",
        for(1,I,80), put(Output_Separator), fail.
write_line.
```

D The "Coupling Expert"

D.1 Start-up Procedure

```
# This command file starts up the "Coupling Expert" in a
# Unix environment by consulting all the components

ifprolog -c drive -c load -c assembly -c coupling \
        -c frame -c gen_frames -c reading \
        -c show -c fillout -c constraints \
        -c procedures -c requirement -c controlling \
        -c auxiliary_pred -c explanation -c metaknowledge
```

D.2 Module "drive"

```
frame(drive,general,
      rpm_independent_drive_frequency,
      value,[0]).


frame(drive,1,
      identifying_name,value,['AC_Motor I']).
frame(drive,1,
      ako,value,[general]).
frame(drive,1,
      torque_rating,value,[55]).
frame(drive,1,
      continuous_rpm,value,[710]).
frame(drive,1,
      angular_momentum,value,[0.064]).

frame(drive,2,
      identifying_name,value,['Rotary_Current_Motor 160 M4']).
frame(drive,2,
      ako,value,[general]).
frame(drive,2,
      torque_rating,value,[72.5]).
```

```
frame(drive,2,
      continuous_rpm,value,[1450]).
frame(drive,2,
      angular_momentum,value,[0.0735]).

frame(drive,3,
      identifying_name,value,['AC_Motor II']).
frame(drive,3,
      ako,value,[general]).
frame(drive,3,
      torque_rating,value,[100]).
frame(drive,3,
      continuous_rpm,value,[1450]).
frame(drive,3,
      angular_momentum,value,[0.06]).

frame(drive,4,
      identifying_name,value,['Dieselmotor 4 Cylinder']).
frame(drive,4,
      ako,value,[general]).
frame(drive,4,
      torque_rating,value,[162]).
frame(drive,4,
      continuous_rpm,value,[2500]).
frame(drive,4,
      angular_momentum,value,[0.089]).

frame(drive,5,
      identifying_name,value,['DC_Motor 160M']).
frame(drive,5,
      ako,value,[general]).
frame(drive,5,
      torque_rating,value,[191]).
frame(drive,5,
      continuous_rpm,value,[1000]).
frame(drive,5,
      angular_momentum,value,[5]).
```

D.3   Module "load"

```
frame(load,general,
      rpm_independent_drive_frequency,
      value,[0]).
```

```
frame(load,1,
      identifying_name,value,['Fan']).
frame(load,1,
      ako,value,[general]).
frame(load,1,
      torque_rating,value,[38]).
frame(load,1,
      angular_momentum,value,[5]).

frame(load,2,
      identifying_name,value,['Rotary_Pump']).
frame(load,2,
      ako,value,[general]).
frame(load,2,
      torque_rating,value,[69]).
frame(load,2,
      angular_momentum,value,[0.53]).

frame(load,3,
      identifying_name,value,['Rotary_Current_Generator I']).
frame(load,3,
      ako,value,[general]).
frame(load,3,
      torque_rating,value,[102]).
frame(load,3,
      angular_momentum,value,[0.56]).

frame(load,4,
      identifying_name,value,['Marine_Propeller']).
frame(load,4,
      ako,value,[general]).
frame(load,4,
      torque_rating,value,[150]).
frame(load,4,
      angular_momentum,value,[18]).

frame(load,5,
      identifying_name,value,['Rotary_Current_Generator II']).
frame(load,5,
      ako,value,[general]).
frame(load,5,
      torque_rating,value,[181]).
frame(load,5,
      angular_momentum,value,[242]).
```

D.4   Module "assembly"

```
frame(assembly,general,
      type_of_mounting,value,[axial]).



frame(assembly,1,
      identifying_name,value,['Assembly 1']).
frame(assembly,1,
      ako,value,[general]).
frame(assembly,1,
      temperature,value,[30]).
frame(assembly,1,
      axial_shaft_alignment,value,[0.5]).
frame(assembly,1,
      radial_shaft_alignment,value,[0.7]).
frame(assembly,1,
      angular_shaft_alignment,value,[1]).
frame(assembly,1,
      length_of_housing,value,[500]).
frame(assembly,1,
      diameter_of_housing,value,[400]).

frame(assembly,2,
      identifying_name,value,['Assembly 2']).
frame(assembly,2,
      ako,value,[general]).
frame(assembly,2,
      temperature,value,[50]).
frame(assembly,2,
      axial_shaft_alignment,value,[0.7]).
frame(assembly,2,
      radial_shaft_alignment,value,[0.9]).
frame(assembly,2,
      angular_shaft_alignment,value,[1.1]).
frame(assembly,2,
      length_of_housing,value,[200]).
frame(assembly,2,
      diameter_of_housing,value,[700]).


frame(assembly,3,
      identifying_name,value,['Assembly 3']).
frame(assembly,3,
      ako,value,[general]).
```

```
frame(assembly,3,
     temperature,value,[10]).
frame(assembly,3,
     axial_shaft_alignment,value,[0.2]).
frame(assembly,3,
     radial_shaft_alignment,value,[0.3]).
frame(assembly,3,
     angular_shaft_alignment,value,[0.8]).
frame(assembly,3,
     length_of_housing,value,[100]).
frame(assembly,3,
     diameter_of_housing,value,[100]).
```

D.5   Module "coupling"

```
frame(coupling,general,
     type_of_mounting,value,[axial]).


frame(coupling,'Series Stromag gr',
     ako,value,[general]).
frame(coupling,'Series Stromag gr',
     memory_function,value,[0.5]).
frame(coupling,'Series Stromag gr',
     semi_static_friction,value,[0.8]).
frame(coupling,'Series Stromag gr',
     characteristic,value,[1.1]).
frame(coupling,'Series Stromag gr',
     nominal_twisting_angle,value,[3.5]).
frame(coupling,'Series Stromag gr',
     angular_clearance,value,[2]).
frame(coupling,'Series Stromag gr',
     radial_clearance,value,[1]).
frame(coupling,'Series Stromag gr',
     axial_clearance,value,[4]).

frame(coupling,'Series Stromag pna',
     ako,value,[general]).
frame(coupling,'Series Stromag pna',
     memory_function,value,[0.515]).
frame(coupling,'Series Stromag pna',
     semi_static_friction,value,[0.416]).
frame(coupling,'Series Stromag pna',
     characteristic,value,[1.03]).
```

```
frame(coupling,'Series Stromag pna',
      nominal_twisting_angle,value,[28]).
frame(coupling,'Series Stromag pna',
      angular_clearance,value,[4]).
frame(coupling,'Series Stromag pna',
      radial_clearance,value,[4]).
frame(coupling,'Series Stromag pna',
      axial_clearance,value,[8]).
frame(coupling,'Series Stromag pna',
      type_of_mounting,value,[radial]).


frame(coupling,'Series Kauermann e',
      ako,value,[general]).
frame(coupling,'Series Kauermann e',
      memory_function,value,[0.79]).
frame(coupling,'Series Kauermann e',
      semi_static_friction,value,[0.4]).
frame(coupling,'Series Kauermann e',
      characteristic,value,[1.3]).
frame(coupling,'Series Kauermann e',
      nominal_twisting_angle,value,[4.8]).
frame(coupling,'Series Kauermann e',
      angular_clearance,value,[1]).
frame(coupling,'Series Kauermann e',
      radial_clearance,value,[0.8]).
frame(coupling,'Series Kauermann e'
      axial_clearance,value,[2]).


frame(coupling,'Series Rotex 80a',
      ako,value,[general]).
frame(coupling,'Series Rotex 80a',
      memory_function,value,[0.43]).
frame(coupling,'Series Rotex 80a',
      semi_static_friction,value,[0.59]).
frame(coupling,'Series Rotex 80a',
      characteristic,value,[1.5]).
frame(coupling,'Series Rotex 80a',
      nominal_twisting_angle,value,[3.2]).
frame(coupling,'Series Rotex 80a',
      angular_clearance,value,[1.5]).
frame(coupling,'Series Rotex 80a',
      radial_clearance,value,[0.8]).
frame(coupling,'Series Rotex 80a',
      axial_clearance,value,[2]).
```

```
frame(coupling,10,
      identifying_name,value,['Stromag gr 2']).
frame(coupling,10,
      ako,value,['Series Stromag gr']).
frame(coupling,10,
      torque_rating,value,[25]).
frame(coupling,10,
      angular_momentum,value,[0.03]).
frame(coupling,10,
      diameter,value,[75]).
frame(coupling,10,
      length,value,[80]).


frame(coupling,11,
      identifying_name,value,['Stromag gr 10']).
frame(coupling,11,
      ako,value,['Series Stromag gr']).
frame(coupling,11,
      torque_rating,value,[100]).
frame(coupling,11,
      angular_momentum,value,[0.22]).
frame(coupling,11,
      diameter,value,[112]).
frame(coupling,11,
      length,value,[125]).


frame(coupling,12,
      identifying_name,value,['Stromag gr 25']).
frame(coupling,12,
      ako,value,['Series Stromag gr']).
frame(coupling,12,
      torque_rating,value,[250]).
frame(coupling,12,
      angular_momentum,value,[0.89]).
frame(coupling,12,
      diameter,value,[150]).
frame(coupling,12,
      length,value,[155]).


frame(coupling,13,
      identifying_name,value,['Stromag gr 63']).
frame(coupling,13,
      ako,value,['Series Stromag gr']).
frame(coupling,13,
      torque_rating,value,[630]).
```

```
frame(coupling,13,
       angular_momentum,value,[4.13]).
frame(coupling,13,
       diameter,value,[210]).
frame(coupling,13,
       length,value,[215]).

frame(coupling,14,
       identifying_name,value,['Stromag gr 100']).
frame(coupling,14,
       ako,value,['Series Stromag gr']).
frame(coupling,14,
       torque_rating,value,[1000]).
frame(coupling,14,
       angular_momentum,value,[9.42]).
frame(coupling,14,
       diameter,value,[240]).
frame(coupling,14,
       length,value,[270]).


frame(coupling,20,
       identifying_name,value,['Stromag pna 1']).
frame(coupling,20,
       ako,value,['Series Stromag pna']).
frame(coupling,20,
       torque_rating,value,[10]).
frame(coupling,20,
       angular_momentum,value,[0.01]).
frame(coupling,20,
       diameter,value,[86]).
frame(coupling,20,
       length,value,[60]).

frame(coupling,21,
       identifying_name,value,['Stromag pna 6']).
frame(coupling,21,
       ako,value,['Series Stromag pna']).
frame(coupling,21,
       torque_rating,value,[60]).
frame(coupling,21,
       angular_momentum,value,[0.11]).
frame(coupling,21,
       diameter,value,[136]).
frame(coupling,21,
       length,value,[110]).
```

```
frame(coupling,22,
      identifying_name,value,['Stromag pna 40']).
frame(coupling,22,
      ako,value,['Series Stromag pna']).
frame(coupling,22,
      torque_rating,value,[320]).
frame(coupling,22,
      angular_momentum,value,[1.4]).
frame(coupling,22,
      diameter,value,[210]).
frame(coupling,22,
      length,value,[160]).

frame(coupling,23,
      identifying_name,value,['Stromag pna 125']).
frame(coupling,23,
      ako,value,['Series Stromag pna']).
frame(coupling,23,
      torque_rating,value,[1200]).
frame(coupling,23,
      angular_momentum,value,[9.6]).
frame(coupling,23,
      diameter,value,[310]).
frame(coupling,23,
      length,value,[240]).

frame(coupling,30,
      identifying_name,value,['Kauermann 0004 e']).
frame(coupling,30,
      ako,value,['Series Kauermann e']).
frame(coupling,30,
      torque_rating,value,[28.1]).
frame(coupling,30,
      angular_momentum,value,[0.013]).
frame(coupling,30,
      diameter,value,[82]).
frame(coupling,30,
      length,value,[92]).

frame(coupling,31,
      identifying_name,value,['Kauermann 0012 e']).
frame(coupling,31,
      ako,value,['Series Kauermann e']).
frame(coupling,31,
      torque_rating,value,[84.3]).
```

```
frame(coupling,31,
      angular_momentum,value,[0.062]).
frame(coupling,31,
      diameter,value,[115]).
frame(coupling,31,
      length,value,[112]).

frame(coupling,32,
      identifying_name,value,['Kauermann 003 e']).
frame(coupling,32,
      ako,value,['Series Kauermann e']).
frame(coupling,32,
      torque_rating,value,[211]).
frame(coupling,32,
      angular_momentum,value,[0.321]).
frame(coupling,32,
      diameter,value,[165]).
frame(coupling,32,
      length,value,[132]).

frame(coupling,33,
      identifying_name,value,['Kauermann 008 e']).
frame(coupling,33,
      ako,value,['Series Kauermann e']).
frame(coupling,33,
      torque_rating,value,[562]).
frame(coupling,33,
      angular_momentum,value,[1.1]).
frame(coupling,33,
      diameter,value,[217]).
frame(coupling,33,
      length,value,[163]).

frame(coupling,34,
      identifying_name,value,['Kauermann 02 e']).
frame(coupling,34,
      ako,value,['Series Kauermann e']).
frame(coupling,34,
      torque_rating,value,[1405]).
frame(coupling,34,
      angular_momentum,value,[3.2]).
frame(coupling,34,
      diameter,value,[272]).
frame(coupling,34,
      length,value,[223]).
```

```
frame(coupling,40,
      identifying_name,value,['Rotex 80a 9']).
frame(coupling,40,
      ako,value,['Series Rotex 80a']).
frame(coupling,40,
      torque_rating,value,[1.8]).
frame(coupling,40,
      angular_momentum,value,[0.00003]).
frame(coupling,40,
      diameter,value,[20]).
frame(coupling,40,
      length,value,[30]).


frame(coupling,41,
      identifying_name,value,['Rotex 80a 19']).
frame(coupling,41,
      ako,value,['Series Rotex 80a']).
frame(coupling,41,
      torque_rating,value,[4.9]).
frame(coupling,41,
      angular_momentum,value,[0.0005]).
frame(coupling,41,
      diameter,value,[40]).
frame(coupling,41,
      length,value,[66]).


frame(coupling,42,
      identifying_name,value,['Rotex 80a 28']).
frame(coupling,42,
      ako,value,['Series Rotex 80a']).
frame(coupling,42,
      torque_rating,value,[46]).
frame(coupling,42,
      angular_momentum,value,[0.004]).
frame(coupling,42,
      diameter,value,[65]).
frame(coupling,42,
      length,value,[90]).


frame(coupling,43,
      identifying_name,value,['Rotex 80a 42']).
frame(coupling,43,
      ako,value,['Series Rotex 80a']).
frame(coupling,43,
      torque_rating,value,[130]).
```

```
frame(coupling,43,
      angular_momentum,value,[0.04]).
frame(coupling,43,
      diameter,value,[95]).
frame(coupling,43,
      length,value,[126]).

frame(coupling,44,
      identifying_name,value,['Rotex 80a 55']).
frame(coupling,44,
      ako,value,['Series Rotex 80a']).
frame(coupling,44,
      torque_rating,value,[180]).
frame(coupling,44,
      angular_momentum,value,[0.12]).
frame(coupling,44,
      diameter,value,[120]).
frame(coupling,44,
      length,value,[160]).

frame(coupling,45,
      identifying_name,value,['Rotex 80a 75']).
frame(coupling,45,
      ako,value,['Series Rotex 80a']).
frame(coupling,45,
      torque_rating,value,[475]).
frame(coupling,45,
      angular_momentum,value,[0.54]).
frame(coupling,45,
      diameter,value,[160]).
frame(coupling,45,
      length,value,[210]).
```

D.6   Module "frame"

```
search_for(Type,Frame,Slot,Facet,Data_Item) :-
      clause(frame(Type,Frame,Slot,Facet,Data_Item),_).


is_instance(Type,Name) :-
      search_for(Type,Name,identifying_name,_,_).
```

```
ask(Type,Frame,Slot,Data_Item) :-
    (    search_for(Type,Frame,Slot,value,Data_Item)
    ;    search_for(Type,gen_Frame,Slot,if_needed,Proc),
         execute(Proc,Type,Frame,Slot,Data_Item)
    ;    search_for(Type,Frame,ako,value,[Parent_Frame]),
         ask(Type,Parent_Frame,Slot,Data_Item)
    ),
    !.

ask_coupling(Slot,Data_Item) :-
    current(coupling,Name),
    ask(coupling,Name,Slot,[Data_Item]).

ask_drive(Slot,Data_Item) :-
    current(drive,Name),
    ask(drive,Name,Slot,[Data_Item]).

ask_load(Slot,Data_Item) :-
    current(load,Name),
    ask(load,Name,Slot,[Data_Item]).

ask_assembly(Slot,Data_Item) :-
    current(assembly,Name),
    ask(assembly,Name,Slot,[Data_Item]).

ask_requirement(Slot,Data_Item) :-
    ask(requirement,current,Slot,[Data_Item]).


add(Type,Frame,Slot,Facet,Data_Item) :-
    (        retract(frame(Type,Frame,Slot,Facet,Old)),
             asserta(frame(Type,Frame,Slot,
                           Facet,[Data_Item|Old]))
    ;        asserta(frame(Type,Frame,Slot,
                           Facet,[Data_Item]))
    ),
    (        Facet = value,
             frame(Type,gen_Frame,Slot,if_added,Proc),
             execute(Proc,Type,Frame,Slot,[Data_Item])
    ;        true
    ),
    !.
```

```
delete(Type,Frame,Slot,Facet) :-
        (          retract(frame(Type,Frame,Slot,
                              Facet,Data_Item)),
                   (       Facet = value,
                           frame(Type,gen_Frame,Slot,
                                 if_removed,Proc),
                           execute(Proc,Type,Frame,
                                     Slot,Data_Item)
                   ;       true
                   )
        ;          true
        ).

delete(Type,Frame,Slot) :-
        (          delete(Type,Frame,Slot,Facet),
                   fail
        ;          true
        ).

delete(Type,Frame) :-
        (          delete(Type,Frame,Slot),
                   fail
        ;          true
        ).

execute([Proc],Type,Frame,Slot,[Data_Item]) :-
        Attachment =.. [Proc,Type,Frame,Slot,Data_Item],
        Attachment.


examine(Name,Result) :-
        note(coupling,Name,current),
        delete(requirement,current),
        criteria(List),
        member(Criterion,List),
        examine_constraint(Criterion,Result),
        Result = [],
        !.

examine(_,[]).

examine_constraint(Criterion,Result) :-
        constraint(Criterion,Result),
        !.
```

D.7 Module "gen_frames"

```
frame(drive,gen_Frame,
      identifying_name,
      default,[new_drive]).

frame(drive,gen_Frame,
      identifying_name,
      prefer,[]).

frame(drive,gen_Frame,
      identifying_name,
      require,[]).

frame(drive,gen_Frame,
      ako,
      default,[general]).

frame(drive,gen_Frame,
      ako,
      prefer,[in_list([general])]).

frame(drive,gen_Frame,
      ako,
      require,[in_list([general])]).

frame(drive,gen_Frame,
      rpm_independent_drive_frequency,
      default,[0]).

frame(drive,gen_Frame,
      rpm_independent_drive_frequency,
      prefer,[less_than_or_equal_to(2000)]).

frame(drive,gen_Frame,
      rpm_independent_drive_frequency,
      require,[less_than_or_equal_to(5000)]).

frame(drive,gen_Frame,
      angular_momentum,
      default,[1]).

frame(drive,gen_Frame,
      angular_momentum,
      prefer,[between(0.5,500)]).
```

```
frame(drive,gen_Frame,
      angular_momentum,
      require,[less_than_or_equal_to(12000)]).

frame(drive,gen_Frame,
      continuous_rpm,
      default,[1500]).

frame(drive,gen_Frame,
      continuous_rpm,
      prefer,[between(500,4000)]).

frame(drive,gen_Frame,
      continuous_rpm,
      require,[less_than_or_equal_to(10000)]).

frame(drive,gen_Frame,
      torque_rating,
      default,[150]).

frame(drive,gen_Frame,
      torque_rating,
      prefer,[between(50,200)]).

frame(drive,gen_Frame,
      torque_rating,
      require,[less_than_or_equal_to(100000)]).


frame(load,gen_Frame,
      identifying_name,
      default,[new_load]).

frame(load,gen_Frame,
      identifying_name,
      prefer,[]).

frame(load,gen_Frame,
      identifying_name,
      require,[]).

frame(load,gen_Frame,
      ako,
      default,[general]).
```

```
frame(load,gen_Frame,
      ako,
      prefer,[in_list([general])]).

frame(load,gen_Frame,
      ako,
      require,[in_list([general])]).

frame(load,gen_Frame,
      rpm_independent_drive_frequency,
      default,[0]).

frame(load,gen_Frame,
      rpm_independent_drive_frequency,
      prefer,[less_than_or_equal_to(2000)]).

frame(load,gen_Frame,
      rpm_independent_drive_frequency,
      require,[less_than_or_equal_to(5000)]).

frame(load,gen_Frame,
      angular_momentum,
      default,[1]).

frame(load,gen_Frame,
      angular_momentum,
      prefer,[between(0.5,500)]).

frame(load,gen_Frame,
      angular_momentum,
      require,[less_than_or_equal_to(12000)]).

frame(load,gen_Frame,
      torque_rating,
      default,[0]).

frame(load,gen_Frame,
      torque_rating,
      prefer,[less_than_or_equal_to(10000)]).

frame(load,gen_Frame,
      torque_rating,
      require,[less_than_or_equal_to(100000)]).
```

```
frame(coupling,gen_Frame,
      identifying_name,
      default,[new_coupling]).

frame(coupling,gen_Frame,
      identifying_name,
      prefer,[]).

frame(coupling,gen_Frame,
      identifying_name,
      require,[]).

frame(coupling,gen_Frame,
      ako,
      default,['Series Stromag gr']).

frame(coupling,gen_Frame,
      ako,
      prefer,[in_list(['Series Stromag gr',
                       'Series Stromag pna',
                       'Series Kauermann e',
                       'Series Rotex 80a'
                      ])]).

frame(coupling,gen_Frame,
      ako,
      require,[in_list(['Series Stromag gr',
                        'Series Stromag pna',
                        'Series Kauermann e',
                        'Series Rotex 80a'
                       ])]).

frame(coupling,gen_Frame,
      type_of_mounting,
      default,[axial]).

frame(coupling,gen_Frame,
      type_of_mounting,
      prefer,[in_list([axial,pluggable,radial])]).

frame(coupling,gen_Frame,
      type_of_mounting,
      require,[in_list([axial,pluggable,radial])]).

frame(coupling,gen_Frame,
      torque_rating,
      default,[150]).
```

```
frame(coupling,gen_Frame,
      torque_rating,
      prefer,[between(50,200)]).

frame(coupling,gen_Frame,
      torque_rating,
      require,[less_than_or_equal_to(100000)]).

frame(coupling,gen_Frame,
      angular_momentum,
      default,[1]).

frame(coupling,gen_Frame,
      angular_momentum,
      prefer,[between(0.5,500)]).

frame(coupling,gen_Frame,
      angular_momentum,
      require,[less_than_or_equal_to(12000)]).

frame(coupling,gen_Frame,
      diameter,
      default,[2000]).

frame(coupling,gen_Frame,
      diameter,
      prefer,[between(500,2000)]).

frame(coupling,gen_Frame,
      diameter,
      require,[between(10,2000)]).

frame(coupling,gen_Frame,
      length,
      default,[1200]).

frame(coupling,gen_Frame,
      length,
      prefer,[between(500,1500)]).

frame(coupling,gen_Frame,
      length,
      require,[less_than_or_equal_to(2000)]).

frame(coupling,gen_Frame,
      memory_function,
      default,[1.5]).
```

```
frame(coupling,gen_Frame,
      memory_function,
      prefer,[between(0.5,2.5)]).

frame(coupling,gen_Frame,
      memory_function,
      require,[less_than_or_equal_to(3)]).

frame(coupling,gen_Frame,
      semi_static_friction,
      default,[2]).

frame(coupling,gen_Frame,
      semi_static_friction,
      prefer,[less_than_or_equal_to(3)]).

frame(coupling,gen_Frame,
      semi_static_friction,
      require,[less_than_or_equal_to(5)]).

frame(coupling,gen_Frame,
      characteristic,
      default,[1.5]).

frame(coupling,gen_Frame,
      characteristic,
      prefer,[between(1,2)]).

frame(coupling,gen_Frame,
      characteristic,
      require,[between(0.5,2.5)]).

frame(coupling,gen_Frame,
      angular_clearance,
      default,[10]).

frame(coupling,gen_Frame,
      angular_clearance,
      prefer,[between(7,10)]).

frame(coupling,gen_Frame,
      angular_clearance,
      require,[less_than_or_equal_to(10)]).

frame(coupling,gen_Frame,
      axial_clearance,
      default,[20]).
```

```
frame(coupling,gen_Frame,
     axial_clearance,
     prefer,[between(10,20)]).

frame(coupling,gen_Frame,
     axial_clearance,
     require,[less_than_or_equal_to(20)]).

frame(coupling,gen_Frame,
     radial_clearance,
     default,[5]).

frame(coupling,gen_Frame,
     radial_clearance,
     prefer,[between(4,5)]).

frame(coupling,gen_Frame,
     radial_clearance,
     require,[less_than_or_equal_to(5)]).



frame(assembly,gen_Frame,
     identifying_name,
     default,[new_assembly]).

frame(assembly,gen_Frame,
     identifying_name,
     prefer,[]).

frame(assembly,gen_Frame,
     identifying_name,
     require,[]).

frame(assembly,gen_Frame,
     ako,
     default,[general]).

frame(assembly,gen_Frame,
     ako,
     prefer,[in_list([general])]).

frame(assembly,gen_Frame,
     ako,
     require,[in_list([general])]).
```

```
frame(assembly,gen_Frame,
      type_of_mounting,
      default,[axial]).

frame(assembly,gen_Frame,
      type_of_mounting,
      prefer,[in_list([axial,pluggable,radial])]).

frame(assembly,gen_Frame,
      type_of_mounting,
      require,[in_list([axial,pluggable,radial])]).

frame(assembly,gen_Frame,
      diameter_of_housing,
      default,[2000]).

frame(assembly,gen_Frame,
      diameter_of_housing,
      prefer,[between(500,2000)]).

frame(assembly,gen_Frame,
      diameter_of_housing,
      require,[between(10,2000)]).

frame(assembly,gen_Frame,
      length_of_housing,
      default,[1200]).

frame(assembly,gen_Frame,
      length_of_housing,
      prefer,[between(500,1500)]).

frame(assembly,gen_Frame,
      length_of_housing,
      require,[less_than_or_equal_to(2000)]).

frame(assembly,gen_Frame,
      axial_shaft_alignment,
      default,[0]).

frame(assembly,gen_Frame,
      axial_shaft_alignment,
      prefer,[less_than_or_equal_to(5)]).

frame(assembly,gen_Frame,
      axial_shaft_alignment,
      require,[less_than_or_equal_to(20)]).
```

```
frame(assembly,gen_Frame,
     radial_shaft_alignment,
     default,[0]).

frame(assembly,gen_Frame,
     radial_shaft_alignment,
     prefer,[less_than_or_equal_to(2)]).

frame(assembly,gen_Frame,
     radial_shaft_alignment,
     require,[less_than_or_equal_to(5)]).

frame(assembly,gen_Frame,
     angular_shaft_alignment,
     default,[0]).

frame(assembly,gen_Frame,
     angular_shaft_alignment,
     prefer,[less_than_or_equal_to(5)]).

frame(assembly,gen_Frame,
     angular_shaft_alignment,
     require,[less_than_or_equal_to(10)]).

frame(assembly,gen_Frame,
     temperature,
     default,[60]).

frame(assembly,gen_Frame,
     temperature,
     prefer,[between(40,60)]).

frame(assembly,gen_Frame,
     temperature,
     require,[between(-20,80)]).
```

D.8 Module "reading"

```
read_in(Input) :-
     read_till_return(List),
     (        is_a_number(List),
              number(Input,List)
     ;        name(Input,List)
     ),
     !.
```

```
read_till_return([A|B]) :-
        get0(A),
        A = 10,
        !,
        read_till_return(B).

read_till_return([]).

is_a_number([Element]) :-
        Element >= 48,
        Element =< 57.

is_a_number([Element|Rest]) :-
        Element >= 48,
        Element =< 57,
        is_a_number(Rest).
```

D.9   Module "show"

```
display_instances(Type,Name) :-
        display_instances(Type,Name,1).

display_instances(Type,Name,I) :-
        search_for(Type,Name,_,_,_),
        !, nl,
        I8 is I * 8,
        tab(I8),
        write(Name),
        (       search_for(Type,Instance,ako,value,[Name]),
                J is I + 1,
                display_instances(Type,Instance,J),
                fail
        ;       true
        ).


display_frame(Type,Name) :-
        (       search_for(Type,Name,Slot,value,Data_Item),
                nl,
                write(Slot),
                write(' :'),
                write_list(Data_Item),
                fail
        ;       true
        ).
```

```
write_list([]).

write_list([Element|Rest]) :-
        write(' '),
        write(Element),
        write_list(Rest).


display_existing_objects(Type) :-
        (       nl,nl,
                search_for(Type,Name,identifying_name,
                                    value,[Data_Item]),
                write(Name),
                tab(5),
                write(Data_Item),
                nl,
                fail
        ;       true
        ).
```

D.10   Module "fillout"

```
new_frame(Type,Name) :-
        (       frame(Type,gen_Frame,Slot,default,Data_Item),
                read_value_entered(Type,Name,Slot),
                fail
        ;       nl,
                write('New frame: '),
                write(Name),
                display_frame(Type,Name)
        ).

read_value_entered(Type,Name,Slot) :-
        nl,
        write(Slot),
        write(': '),
        read_in(Input),
        recognize(Input,Type,Name,Slot),
        !.

recognize(Input,Type,Name,Slot) :-
        member(Input,[abort,break,bye,end]),
        !,
        Input,
        read_value_entered(Type,Name,Slot).
```

```
recognize(Input,Type,Name,Slot) :-
        member(Input,[help,assistance,info]),
        !,
        write_help_list,
        read_value_entered(Type,Name,Slot).


recognize('',Type,Name,Slot) :-
        !.


recognize('.',Type,Name,Slot) :-
        !,
        frame(Type,gen_Frame,Slot,default,[Data_Item]),
        add(Type,Name,Slot,value,Data_Item).


recognize('*',Type,Name,Slot) :-
        !,
        nl,
        frame(Type,gen_Frame,Slot,default,Data_Item),
        write('Default-Value : '),
        write_list(Data_Item),
        nl,
        read_value_entered(Type,Name,Slot).


recognize(?,Type,Name,Slot) :-
        !,
        nl,
        (       frame(Type,gen_Frame,Slot,prefer,Data_Item),
                write_constraint(Data_Item)
        ;       write('No preferred value present.')
        ),
        nl,
        read_value_entered(Type,Name,Slot).


recognize(??,Type,Name,Slot) :-
        !,
        nl,
        (       frame(Type,gen_Frame,Slot,require,Data_Item),
                write_constraint(Data_Item)
        ;       write('No required values present.')
        ),
        nl,
        read_value_entered(Type,Name,Slot).
```

```prolog
recognize(Input,Type,Name,Slot) :-
        !,
        frame(Type,gen_Frame,Slot,require,Data_Item),
        (       check_these_constraints(Input,Data_Item),
                !,
                add(Type,Name,Slot,value,Input)
        ;       write_constraint(Data_Item),
                read_value_entered(Type,Name,Slot)
        ).


write_help_list :-
        nl,
        write('Possible commands :'),
        nl,
        write('assistance,help,info  ==> '),
        write('display this list.'),
        nl,
        write('?                      ==> '),
        write('display some typical values.'),
        nl,
        write('??                     ==> '),
        write('display the limits on values.'),
        nl,
        write('*                      ==> '),
        write('display the default value.'),
        nl,
        write('.                      ==> '),
        write('take the default value.'),
        nl,
        write('<return>               ==> '),
        write('omit this slot.'),
        nl.

write_constraint([]).

write_constraint([Constraint|Rest]) :-
        write_this_constraint(Constraint),
        write_constraint(Rest).

write_this_constraint(in_list(L)) :-
        nl,
        write('Possible inputs :'),
        nl,
        write_list(L).
```

```
write_this_constraint(between(A,B)) :-
        nl,
        write('The value must lie between '),
        write(A),
        write(' and '),
        write(B),
        write('.').


write_this_constraint(greater_than(A)) :-
        nl,
        write('The value must be greater than '),
        write(A),
        write('.').


write_this_constraint(less_than(A)) :-
        nl,
        write('The value must be less than '),
        write(A),
        write('.').

write_this_constraint(less_than_or_equal_to(A)) :-
        nl,
        write('The value must be less than or equal to '),
        write(A),
        write('.').


check_these_constraints(_,[]).

check_these_constraints(Input,[Constraint|Rest]) :-
        check_this_constraint(Input,Constraint),
        check_these_constraints(Input,Rest).


check_this_constraint(Input,in_list(L)) :-
        member(Input,L).

check_this_constraint(Input,between(A,B)) :-
        numeric(Input),
        Input >= A,
        Input =< B.

check_this_constraint(Input,greater_than(A)) :-
        numeric(Input),
        Input > A.
```

```
check_this_constraint(Input,less_than(A)) :-
      numeric(Input),
      Input ‹ A.

check_this_constraint(Input,less_than_or_equal_to(A)) :-
      numeric(Input),
      Input =‹ A.
```

D.11   Module "constraints"

```
constraint(type_of_mounting,[]) :-
      ask_assembly(type_of_mounting,Assembly_Type),
      ask_coupling(type_of_mounting,Coupling_Type),
      Assembly_Type == Coupling_Type.

constraint(axial_shaft_alignment,[]) :-
      ask_assembly(axial_shaft_alignment,S_ax),
      ask_coupling(axial_clearance,C_ax),
      S_ax ‹ C_ax.

constraint(radial_shaft_alignment,[]) :-
      ask_assembly(radial_shaft_alignment,S_r),
      ask_coupling(radial_clearance,C_r),
      S_r ‹ C_r.

constraint(angular_shaft_alignment,[]) :-
      ask_assembly(angular_shaft_alignment,S_ang),
      ask_coupling(angular_clearance,C_ang),
      S_ang ‹ C_ang.

constraint(length_of_housing,[]) :-
      ask_assembly(length_of_housing,L_max),
      ask_coupling(length,L_C),
      L_C ‹ L_max.

constraint(diameter_of_housing,[]) :-
      ask_assembly(diameter_of_housing,D_max),
      ask_coupling(diameter,D_C),
      D_C ‹ D_max.

constraint(coupling_torque_rating,[]) :-
      ask_coupling(torque_rating,T_CN),
      ask_requirement(temperature_factor,S_theta),
      ask_requirement(torque,T_N),
      T_CN › T_N * S_theta.
```

```
constraint(drive_frequency,[]) :-
        ask_requirement(intrinsic_oscillation_at_nominal_load,
                        F_e),
        ask_drive(rpm_independent_drive_frequency,F),
        (       F_e < 0.9 * F
        ;       F_e > 1.1 * F
        ).

constraint(load_frequency,[]) :-
        ask_requirement(intrinsic_oscillation_at_nominal_load,
                        F_e),
        ask_load(rpm_independent_drive_frequency,F),
        (       F_e < 0.9 * F
        ;       F_e > 1.1 * F
        ).

constraint(rated_frequency,[]) :-
        ask_requirement(intrinsic_oscillation_at_nominal_load,
                        F_e),
        ask_requirement(rated_frequency,F),
        (       F_e < 0.9 * F
        ;       F_e > 1.1 * F
        ).

constraint(Criterion,[Criterion]).
```

D.12   Module "procedures"

```
calculate_dynamic_coupling_stiffness(Type,Frame,Slot,
                                     Data_Item) :-
        ask_coupling(nominal_twisting_angle,Phi),
        ask_coupling(torque_rating,T_CN),
        ask_coupling(semi_static_friction,Gdr),
        ask_coupling(memory_function,Mma),
        ask_requirement(elastic_coupling_stiffness,C_Tel),
        Data_Item is (Gdr + Mma) * T_CN / Phi + C_Tel,
        asserta(frame(Type,Frame,Slot,value,[Data_Item])).

calculate_elastic_coupling_stiffness(Type,Frame,Slot,
                                     Data_Item) :-
        ask_coupling(nominal_twisting_angle,Phi),
        ask_coupling(torque_rating,T_CN),
        ask_requirement(characteristic_curve_factor,M_1),
        ask_requirement(stretching,Epsilon),
```

```
          Data_Item is (Epsilon ^ 2 * (1 - M_1) * 3 + M_1)
                          * T_CN / Phi,
          asserta(frame(Type,Frame,Slot,value,[Data_Item])).

calculate_stretching(Type,Frame,Slot,Data_Item) :-
          ask_coupling(characteristic,Lambda),
          ask_requirement(normed_nominal_moment,T),
          (    Lambda = 1,
               !,
               Data_Item is T
          ;    ask_requirement(characteristic_curve_factor,M_1),
               P is M_1 / (1 - M_1),
               Q is T / (M_1 - 1) / 2,
               D is sqrt(P ^ 3 / 27 + Q x5E 2),
               U is (D - Q) ^ (1 / 3),
               ZZ is (D * Q) * (-1),
               S is sign(ZZ),
               Z is abs(ZZ),
               V is (Z ^ (1 / 3)) * S,
               Data_Item is U + V
          ),
          asserta(frame(Type,Frame,Slot,value,[Data_Item])).

calculate_intrinsic_oscillation_at_nominal_load(
                        Type,Frame,Slot,Data_Item) :-
          Pi is 3.1416,
          ask_requirement(
          total_drive_angular_momentum,I_Dtot),
          ask_requirement(
          total_load_angular_momentum,I_Ltot),
          ask_requirement(
          dynamic_coupling_stiffness,C_Tdyn),
          Data_Item is sqrt((C_Tdyn/I_Dtot)+(C_Tdyn/I_Ltot))
                                          /2/Pi,
          asserta(frame(Type,Frame,Slot,value,[Data_Item])).

calculate_nominal_frequency(Type,Frame,Slot,Data_Item) :-
          ask_drive(continuous_rpm,N),
          Data_Item is N / 60,
          asserta(frame(Type,Frame,Slot,value,[Data_Item])).

calculate_total_drive_angular_momentum(
          Type,Frame,Slot,Data_Item) :-
          ask_drive(angular_momentum,I_D),
          ask_coupling(angular_momentum,I_C),
```

```
                Data_Item is I_C / 2 + I_D,
                asserta(frame(Type,Frame,Slot,value,[Data_Item])).

        calculate_total_load_angular_momentum(
                Type,Frame,Slot,Data_Item) :-
                ask_load(angular_momentum,I_L),
                ask_coupling(angular_momentum,I_C),
                Data_Item is I_C / 2 + I_L,
                asserta(frame(Type,Frame,Slot,value,[Data_Item])).

        calculate_characteristic_factor(Type,Frame,Slot,Data_Item) :-
                ask_coupling(characteristic,Lambda),
                Data_Item is (3 - Lambda) / 2,
                asserta(frame(Type,Frame,Slot,value,[Data_Item])).

        calculate_temperature_factor(Type,Frame,Slot,Data_Item) :-
                ask_assembly(temperature,Theta),
                (       Theta < 30,
                        !,
                        Data_Item is 1
                ;       Theta < 40,
                        !,
                        Data_Item is 1.1
                ;       Theta < 60,
                        !,
                        Data_Item is 1.4
                ;       Data_Item is 1.8
                ),
                asserta(frame(Type,Frame,Slot,value,[Data_Item])).

        calculate_normed_nominal_moment(Type,Frame,Slot,Data_Item) :-
                ask_coupling(torque_rating,T_CN),
                ask_requirement(torque,T_N),
                Data_Item is T_N / T_CN,
                asserta(frame(Type,Frame,Slot,value,[Data_Item])).

        calculate_torque(Type,Frame,Slot,Data_Item) :-
                ask_drive(torque_rating,T_DN),
                ask_load(torque_rating,T_LN),
                (       T_DN < T_LN,
                        !,
                        Data_Item is T_DN
                ;       Data_Item is T_LN
                ),
                asserta(frame(Type,Frame,Slot,value,[Data_Item])).
```

D.13   Module "requirement"

```
frame(requirement,gen_Frame,
      dynamic_coupling_stiffness,if_needed,
      [calculate_dynamic_coupling_stiffness]).

frame(requirement,gen_Frame,
      elastic_coupling_stiffness,if_needed,
      [calculate_elastic_coupling_stiffness]).

frame(requirement,gen_Frame,
      stretching,if_needed,
      [calculate_stretching]).

frame(requirement,gen_Frame,
      intrinsic_oscillation_at_nominal_load,if_needed,
      [calculate_intrinsic_oscillation_at_nominal_load]).

frame(requirement,gen_Frame,
      rated_frequency,if_needed,
      [calculate_nominal_frequency]).

frame(requirement,gen_Frame,
      total_drive_angular_momentum,if_needed,
      [calculate_total_drive_angular_momentum]).

frame(requirement,gen_Frame,
      total_load_angular_momentum,if_needed,
      [calculate_total_load_angular_momentum]).

frame(requirement,gen_Frame,
      characteristic_curve_factor,if_needed,
      [calculate_characteristic_factor]).

frame(requirement,gen_Frame,
      temperature_factor,if_needed,
      [calculate_temperature_factor]).

frame(requirement,gen_Frame,
      normed_nominal_moment,if_needed,
      [calculate_normed_nominal_moment]).

frame(requirement,gen_Frame,
      torque,if_needed,
      [calculate_torque]).
```

D.14   Module "controlling"

```prolog
start :-
        repeat,
        main_menu(Code_Number),
        Code_Number = end.

main_menu(Code_Number) :-
        menu_title('Main Menu'),
        nl,write('1                      enter objects
        nl,write('2                      select object
        nl,write('3                      display objec
        nl,
        nl,write('end                    end'),
        end_of_menu,
        read_in(Code_Number),
        deal_with(main_menu,Code_Number),
        !.

deal_with(main_menu,Code_Number) :-
        transform(main_menu,Code_Number,Function),
        Function,
        !.

transform(main_menu,1,enter).
transform(main_menu,2,select).
transform(main_menu,3,display_it).
transform(main_menu,end,true).

transform(menu,1,drive).
transform(menu,2,load).
transform(menu,3,assembly).
transform(menu,4,coupling).
transform(menu,end,back).

transform(_,_,invalid).



enter :-
        repeat,
        enter(Code_Number),
        Code_Number = end.
```

```
enter(Code_Number) :-
        menu_title('Compiling Objects'),
        nl,write('1             Drive Side'),
        nl,write('2             Load Side'),
        nl,write('3             Assembly'),
        nl,write('4             Coupling'),
        nl,
        nl,write('end           back to the Main Menu'),
        end_of_menu,
        read_in(Code_Number),
        deal_with(enter,Code_Number),
        !.

deal_with(enter,Code_Number) :-
        transform(menu,Code_Number,Type),
        enter_object(Type),
        !.

enter_object(back) :-
        !.

enter_object(invalid) :-
        invalid,
        !.

enter_object(Type) :-
        nl,nl,
        write('Number : '),
        read_in(Name),
        new_frame(Type,Name).



select :-
        repeat,
        select(Code_Number),
        Code_Number = end.

select(Code_Number) :-
        menu_title('Object Selection'),
        nl,write('1             Drive Side'),
        nl,write('2             Load Side'),
        nl,write('3             Assembly'),
        nl,write('4             Coupling'),
        nl,
```

```
                nl,write('end                 back to the Main Me
                end_of_menu,
                read_in(Code_Number),
                deal_with(select,Code_Number),
                !.

    deal_with(select,Code_Number) :-
                transform(menu,Code_Number,Type),
                select_objects(Type).

    select_objects(back) :-
                !.

    select_objects(invalid) :-
                invalid,
                .!.


    select_objects(coupling) :-
            (           current(assembly,0),
                        nl,nl,
                        write('The assembly'),
                        write(' remains to be selected')
            ;           current(drive,0),
                        nl,nl,
                        write('The drive side'),
                        write(' remains to be selected')
            ;           current(load,0),
                        nl,nl,
                        write('The load side'),
                        write(' remains to be selected')
            ),
            nl,nl,
            !.

    select_objects(coupling) :-
            repeat,
            select_objects(coupling,Code_Number),
            Code_Number = end.

    select_objects(coupling,Code_Number) :-
            menu_title('Coupling Selection'),
            nl,write('p          primitive selection'),
            nl,write('m          selection using metakno
```

```
        nl,
        nl,write('end          end'),
        end_of_menu,
        read_in(Code_Number),
        deal_with(select_objects,coupling,Code_Number),
        !.


deal_with(select_objects,coupling,end) :-
        !.


deal_with(select_objects,coupling,m) :-
        metaknowledge,
        !.


deal_with(select_objects,coupling,p) :-
        !,
        (       is_instance(coupling,Name),
                examine(Name,List),
                write_protocol(partial,List),
                List == [],
                !,
                write_result(Name)
        ;       nl,
                write('A suitable coupling could '),
                write('not be found !'),
                nl
        ).


deal_with(select_objects,coupling,Name) :-
        (       not is_instance(coupling,Name),
                nl,write('No such coupling exists'),
                nl
        ;       examine_coupling(Name)
        ).




select_objects(Type) :-
        menu_title('Available ',Type),
        display_existing_objects(Type),
        end_of_menu,
        read_in(Code_Number),
        note(Type,Code_Number,current),
```

```
display_it :-
      repeat,
      display_it(Code_Number),
      Code_Number = end.

display_it(Code_Number) :-
      menu_title('Display Objects'),
      nl,write('1              Drive Side'),
      nl,write('2              Load Side'),
      nl,write('3              Assembly'),
      nl,write('4              Coupling'),
      nl,
      nl,write('end            back to the Main Me
      end_of_menu,
      read_in(Code_Number),
      deal_with(display_it,Code_Number),
      !.

deal_with(display_it,Code_Number) :-
      transform(menu,Code_Number,Type),
      display_objects(Type),
      !.

display_objects(back) :-
      !.

display_objects(invalid) :-
      invalid.

display_objects(Type) :-
      repeat,
      display_objects(Type,Code_Number),
      Code_Number = end.

display_objects(Type,Code_Number) :-
      menu_title('Display ',Type),
      nl,write('all        show all instances'),
      nl,write('current    show current object'),
      nl,write('N          show object N'),
      nl,
      nl,write('end            back to the Main Menu'
      end_of_menu,
      read_in(Code_Number),
      deal_with(display_objects,Type,Code_Number),
```

```
write_out(drive) :-
        write('Drive Sides').

write_out(load) :-
        write('Load Sides').

write_out(assembly) :-
        write('Assembly').

write_out(coupling) :-
        write('Couplings').



deal_with(display_objects,Type,end).

deal_with(display_objects,Type,all) :-
        display_instances(Type,general,1).

deal_with(display_objects,Type,current) :-
        current(Type,Name),
        display_frame(Type,Name).

deal_with(display_objects,Type,Name) :-
        (       not is_instance(Type,Name),
                nl,write('No such object exists'),
                nl
        ;       display_frame(Type,Name)
        ).
```

D.15 Module "auxiliary_pred"

```
assistance :-
        nl,
        write('Please enter the word "start."').

note(Type,Name,current) :-
        retract(current(Type,_)),
        asserta(current(Type,Name)).

current(coupling,0).
current(drive,0).
current(load,0).
current(assembly,0).
```

```
protocol(0,0,0,0,_,[]).

line :-
        write('*************************'),
        write('*************************').

menu_title(Text) :-
        nl,line,
        nl,tab(14),
        write(Text),
        nl,line,nl,nl.

menu_title(Text,Type) :-
        nl,line,
        .nl,tab(14),
        write(Text),
        write_out(Type),
        nl,line,nl,nl.

end_of_menu :-
        nl,line,
        nl,write('Please enter your choice ==> ').

indent(Text) :-
        nl,tab(10),
        write(Text).

invalid :-
        nl,write('Input is invalid !').


criteria(
        [
        type_of_mounting,
        axial_shaft_alignment,
        radial_shaft_alignment,
        angular_shaft_alignment,
        length_of_housing,
        diameter_of_housing,
        coupling_torque_rating,
        drive_frequency,
        load_frequency,
        rated_frequency
```

```
criteria(1,
        [
        type_of_mounting,
        axial_shaft_alignment,
        radial_shaft_alignment,
        angular_shaft_alignment
        ]).

criteria(2,
        [
        length_of_housing,
        diameter_of_housing,
        coupling_torque_rating,
        drive_frequency,
        load_frequency,
        rated_frequency
        ]).


write_result(Coupling) :-
        nl,nl,
        write('The coupling selected is '),
        write(Coupling),
        search_for(coupling,Coupling,identifying_name,
                                  value,[Name]),
        nl,
        write('with the designation '),
        write(Name),
        nl,nl.

write_protocol(Type,Result) :-
        current(drive,Drive),
        current(load,Load),
        current(assembly,Assembly),
        current(coupling,Coupling),
        !,
        store_protocol(
        Drive,Load,Assembly,Coupling,Type,Result).

store_protocol(
        Drive,Load,Assembly,Coupling,complete,Result) :-
        (       retract(protocol(
                Drive,Load,Assembly,Coupling,_,_))
        ;       true
        ),
```

```
            asserta(protocol(
            Drive,Load,Assembly,Coupling,complete,Result)).

store_protocol(
            Drive,Load,Assembly,Coupling,partial,Result) :-
            (       protocol(
                    Drive,Load,Assembly,Coupling,_,_)
            ;       asserta(protocol(
                    Drive,Load,Assembly,Coupling,partial,Result))
            ).
```

D.16   Module "explanation"

```
examine_coupling(Coupling) :-
            retract(current(coupling,Current)),
            asserta(current(coupling,Coupling)),
            criteria(List),
            compare(Coupling,List,Result),
            write_protocol(complete,Result),
            explain(Coupling,Result),
            note(coupling,Current,current).

compare(Coupling,[],[]).

compare(Coupling,[Criterion|Rest],Result) :-
            constraint(Criterion,Partial_Result),
            compare(Coupling,Rest,Final_Result),
            append(Partial_Result,Final_Result,Result).

explain(Coupling,[]) :-
            nl,
            write('The coupling '),
            write(Coupling),
            write(' is suitable!'),
            nl,nl.

explain(Coupling,Result) :-
            nl,
            write('The coupling '),
            write(Coupling),
            write(' is not suitable:'),
            nl,
            write_explanations(Result),
            nl,nl.
```

```
write_explanations([]).

write_explanations([Constraint|Rest]) :-
      write_this_explanation(Constraint),
      write_explanations(Rest).

write_this_explanation(type_of_mounting) :-
      indent('- The mounting of the coupling and'),
      indent('  the assembly do not match').

write_this_explanation(axial_shaft_alignment) :-
      indent('- The axial clearance of the'),
      indent('  coupling is less than the axial'),
      indent('  shaft alignment of the assembly').

write_this_explanation(radial_shaft_alignment) :-
      indent('- The radial clearance of the'),
      indent('  coupling is less than the radial'),
      indent('  shaft alignment of the assembly').

write_this_explanation(angular_shaft_alignment) :-
      indent('- The angular clearance of the'),
      indent('  coupling is less than the angular'),
      indent('  shaft alignment of the assembly').

write_this_explanation(length_of_housing) :-
      indent('- The length of the coupling is greater'),
      indent('  than the length of the housing').

write_this_explanation(diameter_of_housing) :-
      indent('- The diameter of the coupling is greater'),
      indent('  than the diameter of the housing').

write_this_explanation(coupling_torque_rating) :-
      indent('- The torque rating of the coupling'),
      indent('  is too low').

write_this_explanation(drive_frequency) :-
      indent('- The drive frequency of the drive side'),
      indent('  is too close to the intrinsic oscillation').

write_this_explanation(load_frequency) :-
      indent('- The drive frequency of the load side'),
      indent('  is too close to the intrinsic oscillation').
```

```
write_this_explanation(rated_frequency) :-
        indent('- The nominal frequency is too close'
        indent('  to the intrinsic oscillation').
```

D.17   Module "metaknowledge"

```
metaknowledge :-
        check_if_already_dealt_with.

metaknowledge :-
        examine_groupwise.

metaknowledge :-
        make_suggestion.

check_if_already_dealt_with :-
        current(drive,Drive),
        current(load,Load),
        current(assembly,Assembly),
        protocol(Drive,Load,Assembly,Coupling,_,[]),
        write_result(Coupling).

examine_groupwise :-
        search_for(coupling,Group,ako,_,[general]),
        examine_multilevel(1,Group,Preliminary_Resul
        Preliminary_Result == [],
        search_for(coupling,Coupling,ako,_,[Group]),
        examine_multilevel(2,Coupling,Final_Result),
        write_protocol(partial,Final_Result),
        Final_Result == [],
        write_result(Coupling).


examine_multilevel(Step,Name,Result) :-
        note(coupling,Name,current),
        delete(requirement,current),
        criteria(Step,List),
        member(Criterion,List),
        examine_constraint(Criterion,Result),
        Result = [],
        !.
```

```
make_suggestion :-
        nl,
        write('A suitable coupling was not found.'),
        nl,nl,
        write('Suggestion for an appropriate coupling:'),
        (       suggestion_list(List),
                member(Requirements,List),
                write_suggestion(Requirements),
                fail
        ;       true
        ).

suggestion_list(
        [
        type_of_mounting,
        axial_clearance,
        radial_clearance,
        angular_clearance,
        length,
        diameter,
        torque_rating
        ]).


write_suggestion(type_of_mounting) :-
        ask_assembly(type_of_mounting,Mount_Type),
        write_requirement(
        type_of_mounting,ist,Mount_Type).

write_suggestion(axial_clearance) :-
        ask_assembly(axial_shaft_alignment,S_ax),
        write_requirement(
        axial_clearance,greater_than,S_ax).

write_suggestion(radial_clearance) :-
        ask_assembly(radial_shaft_alignment,S_r),
        write_requirement(
        radial_clearance,greater_than,S_r).

write_suggestion(angular_clearance) :-
        ask_assembly(angular_shaft_alignment,S_ang),
        write_requirement(
        angular_clearance,greater_than,S_ang).
```

```
write_suggestion(length) :-
        ask_assembly(length_of_housing, L_max),
        write_requirement(
        length, less_than, L_max).

write_suggestion(diameter) :-
        ask_assembly(diameter_of_housing, D_max),
        write_requirement(
        diameter, less_than, D_max).

write_suggestion(torque_rating) :-
        ask_requirement(temperature_factor, S_theta),
        ask_requirement(torque, T_N),
        T_max is T_N * S_theta,
        write_requirement(
        torque_rating, greater_than, T_max).


write_requirement(Criterion, Relationship, Data_Item) :
        nl, nl, tab(10),
        write('- '),
        write(Criterion),
        write_relation(Relationship),
        write(Data_Item).

write_relation(is) :-
        write(' is ').

write_relation(greater_than) :-
        write(' must be greater than ').

write_relation(less_than) :-
        write(' must be less than ').
```

Further Reading

We hope that this book has given you sufficient incentive to pursue your interest in Prolog. Should you desire more information on this subject we suggest you examine the following literature for possible assistance.

The standard text on Prolog is, of course,

W.F. Clocksin and *C.S. Mellish*, **Programming in Prolog**, Springer, Berlin Heidelberg New.York (1981).

It has become the de facto standard definition of a language characterized by many different implementations. Almost every Prolog system of mention on the market today orients itself on the "Clocksin-Mellish" syntax.

A textbook which focuses on the practical aspects of applications programming with Prolog and the techniques involved in implementing large systems is

P. Schnupp and *L.W. Bernhard*, **Productive Prolog Programming**, Prentice-Hall International (UK) Ltd., London and Hanser, Munich and Vienna (1987).

A book which we can also recommend as a textbook and reference work is

I. Bratko, **Prolog Programming for Artificial Intelligence**, Addison-Wesley, Reading, Mass. (1986).

This book is didactically well-structured and carefully written. It contains numerous useful Prolog procedures, particularly for searching and processing data structures commonly used in knowledge-based applications, such as trees and graphs in general. A great deal of emphasis is placed on such issues as complexity and the advantages and disavantages of various strategies for searching the solution space, a topic which we touched upon in various examples, but did not deal with in as much detail.

As a survey of the area of expert systems we highly recommend

F. Hayes-Roth, D.A. Waterman and *D.B. Lenat*, **Building Expert Systems**, Addison-Wesley, Reading, Mass. (1983).

It also provides a very comprehence bibliography which is sure to be of interest to the reader.

For a very useful, practical introduction to the programming of expert systems and the overall issues involved one might read

S.M. Weiss and *C.A. Kulikowski*, **A Practical Guide to Designing Expert Systems**, Rowman & Allenheld, New Jersey (1984)

and

D.A. Waterman, **A Guide to Expert Systems**, Addison-Wesley, Reading, Mass. (1986).

For a more business-oriented introduction to the field we suggest

P. Harmon and *D. King*, **Expert Systems - Artificial Intelligence in Business**, Wiley, New York (1985)

which provides an excellent discussion and survey of the "Shells" and similar tools available on the market. We particularly recommend this book to those readers who do not share our "prejudice" against this sort of expert system development.
A technically more difficult and yet still very readable work is

P. Jackson, **Introduction to Expert Systems**, Addison-Wesley, Wokingham, Mass. (1986).

In contrast to the appications-oriented focus of Harmon and King's book, Jackson places more emphasis on the software methodological aspects and techniques of implementation.
One topic which we did not discuss in this book, which is an issue of increasing interest is that of "fuzzy" rules and concepts. Should the reader care to pursue her inquiry into its meaning and potential, we suggest starting with the article

L.A. Zadeh, **Commonsense Knowledge Representation Based on Fuzzy Logic**, Computer **16**, No. 10 (Oct 1983), p.61.

A very comprehensive survey of the field of artificial intelligence can be found in the three volume set

A. Barr, P.R. Cohen and *E.A. Feigenbaum* (eds.), **The Handbook of Artificial Intelligence**, Volumes 1-3, William Kaufman (1982).

This contains a very complete collection of original articles and contributions from scientists active in the development of artificial intelligence.
Two further introductory works we can recommend are

E.A. Rich, **Artificial Intelligence**, McGraw-Hill, New York (1983)

and

P.H. Winston, **Artificial Intelligence** (2nd edition), Addison-Wesley, Reading, Mass. (1984).

Both provide the reader with practical information regarding the techniques of expert system development. The authors present their technical guidance in a "language independent" fashion, unlike many earlier books which required, for examples, an understanding of Lisp in order to follow the examples.

A discussion of the role of Prolog in Japan's Fifth Generation project can be found in

E.A. Feigenbaum and *P. McCorduck,* **The Fifth Generation: Artificial Intelligence and Japan's Computer Challenge to the World,** Addison-Wesley, Reading, Mass. (1983).

For those readers more interested in software technological issues,

J. Doyle, **Expert Systems and the "Myth" of Symbolic Reasoning,** IEEE Trans. on Software Engineering, **SE-11,** No. 11 (Sept. 1985), p. 1386

presents a highly readable discussion of the close relationship between the development of expert systems and the formal specification and prototyping of software systems.

A very comprehensive bibliography with 336 citations regarding existing expert systems can be found in

B.G. Buchanan, **Expert Systems: Working Systems and the Research Literature, Expert Systems 3,** No. 1 (Jan. 1986), p. 32.

Over 60 expert systems are surveyed, which at the time of publication were actually installed and in use outside of the original development environments.

Given the rapid growth in this field we cannot possibly do justice to all the literature available, but we hope these recommendations will help you further in your endeavors.

Bibliography

ADAM84   J.B. Adams, "Probabilistic Reasoning and Certainty Factors" [BUCH84], p. 263

ANON86   "The MCC Experiment", Scientific American **254**, No. 4 (April 1986), p. 54

BRAT86   I. Bratko, "Prolog Programming for Artificial Intelligence", Addison-Wesley, Reading, Mass. (1986)

BUCH84   B.G. Buchanan, E.H. Shortliffe (eds.), "Rule-Based Expert Systems", Addison-Wesley, Reading, Mass. (1984)

BUCH86   B.G. Buchanan, "Expert Systems: Working Systems and the Research Literature", Expert Systems **3**, No. 1 (Jan. 1986), p. 32

CHRI85   J. Christ, "Etablierung eines Vagabunden oder: Wie aus einem Computerspiel ein Expertensystem wird", unix/mail **4** (1985) 1, p. 26

CLOC81   W.F. Clocksin, C.S. Mellish, "Programming in Prolog", Springer, Berlin Heidelberg New York (1981)

CUAD85   C.Y. Cuadrado, J.L. Cuadrado, "Prolog Goes to Work", Byte **10** (Aug. 1985), p. 151

DOYL85   J. Doyle, "Expert Systems and the 'Myth' of Symbolic Reasoning", IEEE Trans. on Software Eng., **SE-11**, No. 11 (Sept. 1985), p. 1386

FEIG84   E.A. Feigenbaum, P. McCorduck, "The Fifth Generation – Artificial Intelligence and Japan's Computer Challenge to the World", Pan Books, London and Sidney (1984)

FIKE85   R. Fikes, T. Kehler, "The Role of Frame-Based Representation in Reasoning", Comm. ACM **28** (Sept. 1985), p. 905

FLOY81   Ch. Floyd, "A Process-Oriented Approach to Software Development", in: "Systems Architecture", Proc. ICS 81, Westbury House, London (1981), p. 285

FRIE85   P. Friedland, L.H. Kedes, "Discovering the Secrets of DNA", CACM **28** (Nov. 1985), p. 1164

GREE84   St. Greenwood, "A Menu Driven Shell for Use with Any Prolog Program", Logic Programming Newsletter (Winter 84/85), p. 8

GRUN86   St. Grundmann, W. Schönfeld, "Ein juristisches Expertensystem", State of the Art: Expertensysteme **1/86**, p. 46

GSCH85   A. Gschwind, C.T. Nguyen Huu, "Fehlerdiagnose und Störungsbeseitigung mit wissensbasierten Systemen", Newsletter of GI

FA 1.2 'Künstliche Intelligenz & Mustererkennung', No. 39 (Oct. 1985), p. 33

GÜNT85   U. Güntzer, G. Huber, "Ein Expertensystem zur Unterstützung der Filialanalyse bei der HYPO-Bank", GI/OCG/ÖGI-Jahrestagung 1985 (H.R. Hansen, ed.), Springer, Berlin Heidelberg New York Tokyo (1985), p. 839

GÜNT86   U. Güntzer, G. Huber, G. Jüttner, K.-R. Moll, "Filialanalyse bei der HYPO-Bank", State of the Art: Expertensysteme 1/86, p. 38

HALL59   E.T. Hall, "The Silent Language", Doubleday (1959), paperback edition, Anchor Press, Garden City, N.Y. (1973)

HARM85   P. Harmon, D. King, "Expert Systems - Artificial Intelligence in Business", Wiley, New York (1985)

HARM86   P. Harmon, D. King, "Expertensysteme in der Praxis", Oldenbourg, Munich and Vienna (1985)

HUKE86   Ch.T. Nguyen Huu, U. Kekeritz, "Eine Frame-Implementation in Prolog", Newsletter of GI FA 1.2 'Künstliche Intelligenz & Mustererkennung', No. 41 (April 1986), p. 19

INCE84   D.C. Ince, "Module Interconnection LAnguages and Prolog", acm SIGPLAN Notices 19, No. 8 (Aug. 1984), p. 89

JACK86   P. Jackson, "Introduction to Expert Systems", Addison-Wesley, Wokingham (1986)

KEMP86   P. Kemppainen, E. Reilio, "XCM - A Configuration Management Expert System for Mass Production of Embedded Software", in: Proc. 6th Int'l Workshop on Expert Systems & Their Applications, Avignon, 28-30. April 1986), p. 389

KIMM79   R. Kimm, W. Koch, W. Simonsmeier, F. Tontsch, "Einführung in Software Engineering", de Gruyter, Berlin and New York (1979)

KOWA79   R. Kowalski, "Logic for Problem Solving", Elsevier, New York (1979)

KOWA85   R. Kowalski, "Logic Programming", Byte 10 (Aug. 1985), p. 161

LENA84   D.B. Lenat, "Computer Software for Intelligent Systems", Scientific American 251, No. 3 (Sept 1984), p. 152

MALP85   J. Malpass, "Prolog as a Unix System Tool", Unix/World (July 1985), p. 48

MENS85   G. Mensel, J. Michel, "Entwicklung und Konstruktion eines wissensbasierten betriebswirtschaftlichen Beratungs- und Konfigurationssystems im Bereich der Lagerwirtschaft und Fertigungsorganisation", in: Compas '85, VDE-Verlag, Berlin (1985), p. 981

PESC85   H. Pesch, P. Schnupp, H. Schaller, A.P. Spirk, "Test Case Preparation Using Prolog", Proc. 8th Int. Conf. Software Engineering, London (Aug. 28-30, 1985), p. 252

PUPP85   F. Puppe, H. Puppe, M. Beetz, "MED1 - ein Werkzeug für Diagnostik-Expertensysteme", Nachr. f. Dokum. 36, Nr. 1 (1985), p. 28

PUPP86	F. Puppe, "Expertensysteme", Informatik-Spektrum **9**, (1986), p. 1
REIS85	W. Reisig, "Systementwurf mit Netzen", Springer, Berlin Heidelberg New York Tokyo (1985)
RICH83	E. Rich, "Artificial Intelligence", MacGraw-Hill, New York (1983)
SAVO85	St.E. Savory (ed.), "Künstliche Intelligenz und Expertensysteme – ein Forschungsbericht der Nixdorf Computer AG", Oldenbourg, Munich (1985)
SCHN83	P. Schnupp, "Prolog – eine nichtprozedurale Sprache zur Programmierung von Expertensystemen und zum 'rapid prototyping'", in: "Intelligenztechnologie" (M. Schulze-Vorberg, ed.), Teubner, Stuttgart (1983), p. 86
SCHN83a	P. Schnupp, "Prolog als Spezifikations- und Modellierungswerkzeug", in: "Requirements Engineering" (G. Hommel, D. Krönig eds.), Informatik Fachberichte **74**, Springer, Heidelberg (1983), p. 173
SCHN85	P. Schnupp, U. Leibrandt, "Expertensysteme", Springer, Berlin Heidelberg New York (1985)
SCHN87	P. Schnupp, L.W. Bernhard, "Productive Prolog Programming", Prentice-Hall International (UK) Ltd., London and Hanser, Munich and Vienna (1987)
SCHR86	U. Schreier, "Die Beziehungen zwischen Datenbank- und Expertensystemen", State of the Art: Expertensysteme **1/86**, p. 30
SHAP83	Y. Shapiro, "Algorithmic Program Debugging", MIT Press, Cambridge, Mass. (1983)
SHEI85	B. Sheil, "Programming the Uncertain with Exploratory Systems", Computer Design (March 1985), p. 133
SHOR84	E.H. Shortliffe, B.G. Buchanan, "A Model of Inexact Reasoning in Medicine" [BUCH84], p. 233
SIMO86	G. Simons, "Die Fünfte Computer-Generation", Hanser, Munich (1986)
TRUM86	P. Trum, "Automatische Generierung von Arbeitsplänen", State of the Art: Expertensysteme **1/86**, p. 69
WINS84	P.H. Winston, "Artificial Intelligence" (2nd edition), Addison-Wesley, Reading, Mass. (1984)
ZADE83	L.A. Zadeh, "Commonsense Knowledge Representation Based on Fuzzy Logic", Computer **16**, No. 10 (Oct. 1983), p. 61
ZANI84	C. Zaniolo, "Object-oriented Programming in Prolog", IEEE International Symposion on Logic Programming, Atlantic City, N.J. (1984), p. 265

Subject Index